AND HE LEADS THEM

THE MIND AND THE HEART OF PHILIP SALIBA

"The Shepherd calls His own sheep by name, and He leads them." —John 10:2, 3

**JOSEPH J. ALLEN,
EDITOR**

The Thirty-Fifth Anniversary
of the Episcopate of Metropolitan PHILIP

Conciliar Press
Ben Lomond, California

Copyright © 2001 by Metropolitan Philip Saliba

All Rights Reserved.

ISBN 1-888212-29-2 (paperback)
ISBN 1-888202-30-6 (hardcover)

Conciliar Press
P.O. Box 76
Ben Lomond, California 95005

Printed in the United States of America

Cover design by Fr. Paul Albert of St. John Studio

The icon of The Good Shepherd appears courtesy of Margaret Apergis & Sons Co., of Athens, Greece. Icon written by the Hagiographers of the Holy Monastery of the Transfiguration, Kymi, Greece.

This book is dedicated to the faithful
of the Antiochian Orthodox
Christian Archdiocese of North America
who have helped me fulfill some of my dreams
and who shared my joy and sorrow
during the past thirty-five years.

Table of Contents

Acknowledgments 5

Part I
The First Decade: The Late 1960s and the 1970s
1 The Man, the Bishop: Philip Saliba 9
2 For This Purpose 21
3 Laborers Together 29
4 Pray to the Lord of the Harvest 55
5 This Home Is Your Home 67
6 Changed from Glory to Glory 85
7 Is Life Not More than Food? 123
8 Make Disciples of All Nations:
    A Struggle Not to Be Abandoned 151
9 Be Doers of the Word 187

Part II
The Second Decade: The 1980s
10 Behold the New Has Come:
    New Challenges for the 1980s 213
11 Incarnating Theology:
    The Roots of Pastoral Ministry 235
12 The Whole People of God 247
13 Tenderness and Joy:
    Speaking from the Heart 281
14 Looking to New Horizons 315
15 Bearing Witness to the Light 329

Part III
The Third Decade: The 1990s
16 To Thy Name Give Glory:
    The Twenty-fifth Anniversary 347
17 Mission and Evangelism 371
18 The Legacy of Antioch for North America 389

19 Faith and Works:
   Whose Feet Will I Wash?................................... 413
20 Keeping Hearts and Minds in Christ Jesus:
   Endings and Beginnings; a New Millennium 435

Appendix:
Selected Letters of Metropolitan Philip 453

Acknowledgments

This book, published on the occasion of the thirty-fifth anniversary of the episcopate of Metropolitan Philip, could not have been accomplished without the dedication and hard work of the following persons. In alphabetical order, they are:

> Father Paul Alberts, Father Elias Bitar, Royal Giffen, Father Peter Gillquist, Kathy Meyer, Leslie Saliba, Carolyn Tanguay, Carla Zell, Deacon Thomas Zell, and Refa Zouzoulas.

Their contribution to this book is an expression of their love for His Eminence. They deserve our fondest acknowledgment, and they join in a chorus of voices which proclaims:

> "Eis Pola Eti Dhespota!"
> "Many Years to you, Master!"

Part I

The First Decade
The late 1960s and the 1970s

Chapter 1

THE MAN, THE BISHOP: PHILIP SALIBA

> *We may know the human only when we are confronted by the divine. We may know the temporal only when we ponder the eternal. And we may know the depth of the valley only when we look at the peak of the mountain. We are sick and paralyzed by fear and will never be healed without a true encounter with Christ.*
> Metropolitan Philip

- *Reflections on the Episcopate of Philip Saliba*

AND HE LEADS THEM

This book is written on the occasion of the thirty-fifth anniversary of the episcopate of Metropolitan Philip Saliba. It is a compilation of his writings and addresses, although certainly not inclusive of all of that he wrote and spoke as Metropolitan Archbishop of the Antiochian Orthodox Christian Archdiocese of North America.

*We begin in this first chapter, however, by opening the mind and heart of the man. In this way, we offer to the reader a gateway into understanding his episcopal ministry. This opening chapter, therefore, focuses upon the four characteristics which will best introduce the reader to the text which follows: Philip as **administrator, philanthropist, builder** and **father**. Those who know the Metropolitan would readily agree that history will best remember him according to these four descriptive titles.*

*In the immediate sense, then, the following brief meditation **on the man and on the bishop** will prepare the reader to appreciate more fully the text which follows.*

J. J. A.

Reflections on the Episcopate of Philip Saliba

"The Shepherd calls his own sheep by name *and He leads them*" (John 10:2, 3). There are no better words than these to guide us in our opening reflection on the episcopate of Metropolitan Philip.

However, to write about either the man or the episcopacy of Philip Saliba is not to begin with him, nor to end with him. One must begin with Christ: Metropolitan Philip's life and faith explicate this truth; his ministry proves it. The reader will see this truth throughout the book.

We can take our lead by remembering that our chosen words from John's Gospel, the title of this book, show us our Lord is being "self-reflective"; Jesus is referring to Himself. No one should forget that. He makes this only too clear when He later says, "I am the door of the sheep" (John 10:7). Now, if Christ is the only Shepherd, the door of the sheep, how then does this quote properly apply to the person and ministry of Philip Saliba? Said in another way, how is his ministry linked to that quote? As we shall see, it is Christ's ministry as Shepherd which Philip has made his own—and with intention and purpose.

Regarding this very truth, if anyone has known what the Great Apostle Paul meant with his critical instruction on ministry, it is Metropolitan Philip.

> Not that we are sufficient of ourselves . . . our sufficiency is of God, who has made us ministers of the new testament: not of the letter, but the spirit; for the letter kills, but the spirit gives life . . . Therefore, seeing that we have this ministry, as we have received mercy, we faint not . . . for we preach not ourselves but Christ Jesus the Lord, and ourselves as your servant for Jesus' sake (2 Corinthians 3:5, 6; 4:1, 5).

Patristic Sources

There are also many patristic sources which, taking their lead from the Scripture, seek to show this same linkage and identification. In each case, the point is constant: one such as Metropolitan Philip must properly reflect—be transparent to—"the sole priest and mediator between God and man," Jesus Christ (cf. 1 Timothy 2:1–6). This is the case since the more responsibility accepted by the shepherd of any church, the more he must be transparent to the One Shepherd, i.e., the one "who entered once for all into the Holy Place" (Hebrews 9:12). In this way, the fathers of theology, when referring to the pastoral ministry, say that one in Philip's position is acting *in persona christi*. And so he has, and so he does.

When these patristic sources refer to this identification with Christ's ministry in a liturgical and sacramental mode, they point us to the succinct definition found in the Epistle to the Hebrews: "For every high priest, taken from men, is ordained for men in the things pertaining to God, that he may offer both gifts and sacrifices for our sins" (Hebrews 5:1). Philip the bishop, the high priest, has always known the truth of this identification, now given a liturgical orientation. Again, the linkage of his ministry with that of Christ is confirmed.

But these fathers not only speak of this linkage in terms of liturgy, they also speak of it in terms of the pastoral praxis as it engages everyday life, drawing closely on the analogy of "the shepherd and the flock." Indeed, St. Ephraim the Syrian in the following quotation could well be defining the practical accomplishments of Philip's episcopacy, and in so doing, he again verifies our point of linkage.

> O ye shepherds, be made like unto that diligent Shepherd, chief of the whole flock. He brought nigh those who were afar off. He brought back the wanderers. He visited the sick. He strengthened the weak. He bound up the broken. He gave himself up for the sake of the sheep (*Of Pastors*, P. G. pp. 372, 373).

Finally, however, as we explore the various contents and circumstances in which Metropolitan Philip has gone about this practice of his episcopal ministry, it is St. Gregory the Great who describes that ministry with more specificity. In his *Pastoral Rule*, a touchstone document for all ministry, the great saint and Pope of Rome could well be describing Philip, especially as he refers to the "action" and "voice" of the shepherd.

The shepherd of souls should always be chief in action, that by living he may point out the way of life to those that are put under him, and that the flock which follows the voice . . . of the shepherd, may learn how to walk better through example than through words . . . For that voice more readily penetrates the hearer's heart . . . since what he commands by speaking, he helps the doing of by showing (*The Pastoral Rule*, P. L. II: 2, 77, 27).

Metropolitan Philip has been, above all, "chief in action," and thus the "flock which follows his voice" does so because that voice more readily "penetrates the hearer's heart."

We see, then, from such patristic sources, just how our chosen words from St. John's Gospel describe the veritable ministry of Metropolitan Philip. All that he has done—and which we will now, even if feebly, attempt to describe—can be subsumed under these words: "The Shepherd calls His own sheep by name *and He leads them.*"

Philip, the Administrator

The issues and problems that faced the young Metropolitan when he was consecrated in 1966 were met with a vigor that was rooted in both the old and new worlds. Although the ecclesiastical situation at present in Syria and Lebanon seems very different from what it was thirty-five years ago, Philip's decisions subsequent to his consecration were often a response to what he had seen in those countries as a young seminarian and deacon. Indeed, he was openly disappointed—and as a result, sometimes angry, sometimes critical—of what was at that time prevailing in the Church administration.

Philip was but fourteen when he entered the Balamand Seminary at Tripoli, Lebanon. He later attended and graduated from the Orthodox Secondary School in Homs, Syria, and the Assiyeh Orthodox College in Damascus, Syria. At the tender age of eighteen, he was ordained to the holy diaconate in 1949 and was assigned to serve as secretary to His Beatitude, Alexander III (Tahan), Patriarch of Antioch and All the East. In 1952, he was appointed to teach in the department of Arabic Language and Literature at the Balamand Seminary.

He never forgot what he saw during these years: a lack of integrity on the part of some of the hierarchy; a diminution of solid Orthodox theological training into robotic forms; a lack of organized programs for the future generations of Orthodox youth; an abuse of the clergy and their families in terms of dignity and security; a patriarchate which still, since the Ottoman Empire, remained dependent upon other local Orthodox churches, e.g., Greece and Russia. These conditions—and there were more—demonstrated a general lack in the proper leadership and administration of ecclesiastical life.

This initial and negative perception was only exacerbated when the young Philip began his academic studies in the West: first at the Kelham School of Theology and London University in England where he spent three years; then in 1956, when he entered the Holy Cross Greek Orthodox School of Theology in Brookline, Massachusetts. This latter exposure presented a "contour" by which Philip was better able to measure the prevailing conditions in the Orthodox Church in the Middle East. Furthermore, this same contour taught Philip about the need for a more organized and integrated administration, one which confronted the reality and context of the day, but remained rooted in the Gospel of Jesus Christ. Philip knew he had to be the scribe described by Our Lord in St. Matthew:

Therefore every scribe who is instructed in the kingdom of heaven, is like a householder who brings forth out of his treasure things old and things new (Matthew 13:52).

"Things old": this meant both what he learned from his mother and father in Abou-Mizan, Lebanon, where he was raised in a traditional Orthodox family, and then as he more formally studied theology at the Balamand Seminary. "Things new": this meant what he learned by this "contour" while studying in the West. Both experiences—old and new—made a lasting impression upon the manner in which Philip would later administrate: he now understood the need to discern between custom(s) and the Apostolic Tradition; between empty forms and true forms (which are not disconnected from meaning); between a rigid, pharisaic *status quo* and a creative, evangelical vision. Such discernment, which is known in the desert literature as "the mother of all virtues," is always needed to discover the truth. In terms of hierarchical administration, such discernment, always the hallmark of Metropolitan Philip's administrative policy, creates equilibrium rather than irresponsibility, care rather than carelessness. Philip was schooled in this mix, one which has taken the best from things old and things new.

The final tuning of this mix—in anticipation of his ministry as bishop—was when Deacon Philip passed through two more stages of development; when he was ordained a Presbyter in 1959 to pastor the parish of St. George in Cleveland, Ohio, and then completed his Masters of Divinity degree at St. Vladimir's Orthodox Theological Seminary in Crestwood, New York, in 1965. He was now ready to put into practice as an Orthodox hierarch what he had hitherto experienced and learned.

But where to begin? In what ways can we see the implementation of his administrative capacity?

We can begin with the reorganization of the entire archdiocese into departments, e.g., the Departments of Finance, Christian Education, Information, Legal Affairs, etc., some two dozen of them. Such departments were not "one-man shows," nor products of clericalism; they are a healthy mix of clergy and laity, men and women, the professionally trained and the merely interested.

This same creativity was shown when the young bishop again confronted the *status quo* in 1969. It was at the historic Miami Convention that a model constitution for all parishes was approved. Congregationalism and divisive parochialism would have to give way to a true catholicity, now at an archdiocesan level. At that same convention, the official name of the archdiocese was changed to the Antiochian Orthodox Christian Archdiocese of North America, thus more realistically reflecting the nature of its spiritual and theological heritage. The nomenclature which labeled the archdiocese as "Syrian" was dropped; this was a daring step into the status quo identity at that time, but one which showed an orientation toward a united Orthodox Church in North America.

As the reader will see in the text of this book, this was only the beginning. Again, in the quest for applying things old and things new, the Metropolitan continued to implement vigorously various administrative programs: in the financial area, where he pressed talented and dedicated persons into the service of the Church in order to build a solid financial program; in directing his attention to the Youth, with an emphasis upon the Fellowship of St. John the Divine; in the Antiochian Orthodox Christian Women of North America (AOCWNA); in the creation of the Order of St. Ignatius of Antioch.

But above all, the administrative act which brought joy to the heart of every Antiochian Christian occurred on June 24, 1975. It was on that day that Metropolitan Philip and Archbishop Michael (of the former Toledo, Ohio, diocese) effected administrative and jurisdictional unity of the Antiochian Orthodox faithful of North America. That unity was ratified by the Holy Synod of the Patriarchate on August 19, 1975, wherein Metropolitan Philip was named Primate.

Philip, the Philanthropist and Builder

In both national and international scenarios, Philip Saliba is known as a bishop keenly set upon effecting positive and hopeful change, especially in the implementation of philanthropic and building programs.

Using the same qualities that we noted in the administrative realm, the Metropolitan has applied theology to life in various philanthropic causes. Here one must note the rootedness of Philip in the Antiochian school of theology, a school which has always proposed a radical incarnational approach to theology. One cannot live in an ivory tower, since true theology is never merely theory; it always implies the need to engage people's lives wherever they are found, i.e., in joy and sorrow, in light and darkness. As the reader will note, Philip has always emphasized this incarnational approach, when he addresses both the archdiocesan conventions and local parishes. Thus he falls solidly within the historic approach of Antioch, from St. Ignatius the God-bearer to Ignatius IV, the present Patriarch of Antioch; each abhors the divorce of Christian theology from the life of the people.

The reader will especially see this orientation in international programs such as Philip's creation of the Children's Relief Fund (which has raised over 1.5 million dollars for needy children in the Middle East); in the annual Food for the Hungry campaign, used to relieve suffering not only in the Levant, but throughout North and South America, Europe and Asia; in the campaign which raised one million dollars to rebuild the St. George Orthodox Hospital in Beirut; to provide food and shelter for earthquake victims in Armenia, Iran, Mexico, or for the sick and suffering that resulted out of the Persian Gulf war; etc. The list can go on, and each would simply pile upon the philanthropic deeds of the Metropolitan's ministry.

In terms of building, Philip has always taken the lead. For example, in 1977 he established a $500,000 endowment fund for the support of the Balamand Seminary. And later, in 1999, once the University of Balamand had been established, he granted one million dollars to build a cultural and athletic complex there. And, of course, within the archdiocese, the Metropolitan has been the main spearhead for the building of the Antiochian Village complex, which includes the Summer Camp and the Heritage and Learning Center. One can hardly imagine the Antiochian Archdiocese in the 1980s and 1990s and up to the present without these institutions; they are known throughout all of North America, especially for the vital youth programs undertaken there.

Philip, the Father
An Orthodox bishop is not only an administrator, nor merely a builder and philanthropist; he must also—and always—be a father. From his earliest days in Lebanon and Syria, and then in England and North America, Philip was learning about this crucial dimension: fatherhood. Without this quality, everything realized would fall short.

As the reader will see in the following text, Philip is, first of all, a true father to his clergy. In this capacity, he has established a viable insurance and retirement plan, one which can give to his clergy a sense of dignity and security. In perfect line with this concern, he created the Continuing Theological and Pastoral Education Program which seeks—especially through the biennial symposium, the St. Stephen's Course of Studies and the Antiochian House of Studies programs—to upgrade and renew the ministry of the clergy. It seems he never forgot from his childhood the impoverished life of the clergy; it motivates his deep concern for them. He is truly what some have called him: "a priest's bishop."

But this same fatherhood is again seen in his never-ending concern for the children and youth of his archdiocese. Always searching for new ways, and never settling for less than enthusiastic participation, Philip is always personally involved in these two areas of Church life. He calls various conferences and attempts to dialogue with the directors of such departments. This has been one of the hallmarks of his ministry. The Antiochian

Village and Heritage and Learning Center in Ligonier, Pennsylvania, were founded by Metropolitan Philip, primarily for the youth of our archdiocese.

As is carefully recorded in our text, another dimension of his fatherhood was seen when, just like the father of the prodigal son, he said "welcome home" to the former Evangelical Orthodox Christians. In February, 1987, after searching diligently among the various canonical Orthodox bodies, approximately two thousand of these Christians embraced the canonical Orthodox Church via the Metropolitan's invitation. The Metropolitan gave them the name of the Antiochian Evangelical Orthodox Mission of the archdiocese. Their major task is in the area of missionizing America and Canada and bringing North Americans into the Orthodox Faith. Indeed, throughout the proceedings which led to their full entrance, Philip was a courageous father, willing to undergo the various criticisms hurled at him, because of his fidelity to the Gospel of Jesus Christ.

In these ways—and in many more—Metropolitan Philip is known as a true father to his archdiocese.

And More

It is, of course, impossible to mention every program and emphasis in Metropolitan Philip's thirty-five years as an Orthodox hierarch. This editor knows that he has had to be selective and this always runs the risk of the reader claiming either omission, or subjectivity, or some such accusation. This reflection, however, is just that: a reflection, one written to introduce our readers to this book.

Despite the briefness of this reflection, however, our hope is that in understanding Metropolitan Philip as *administrator, philanthropist, builder* and *father,* we will better understand how history will remember this man. Surely, those who read this book will agree that the words of John's Gospel are well chosen to describe Philip Saliba: ". . . the Shepherd calls His own sheep by name *and He leads them*" (John 10:2, 3).   —*Joseph J. Allen*

Chapter 2

FOR THIS PURPOSE

> *The episcopate, therefore, is not a worldly, vain glory. The episcopate is first and foremost sacrifice, service and love . . . a continuation of the eternal priesthood of Christ in time and space . . . is neither autocratic, nor arbitrary, nor absolute; it is an authority based on the truth that "if anyone would be first, he must be last, and the servant of all" (Mark 9:35).*
>
> Metropolitan Philip

- *The Consecration Address, 1966*

AND HE LEADS THEM

*It was on March 16, 1966, that the thirty-five-year-old priest, Philip Saliba, was nominated and elected Metropolitan from among the ranks of the Antiochian Orthodox clergy in North America. Ilyas Kurban, Metropolitan of Tripoli, Lebanon, was already in North America, administrating the widowed diocese after the death of Metropolitan Antony Bashir in February of 1966. After the nomination by the Holy Synod of Antioch, Kurban elevated Philip to the rank of Archimandrite in Louisville, Kentucky. Thus preparations were already in the making for the consecration to the episcopacy at St. Elias Monastery near Philip's birthplace of Abou Mizan, Lebanon. The following talk, with which we begin this collection of texts, is the young Metropolitan's consecration address. We call the reader to note that although he confesses his unworthiness, Philip's response, which forms the heart of the address, is found in the scriptural words: "for I have appeared to you **for this purpose**, to appoint you to serve and bear witness to the things in which you have seen Me" (Acts 26:16).*

*The many who have read this concise, but poignant, address now realize that it was no mere acceptance speech. Rather, it was also a prophetic address **from** Philip **to** Philip, for in it he challenges himself to respond to God's grace, which "completes that which is wanting," and sets him on the path to the bright future of proclaiming the Gospel of Jesus Christ. For us, the present readers, the remainder of these texts bears the imprint of that challenge.*

J. J. A.

The Consecration Address
1966

Your Beatitude, Brother Members of the Holy Synod and Faithful Orthodox:

With much longing, we left the new world for this good land which was blessed by the footsteps of Jesus of Nazareth. We bring to you greetings, love and sincere obedience from your spiritual children in the United States and Canada. It is indeed a great honor for me, Your Beatitude and beloved brothers, to receive the Grace of the Holy Episcopate through the laying on of your blessed hands which are laboring tirelessly to revive the glory of Antioch which gave Christianity thousands of saints, confessors and martyrs.

On the 16th and 17th of March, 1966, the clergy and laity of the Archdiocese of New York and all North America overwhelmingly nominated me to be their future shepherd. Before the nomination, however, I told the assembled clergy and laity, openly and publicly, that I am not worthy of this divine grace, although that grace "heals the sick and completes that which is wanting," since we human beings are powerless without the help and mercy of God. Yet the pious clergy and faithful laity proceeded with my nomination, despite my weakness and sins which are more numerous than the sand of the seas.

When Metropolitan Antony Bashir of thrice-blessed memory ordained me to the priesthood in 1959, to serve St. George Parish of Cleveland, Ohio, I said in my ordination speech the following:

> In 1948, I left the Balamand Seminary and its quiet life and returned to society and its problems. Thus, an era of doubt, anxiety and rebelliousness began in my life. During this period I lost some of my faith in the Church because I could not differentiate between the Church as a human institution subject to sins and tribulations, and

the Church as a divine institution for which Christ died and was resurrected from the dead, "that He might present her to Himself in splendor, without spot or wrinkle or any such thing, that she might be holy and without blemish" (Ephesians 5:27). Tormented by doubt, despair and confusion, I found refuge in some secular religions, but it was not long before God visited me and said, "Rise and stand upon your feet; for I have appeared to you for this purpose, to appoint you to serve and bear witness to the things in which you have seen Me and to those in which I will appear to you" (Acts 26:16). Thus, I returned to Christ to find in Him the right answer, not only to my personal problems, but also to the problems of humankind and history.

When the Church was as pure as the light that shone on Tabor, the early Christians confessed their sins publicly before the congregation, because the sins which we commit are not against God only, but also against the community. At my priestly ordination, I confessed my sins openly, and today I again confess before God and this congregation that I have sinned more than the publican, more than the prodigal son, more than Paul and more than Augustine. From the depths of my heart, I cry like David, "Have mercy on me, O God, according to Thy steadfast love, according to Thy abundant mercy. Blot out my transgression. Wash me thoroughly from my iniquity and cleanse me from my sins. For I know my transgression, and my sin is ever before me. Against Thee only have I sinned and done evil in Thy sight so that Thou art justified in Thy sentence and blameless in Thy judgment. Behold I was brought forth in iniquity and in sin did my mother conceive me" (Psalm 51).

All of us in the Church of Antioch, clergy and laity alike, must lament our transgressions like David, weep like the adulterous woman, humble ourselves like the publican, confess like the thief on the cross and repent like the prodigal son. This repentance was described by St. Isaac the Syrian as "the trembling of the soul at the gates of paradise." My prayer has been, still is and will always be, the prayer of the Church which knocks on the door of repentance with sinful hands.

I thank God, however, that pharisaism never found a way to my heart, and I have never tried to judge anyone. Only He who knows the secrets of the heart will judge each one of us according to his or her deeds.

In his Epistle to the Hebrews, St. Paul said: "For every high priest chosen from among men is appointed to act on behalf of men in relation to God, to offer gifts and sacrifices for sins" (Hebrews 5:1). The episcopate, therefore, is not a worldly, vain glory. The episcopate is first and foremost sacrifice, service and love. The episcopate is the continuation of the eternal priesthood of Christ in time and space. Thus, the bishop's authority is neither autocratic nor arbitrary nor absolute; it is an authority based on love and service, for "if anyone would be first, he must be last of all and servant of all" (Mark 9:35). Armed with such lofty Christian principles, we launch into our pastoral work in the Archdiocese of New York and North America which is an integral part of the Holy See of Antioch, the See of Peter, Paul and Theodosius IV. All our means in North America are at your disposal, and tomorrow we shall be delighted indeed to accompany His Beatitude to the Holy Hills of Balamand to lay the cornerstone of the theological academy which our predecessor, Metropolitan Antony, has pledged to erect to help the Mother Church.

It is impossible for Antioch to become the bride of Christ and a hymn of praise to Him without a theological institute to breathe life in this Orthodox East where the storms of civil strife, divisiveness, doubt and despair are blowing from all directions. It is impossible for Antioch to recapture its past glory unless it elevates itself from the stagnant swamps of cheap politics to the esplanades of truth, goodness and beauty. We never wanted Antioch to be Eastern or Western in the political sense. We always wanted Antioch to be an Orthodox Christian Church, free, independent, committed to the love of

God and neighbor, obedient to the patriarch, the Holy Synod and canons of ecumenical and local councils; such canons which were written by the blood of martyrs in order to enlighten and guide those who are tempted to rebel against the authority of the Church.

Your Beatitude, we shall never bargain on the truth which liberated us from the bondage of sin. Did the Holy Fathers betray the Church when they were forced to celebrate the Eucharist in the caves and catacombs? Did the martyrs of the twentieth-century Church bargain on the truth when thousands of them went to prisons and gallows in atheistic countries? Anyone who bargains with falsehood and sells his soul to the devil will have to answer to God on the day of judgment!

We promise Your Beatitude that we shall work with you and our venerable brothers to encourage and to promote the youth movements here and in North America, for the faithful youth are the heartbeat of the Church. We assure your Beatitude and our beloved brothers that our doors and hearts will always be open to you, and we hope that you will bless us with your visits from time to time in order to witness the discipline, faith and progress which the Archdiocese of New York and all North America has attained.

We realize that our road is long and difficult, covered with stones and thorns, full of hissing reptiles and howling wolves. But He who has crushed the head of the serpent and calmed the sea will raise us up when we stumble, and lead us on the right path.

(translated from Arabic)

Editor's Endnotes

1. *Philip was ordained to the priesthood in 1959 by Metropolitan Antony Bashir; by that time he had finished his studies at Balamand Orthodox Seminary; Kelham Theological School in Nottingham, England; London University in England; Holy Cross Greek Orthodox School of Theology in Brookline, Massachusetts; and Wayne State University in Detroit, Michigan, where he received his Bachelor of Arts Degree in History.*

2. *In 1949, Philip was already ordained as a deacon by Metropolitan Elia Karam of Mount Lebanon; he served as secretary to Patriarch Alexander III in Damascus; served as deacon in Detroit after he arrived in America; and was assigned as pastor of St. George in Cleveland in 1959. In 1964–65 Philip returned to theological studies at St. Vladimir's Seminary, where he received his Masters of Divinity Degree in 1965.*

Chapter 3

LABORERS TOGETHER

> *For many years, we have been living with two kinds of theologies: one for the church upstairs, and one for the hall downstairs. We do not believe in this "upstairs–downstairs" theology. Nor do we believe in the existence of two classes in the parish opposing each other, namely, clergy versus laity. We are all part of the "whole people of God."*
>
> Metropolitan Philip

- *Laborers Together: Bringing Order, 1968*
- *On the Death of Martin Luther King, 1968*
- *The Scripture and Fathers on Christ: Social Justice and Violence, 1968*
- *A Voice was Heard in Rama, 1968*

AND HE LEADS THEM

*By the time Metropolitan Philip delivered this 1968 State of the Archdiocese address in Pittsburgh, he had spent his first two years traveling, observing and studying the archdiocese. What he found was an archdiocese ill-equipped to meet the challenges of the age. Although he addresses other pertinent issues which will be summarized in the form of editor's endnotes, the main thrust of this address is obvious: "We are **laborers together** with God," he states, challenging each responsible person of the archdiocese to "take heed how he builds" (1 Corinthians 3:9–17). Calling those "who have been sleeping on the job" to awake, he begins to mobilize his archdiocese by bringing a badly needed **order** through a new organization of departments and commissions.*

*Interestingly, we already see forming here an emphasis on Orthodox ecclesiology which will stay foremost in Philip's mind throughout his episcopate: no one man, not the layperson, not the priest, not even the bishop, can do it alone; we need both the clergy and laity, in the fullness of the Body of Christ, to cooperate for the stewardship and growth of the Church. The reader will see this theme throughout Philip's future texts. In the immediate address, he shows this orientation as he seeks to establish the necessary **linkages** which will give his archdiocese the unified structure it eventually achieves: the archdiocese and parish, the pastor and parish council, the clergy and laity, the spiritual and temporal. Only when these components are organically linked, he claims, can we properly become laborers together with God.*

In the wake of Dr. Martin Luther King's assassination in 1968, Philip's second address in this chapter expresses his profound interest in applying the teachings of the Orthodox Faith to contemporary issues. This sad occurrence becomes a pivot toward a more thorough theological exploration into the issue. Thus he plunges into the Scriptures and Fathers to discover the deeper reaches of the issue and writes the third entry in this chapter, "The Scripture and Fathers on Christ, Social Justice and Violence."

Finally, in this chapter, Philip pens the first of his meditations: "A Voice Was Heard in Rama." As the reader will see, his meditations are filled with the pathos of one sincerely teaching love and seeking justice. This meditation is written on the eve of Christmas, 1968.

J. J. A.

Laborers Together; Bringing Order
Pittsburgh, 1968

The biblical theme of my message to you this year is taken from the First Epistle of Saint Paul to the Corinthians, 3:9–17.

We are laborers together with God: you are God's field. You are God's building. But let every man take heed how he builds; for no other foundation can man lay than that which is laid, which is Jesus Christ. Every man's work shall be made manifest, for the day shall declare it. For it shall be manifest by fire, and the fire shall try every man's work, of what sort it is.

Two years have elapsed since my consecration as your archbishop. The first year was spent in intensive traveling and in studying the various problems which we are facing in this particular time. The result of our study was the realization that our archdiocese was not fully equipped to face the challenges of this age, both spiritually and administratively. Therefore, last year in Detroit, Michigan, with your help, we inaugurated a new era by establishing new departments and commissions to help this archdiocese achieve our spiritual and administrative goals. Some of these departments and commissions functioned very well, some not so well because of reasons beyond our control. So, "let every man take heed how he builds!"

I have already stated to you that the work of the Church and this archdiocese cannot be done by one man, and that we urgently need the help of both our clergy and laity in order to fulfill our mission as the Church of Christ in this world. We are most thankful to those of you who have extended to us a helping hand. To those who have been sleeping on the job, we ask them in Christ's name to awake and examine the purpose of their existence. Certainly we do not organize for the sake of organization. We do organize in order to coordinate our efforts so that our vision and dreams for a Christlike Church might be fulfilled and realized. The purpose of all our organizations is to grow spiritually in Christ. If we fail to do so, then all our organizations and all our efforts will have been in vain. "Seek ye first the kingdom of God and His righteousness, and everything else will be added unto you" (Luke 12:31). Despite the many problems which we faced this year, we have made tremendous progress in many areas.

The Current Spiritual Life of the Archdiocese
I am sure all of you agree that we are living in the most turbulent and dangerous time in history. The Church of Christ is attacked by many enemies from without and within. But we can overcome these enemies only if we understand the wealth, the strength and the depth of our faith. Whatever we do during our earthly pilgrimage must help us lift up our hearts unto the Lord. Every step we make must lead us toward heaven and we have the free will to do so.

You have heard reports from the various departments and commissions which we appointed last year, and I would like to thank the chairmen, members, and parish delegates who have contributed to the success of these departments. The two most active departments in the archdiocese this year are the Departments of Christian Education and Sacred Music, because they have a full-time director. We urge you to cooperate with this combined department in order to facilitate its difficult mission. We have combined these two departments, education and music, not only for financial reasons, but because the hymnology and theology of our church are very much related. No Christian education and sacred music materials will be published or sent to our parishes and schools unless they are approved by these departments.

All priests and parish councils are asked to organize effective church schools and church choirs, and every priest is requested to participate in the work of our archdiocese and youth conferences. Any priest who fails to do so without a sound reason will come under canonical discipline. Every priest and parish council must, likewise, abide by our edicts and directives concerning the spiritual and financial matters of the archdiocese.

The Archdiocese and Parish

From this year on, we declare the month of March as the "Archdiocese Month" in the local parishes. This will be an annual event. In January, our parishes will receive a well-published brochure about the archdiocese, its structure, its purpose and its goals. We ask our clergy during this month to deliver homilies related to the life of the archdiocese. We also ask them together with the parish councils to help us increase subscriptions to the *WORD Magazine* which is, in the opinion of many, the best Orthodox publication in this country. March, therefore, is the month to focus on increasing subscriptions, and we will ask our parishes to kindly help us achieve our goal: a subscription in every home of the archdiocese.

Another feature of March will be to undertake a collection in every parish to help our *seminarians*, as they study for service to the Church. It has been our tradition to have this collection on Pentecost Sunday. This is now changed to the last Sunday of March. Our educational endowment fund now gives us about $12,000 a year, but this amount is not enough to cover the expenses of our current fifteen students. We want you to know that each seminarian is costing the archdiocese about $2,000 a year. We need your help since we need well-educated clergy for our archdiocese.

During this past year, we dedicated new churches in Chicago, Illinois, and Portland, Oregon, and the Fellowship Hall and Educational Center in Santa Ana, California. We also broke ground for the new church and community center of Saint Elias Church in Ottawa, Canada, and St. George Cathedral in Worcester, Massachusetts.

Furthermore, the following missions have been established and are functioning to serve the Orthodox faithful:

a. St. Philip's Mission, Fort Lauderdale, Florida;
b. St. Mary's Mission, Yonkers, New York;
c. St. Anne's Western Rite Mission, Burlington, New Jersey;
d. St. Mary's Mission, Baltimore, Maryland;
e. The Antiochian Orthodox Mission in Huntington, West Virginia.

Priests and Parish Councils: No Two Theologies

The following statement is of utmost importance. Please listen and adhere to it strictly and carefully:

For many years we have been administering our local parishes under a false dichotomy, under a dangerous and completely un-Orthodox dualism. Thus we have been preaching two kinds of theologies: one for the church upstairs, and one for the hall downstairs. We do not believe in this "upstairs–downstairs" theology. Nor do we believe in the existence of two classes in the parish opposing each other: namely clergy versus laity. This kind of dualism has caused us many problems.

Some of our clergy do not think that we need organizations and church councils. They think that they can administer the affairs of the parish without help from the laity. Furthermore, they believe that the councils are nothing but an American innovation in our Church and that we do not need them. We completely disagree with this trend of thinking. At the same time, we do have some councils in our archdiocese who believe that the priest can be hired or fired if he is not perfect. The question now is: what human being is perfect? If you are looking for perfect bishops or perfect priests, you are going to look, and look in vain.

I am very reluctant to transfer priests from one parish to another because someone does not like the way a priest combs his hair. I am very reluctant, also, to transfer a priest from one parish to another because his English or Arabic is not perfect. I am further reluctant to transfer a priest from one parish to another because of complaints that he asks questions about the financial affairs of his parish. Priests are appointed and transferred only by the archbishop, after a very thorough investigation about that priest's conduct and behavior, and on the basis of whether or not his ministry in this particular parish is still fruitful.

Likewise, no priest is permitted to submit his resignation to the local council of the parish, and councils are not permitted to go about soliciting priests for their parishes. I believe that we have reached a stage of spiritual maturity when we can look at the parish as the family of God, one which is bound together by the bond of love, and which works together for God's glory.

Saint Peter in his First Epistle, chapter 2 verse 9, wrote:

> You are a chosen generation, a royal priesthood, an holy nation, a peculiar people, that you should show forth the praises of Him who has called you out of darkness into His marvelous light. Which in time past were not a people, but are now the people of God, which had not obtained mercy, but now have obtained mercy.

Thus, my friends, we are no longer living under the yoke of the law but in the grace and fellowship of our Lord and Savior, Jesus Christ. There are no masters and slaves in the parish. The parish is the family of God. This family has a father, who is the priest. Do you mean it when you call him "Father," or not?

The priest who listens to your confessions, who leads you in prayers, who distributes to you the Sacrament of the Holy Eucharist, must be respected as such. At your meetings, he must be given the place of honor. You must listen carefully to his comments and adhere to his recommendations, because who knows better what the parish needs both spiritually and financially than the priest? In his First Epistle to the Corinthians, chapter 4 verse 15, Saint Paul wrote: "For though you have ten thousand instructors in Christ, yet you have not many fathers." The priest, then, is a father to his family and not a dictator. He is the teacher of the faith and must share in the administration of the parish. He must teach his children with love, carefulness, and patience. He must understand that the priesthood is not a vacation, but a vocation. He must understand that the priesthood is a martyrdom for Christ's sake. Any priest who does not believe in these principles will have no place in our archdiocese.

Again and again, my beloved children in Christ, I repeat to you that the parish is the family of God. Our parish councils are elected by the faithful not to fight the priest and find fault with him. They are the elders of the parish and their main function is not to count money downstairs while the priest is preaching upstairs. Rather, their main function is to help the priest insure that the parish is healthy, both spiritually and financially. There is no separation in the life of the parish between the spiritual and financial. Both priests and councils must care for the spiritual and temporal matters of their parishes.

I have served as priest of the archdiocese for eight years and I was very fortunate that I had a board with which to work for the well-being of my parish. I now consider myself very fortunate to have a Board of Trustees to help me administer both the spiritual and financial affairs of the archdiocese.

From Gloom to Glory: The Impossible Dream Continues
My beloved friends, last January 5, while I was preparing for a trip to the Near East, and then to Rome, I suddenly took sick in Washington, D.C. When I discovered the nature of my illness, life seemed gloomy and disappointing. My visions and dreams for a greater future of this archdiocese seemed for a while to be fading away. At that point, I committed myself and my future totally to God. My daily prayer was this:

> The Lord is my Shepherd, I shall not want. . . . Though I walk through the valley of the shadow of death, I fear no evil for Thou art with me. Thy rod and Thy staff, they comfort me (Psalm 23:1–4).

Thank God that my illness was not unto death. Rather, it

was for the glory of God (see John 11:4). After a few weeks in the hospital, I regained my health and strength. The most comforting experience I had while in the hospital was derived from the hundreds of letters and messages which I received from our little children of this archdiocese. I am most thankful to God for their love and your prayers.

Now my physicians say that I am in perfect health, for the scar is completely healed. The gloomy visions and the dark shadows have once again disappeared. The lonely wave which had almost reached the shore turned back to the ocean of life where it belongs, and the impossible dream which we dreamt together last year once again seems possible.

On the Death of Martin Luther King
1968

The martyrdom of Dr. Martin Luther King, Jr., prompted me to write the following article in order to cast away the dark clouds of doubt and confusion hovering over this great nation which we dearly love.

The Devastating Roots of the Problem
The most explosive, devastating and cancerous problem which confronts our society today is racism. This problem is deeply rooted in the history of the United States, and it will never be solved by legislation and demonstration, nor by looting, shooting, burning and destruction.

The tragic relations between black and white people in this country lie not in the structure of the economic system, nor in the mountains, nor in streams, nor valleys, nor in the hamlets and cities of our great nation, but in the heart and conscience of the American people.

After the Second World War, civil rights movements were organized mainly by black leaders to liberate the black people from the prison of illiteracy, ignorance, oppression and poverty.

Such civil rights movements took two different directions: one of hatred and violence led by a militant minority of blacks, and the other of nonviolence and passive resistance spirited by the late Dr. Martin Luther King and the majority of the African-American people.

Despite the fact that the late Dr. King and his followers preached nonviolence in solving the problems of the black people, a few militant blacks resorted to violence and hatred as means of expressing the black people's frustration in America. Thus we witnessed last year one of the hottest summers in the history of this country. Disorder broke out in several large cities, which became victims of lawlessness, looting, killing and burning. The skies of America became darkened by the thick clouds of hatred and bitterness between the black and white citizens.

To the dismay of people of good will, the efforts at keeping the civil rights movement nonviolent failed due to the resistance of so-called Christian leaders who comprised a part of the National Council of Churches.

I was deeply shocked and very disappointed when I read in the religious section of *Time Magazine* (March 16, 1968, issue) an article entitled, "Theology in Defense of Violence."

This article stated, "At the heart of the Christian message is peace on earth, good will to man." In spite of this injunction to concord and reconciliation, the article states that a growing number of theologians and churchmen are willing to endorse violence and even revolution as a means of achieving social justice. In Detroit last October, at a conference on "Church and Society" sponsored by the National Council of Churches, one group of delegates argued that Christians should accept violence as a valid means of attacking the problems of racism and poverty. In the United States, especially among the renewal-minded Catholics, there is a certain amount of sympathy with these views. The Rev. William Cook, a Methodist minister with the Interfaith Council on Religion and International Affairs, thinks that last year's Newark and Detroit riots "were not only understandable, but justifiable."

On April 4, 1968, Dr. Martin Luther King, Jr., was cut down by an assassin's bullet. The next day, April 5, I sent to Mrs. Martin Luther King, Jr., and to my black brothers the following telegram:

> The brutal, cruel, barbaric, and violent assassination of your beloved husband and civil rights leader, Dr. King, who devoted his entire life to nonviolence and social justice, has deeply shocked the conscience of this nation and the entire world. May his innocent blood wash away our guilt and sin and inaugurate a new era in race relations in our country. Although his death was most

untimely, his life and sacrifice will be recorded in history forever. On behalf of myself and the Antiochian Orthodox Archdiocese of New York and All North America, I offer to you my deepest sympathy.

Applying Orthodox Theology

Where do we as Orthodox Christians stand vis-à-vis all of these tragic events? What do God and the Church teach us about social justice, racism, revolution, and violence? According to our Orthodox theology, we fundamentally and drastically disagree with the present trend of the National Council of Churches on the so-called theology of violence. This does not mean that we do not have anything to say about the many social ills which are plaguing our society in this most dangerous time in our history. We strongly condemn racism, segregation, and the exploitation of the poor.

In the Book of Genesis, we read the following: "Then God said, 'Let us make man in our image, after our likeness'" (Genesis 1:26). This does not apply only to the white man, but to all men, regardless of color, race or creed.

The European Christians, against all Christian teaching, have exploited other races throughout history—especially in Africa and Asia, by means of colonization and economic abuses. Today, Asia is revolting and Africa is awakening, and it is time for the white people to realize once and for all that they are a small minority among the races of the world. Woe to them if they do not stop taking advantage of these underdeveloped nations. The Incarnate Logos did not assume only the nature of the white race but the entire nature of men, except sin, regardless of whether they are white, black or yellow.

The whole humanity became one in the God-man, Christ Jesus. "There is neither Jew nor Greek, there is neither slave nor free, there is neither male nor female, for you are all one in Christ Jesus" (Galatians 3:28, 29). Unfortunately, there is a tendency in Orthodox theology to be apathetic toward the world and its social problems. I do not find any biblical foundation for such a trend in our theology. Christ was very much involved with humankind and its problems. His greatness lies in the fact that He identified Himself with the poor, the slave, the oppressed, and the despised. He not only identified Himself with such people, but He went further than that: He died for them and for all mankind. "For God so loved the world that He gave His only Begotten Son, that whoever believes in Him should not perish but have eternal life. For God sent His Son into the world *not* to condemn the world, but that the world might be *saved through him*" (John 3:16, 17). God loved us and this is precisely why He entered history; this is why eternity invaded time and heaven embraced the earth. It was indeed a sad day when Adam and Eve left Paradise. One of the Church Fathers said, "When Adam and Eve left Paradise, they saw the sun set for the first time." According to the Gospel of John, "The Word became flesh" (John 1:2) so that the sun which Adam and Eve saw setting may shine forever.

How We Will Be Judged
On many occasions we hear Christ through the Gospels admonishing the rich to share their wealth with the poor. When He shall come again in His glory to judge the world, He will judge us according to our faith and deeds.

> When the Son of man comes in His glory, and all the angels with Him, then He will sit on His glorious throne. Before Him will be gathered all the nations, and He will separate them one from another as a shepherd separates the sheep from the goats, and He will place the sheep at His right hand, and the goats on His left. There the King will say to those at His right hand, "Come, O blessed of My Father, inherit the Kingdom prepared for you from the foundation of the world; for I was hungry and you gave Me food, I was thirsty and you gave Me drink, I was a stranger and you welcomed Me, I was naked and you clothed Me, I was sick and you visited

Me. I was in prison and you came to Me. . . . (Matthew 25:31–46).

On this, and this alone, we will be judged!

The Scriptures and Fathers on Christ, Social Justice, and Violence
1968

The death of Dr. Martin Luther King haunted me to such an extent that I felt compelled to undertake a deeper look into the phenomena related to our Orthodox Faith in light of social justice and violence. Naturally, I turned to the Scripture and the Fathers. Let us explore their teachings.

Scriptural and Patristic Roots
Christ and the early Church were strong advocates of social justice. They spoke vehemently and frankly against the monopoly of wealth by one man or one class at the expense of others. The Book of Acts points out that the Apostles shared what they had with the early Christian community: ". . . and the multitude of them that believed were of one heart and of one soul: neither said any of them that aught of the things which he possessed was his own; but they had all things in common" (Acts 4:32–33).

The Diaconate in the early Church was established precisely for a social purpose.

> Now in the days when the disciples were increasing in number, the Hellenists murmured against the Hebrews because their widows were neglected in the daily distribution. And the twelve summoned the body of disciples and said, "It is not right that we should give up preaching the word of God to serve tables. Therefore, brethren, pick out from among you seven men of good repute, full of the spirit and of wisdom, whom we may appoint to this duty" (Acts 4:1–5).

The main responsibility of the deacons was to distribute the offerings of the faithful to the poor. In the *Didache* (an early Christian document), we read the following: "Thou must not refuse the needy but share everything with thy brethren. Say not that this is thy property, for if we enjoy together the eternal blessings it should be the more so with temporal ones."

St. John Chrysostom and St. Basil the Great were among the most outspoken Fathers against social injustice and the monopoly of wealth.

> Say not I am spending what is my own, I am enjoying what is my own. No, not your own, but other people's. Precisely because you make an inhuman use of it and say I have a right for my personal enjoyment that which belongs to me. I maintain that those possessions do not belong to you. They belong together to you and your neighbors, just as sunshine, air, earth and all the rest (Chrysostom, *Homily 10 on Corinthians 1*).

To this St. Basil the Great adds:

> Who is covetous? He who is not content with what is sufficient. Who is a robber? He who takes away other people's property. Are you not covetous? Are you not a robber if you make your own that which has been given you in stewardship? He who takes another's clothing is called a thief, he who does not clothe the naked, although he could do so, deserves no better name. The corn which you store belongs to the hungry; the cloak which you keep in your trunk belongs to the naked; the shoes which are rotting in your house belong to those who go barefoot; the silver which you hid in the ground belongs to the needy (St. Basil, *Homily 6:7*).

The courage of the early Fathers in speaking against the indifferent and affluent upper class and injustice in society is quite amazing. I believe that the apostles of eighteenth- and nineteenth-century socialism could have learned a great deal from the Church Fathers, who never hesitated to demonstrate with all honesty and simplicity that we are indeed our brothers' keepers.

Unfortunately, we are living today in the age of the de-Christianization and dehumanization of man. Man has become nothing but an object which can be eliminated if one is powerful enough to make oneself comfortable. We have reached the point where my existence seems to be the limitation of yours. You do not care whether or not I live or die. This is precisely the philosophy of "dog eat dog." Some of us even enjoy watching suicidal scenes. For example, in New York City it has been noted many times that the man on the street was either an excited spectator to suicidal attempts, or indifferent to the tragedies of others.

St. Basil spoke against such an unchristian attitude and way of life:

> Woe unto them that join house to house 'til there be no place for others (Isaiah 5:8). And what do you do? Do you not find a thousand pretexts to rob your neighbor? You say, his house stands in my light; it is too noisy; tramps go there. On one pretext or another you drive him out, persecute him till you force him to move. The sea knows its boundaries; the night does not overstep its appointed limits. But a possessive man has no respect for time, does not recognize boundaries, and like fire he attacks everything and swallows it up (St. Basil, *Homily Against the Rich*).

The Church Fathers were very mindful and fundamentally opposed to social evils. However, there is no evidence of civil disobedience, of inciting class against class, race against race, or nation against nation in their preaching or writings. As a matter of fact, when St. John Chrysostom was ordered by the emperor to leave the city of Constantinople, he chose to leave during the night so that his followers would not see him leave and thus revolt, causing bloodshed and destruction in the imperial city.

The Message of the Gospel Against Social Injustice

Christ and His Church did not compromise with social evils and social injustice, yet they were fundamentally against reducing the eternal message of the Gospel to nothing but social action. The militant Church is struggling in the world, yet she is not of this world. A good Christian must never forget that heaven is his ultimate goal and that he has no permanent city here on earth: "Seek ye first the Kingdom of God and His righteousness; and all these things shall be added unto you" (Matthew 7:33).

The New Testament is full of references to the fact that our Lord did not come to this world to establish an earthly kingdom with the best political system. He made it very clear that his kingdom ". . . is not of this world" (John 18:36). This does not mean that we permit social injustice to reign in society, nor does it mean that we should let the poor, the oppressed and the despised choke in their poverty.

Dietrich Bonhoeffer, a German theologian, wrote in his *Letters From Prison*:

> There are people who are regarded as frivolous, and some Christians think it impious for anyone to hope and prepare for a better earthly future. They think that the meaning of present events is chaos, disorder and catastrophe; and in resignation or pious escapism they surrender all responsibility for reconstruction and for future generations. It may be that the day of judgment will dawn tomorrow, and in that case and not before we shall gladly stop working for a better future (p. 16).

The same author asks, "Are we still of any use?" He answers his own question:

We have been silent witnesses of evil deeds; we have been drenched by many storms; are we still of any use? What we shall need is not geniuses, or cynics, or clever tacticians, but plain, honest and straightforward men. Will our inward power of resistance be strong enough, and our honesty with ourselves remorseless enough for us to find our way back to simplicity and straightforwardness? (pp. 16, 17).

The New Testament never ignored man and his social problems. I believe that Jesus was, still is, and will continue until the end of time to be the most dynamic revolutionary figure in history. In His disdain for social injustice and hypocrisy, He uttered the strongest terms against the scribes and the Pharisees. He never tolerated nor condoned evil.

Now the question is, what form or direction does His revolution take? Did He advocate bloodshed, violence, burning, destruction, hate and animosity in order to reform society and abolish social injustice? The answer to this question can be easily found in the Gospels: "Do violence to no man, neither accuse any falsely" (Luke 3:14). "Then Jesus said unto him, put up again thy sword into its place, for all they that take the sword shall perish by the sword" (Matthew 26:52). "Ye have heard that it hath been said, an eye for an eye, and a tooth for a tooth. But I say unto you that ye resist not evil, but whosoever shall smite thee on thy right cheek, turn to him the other also" (Matthew 6:38, 39). "Blessed are the peacemakers for they shall be called the children of God" (Matthew 2:9). "Recompense to no man evil for evil. Provide things honest in the sight of all men" (Romans 12:17).

Another great example of Christ's resistance to violence and hate is His historic entrance into the city of Jerusalem. The Master on that day had reached the height of His popularity in this world. It could have been very easy for Him to enter the city riding on a horse with a sword in His hand, or riding in a luxurious golden chariot like the Roman emperors. It could have been very easy for Him to order His followers to carry swords and spears. It could have been very easy for Him to crucify all His enemies and cause a great deal of bloodshed in Jerusalem. But instead He entered the city riding a lowly and humble beast. His followers greeted Him and walked with Him carrying no destructive weapons, but palm branches in their hands and songs of peace on their lips.

In Violence, We Profit Nothing
How could any true Christian dare advocate violence as a solution to our social problems? Did the assassination of Martin Luther King, Jr., silence the voice of justice in this land? Did the long hot summer of 1967 with all the shooting, etc., solve the plight of America's deprived citizens?

Many civil rights leaders could be murdered, but their blood throughout this land will continue to cry, "Murderers, assassins, and slaves to your hate and fear!" Many American cities could be burned by the fires of chaos and destruction, but we profit nothing. Unless we burn by the holy fire the hate and the slavery from the American heart, neither the black nor the white will find peace, freedom or justice in this land.

In order to solve the difficult problems which we have been facing, we must concentrate first, and above all, on the human personality, which has been distorted by hate and sin. Instead of directing our efforts to demonstrations, civil disobedience and other violent and negative actions, we must try to rid the American society of its inherited complexes of hate, fear and prejudice.

Therefore, our revolution must begin within the heart of the individual citizen. Harmony and peace in this land must be the reflection of our inner peace and serenity. Unless this inner tranquility is achieved on a personal basis, the might, the wealth, and all the glory of this nation will be reduced to ashes. Violence breeds violence, hate breeds hate, chaos breeds chaos. Ultimately, unless the divine image is restored to the American personality, we will legislate in vain, labor in vain and hope in vain.

A Voice Was Heard in Rama
1968

After Your birth, O beloved of the wretched and the poor,
A voice was heard in Rama,
"Lamentation, weeping, and great mourning, Rachel
Weeping for her children, and would not be comforted
Because they were no more."

O Heavenly Child, Rachel is still weeping
Because the Herod of the twentieth century
Continues to massacre our children
In Rama, Karama and Deir Yaseen.

Rachel is still weeping; Heaven knows whether
Her tears will wash away the innocent blood
Which stains our land. That land which was
Cleansed by Your tears and blood.

How could Rachel be comforted, while Your friends,
The little children, are slain anew, deprived,
Starved and have become strangers and wanderers
On the roads of life.

We, like Rachel, refuse to be consoled until
Herod chokes and justice reigns in the conscience of
    mankind.

Between the manger where You were born and
Calvary where You were killed,
Stretched, hanged on it with You, all of our
People who were crucified by Herod.

We shall not seek You any more in the manger
Of Bethlehem because we know where You are.
You are with us in the tents, in the hills, in the
Valleys and in the narrows of the roads.

Laborers Together

You are with us in our struggle, in our misery,
In our hunger, in our nakedness, in our tears
And in every drop of our blood.

You are a stranger, like us,
Even amongst our own people.

You are a stranger, like us,
Even in the dens and dark caves of the earth.

You are, like us, burned by napalm and
Shattered by bullets.

O friend of the sufferers, after the long dark night,
The dawn of resurrection will break out and the heavy stone
Will be rolled away from the door of the tomb.

After the long dark night, a new day will dawn
Whose sun will never set.

After the long dark night, Rachel will rejoice for her
Children will rise from the grave of history and will
March to their homes, wave after wave
Facing the tanks and rockets of their enemies with the stones
   of their land.

Yes after the long dark night, they will return
To Jaffa and Haifa, to Khaleel and Jaleel,
To Rama and Karama, to Jerusalem and
The Mount of Olives, to Your manger in
Bethlehem and Your deserted home in Nazareth.

O beloved of the oppressed
We have a rendezvous with You in Jerusalem.

Editor's Endnotes

1. Other issues in the 1968 Pittsburgh Convention address with which the Metropolitan deals for the future of the Church and his archdiocese are as follows:

   A. In wishing to uplift the dignity and honor of the clergy, an issue which he continues throughout his episcopate, Metropolitan Philip establishes an insurance plan and calls the local parish to participate in realizing his goal. As part of his new organization of the archdiocese, he appoints an Insurance Committee.

   B. Regarding **the clergy,** Metropolitan Philip addresses the need to financially support **theological education** and Orthodox seminaries; mentions the fact that at that time there were fifteen Antiochian seminarians on complete scholarships; summarizes the priests who were accepted and released from the archdiocese.

   C. Regarding his own **schedule of travel,** Metropolitan Philip reviews his international meetings with former president Dwight D. Eisenhower in which he thanks him for his support of the Arab refugees (after the Arab-Israeli conflict of 1967); reviews the meetings of the Holy Synod 1968 in which the St. George parish of Canton, Ohio, was declared properly in his archdiocese; reviews his meetings with President Charles Helou and Foreign Minister Fuad Butros of Lebanon; reviews his discussions with the Board of Trustees of the Balamand University regarding both the new buildings given by his archdiocese and the future of the Academy; reviews his meeting with Pope Paul VI of Rome regarding the fate of Jerusalem and the millions of Arab refugees.

2. Metropolitan Philip had already met with President Lyndon Johnson in 1967 to discuss the Arab-Israeli conflict.

3. *The reader should know that earlier in the year 1968, the Metropolitan suffered a heart attack that threatened his life (see his closing comments in the 1968 address at Pittsburgh). Those who know him say this radically changed the remainder of his life and ministry.*

Chapter 4

PRAY TO THE LORD OF THE HARVEST

> *Do we have the shoulders of giants and the arms of heroes to carry this yoke? Are we willing to risk our lives so that the small branches may live and reach for the sky? There are two roads in life; one leads to heaven and the other to hell. Which road are we willing to choose?*
> Metropolitan Philip

- *Pray to the Lord of the Harvest: Restless But not Despondent, 1969*
- *Meditation on the Eve of Christmas, 1969*

AND HE LEADS THEM

This State of the Archdiocese address, given in 1969 in Miami, shows the restlessness of the young Metropolitan to get things done, i.e., to move his archdiocese along with more fervor and speed. He is dissatisfied with the response of the archdiocese to his vision of beginning new missions for America, of providing full-time directors for the thirteen new departments, of building a stronger base for future ministries, of helping the poor in this country and abroad, etc.

The reader should especially remember two facts as this text is read. First, this was the height of an American culture steeped in the Vietnam War, the campus revolts, the rallies of a youth anxiously searching for meaning. Indeed, the 1960s and 1970s were a paradoxical age of both anarchy and idealism. The second fact is that, although Philip is trying to grow an archdiocese, in the midst of that restlessness he is himself, as he has always been, a person of restlessness! One can truly sense this in the following text: "Things are moving too slowly ... things must get done ... do not avoid the narrow way ... let us not be satisfied with our nickel per week ... the Holy Synod of Antioch engaging in vain talk and fruitless debate ... Orthodoxy in America is still in a ghetto mentality," etc. Of course, what saves the restlessness from becoming despondency and despair is that Metropolitan Philip, as can be seen here, turns that energy outward, seeking to convert it into a constructive end for the good of the Church. Thus, the restless Metropolitan, in the midst of a restless age, looks to the potential harvest all about him, and calls his people: **"Pray to the Lord of the harvest to send out the laborers."**

In this same year, Philip writes a second meditation on the Nativity of the Lord which we include in this chapter. Like his address in Miami, it demonstrates, even in such a profound and sanctified moment, that that same "restlessness" abounds: "Feed me with your heavenly bread, for the bread of this world will never satisfy my hunger. ... Take me with you to Mount Tabor and let me bathe in your eternal light."

J. J. A.

Pray to the Lord of the Harvest: Restless but Not Despondent
Miami, 1969

We are gathered by the Grace of the Holy Spirit as the Family of God to reassess and reevaluate our life in Christ, and to examine the harvest of the past year. To live in Christ and to spread the good news of His Gospel is not an easy task, especially in this violent and critical time in history. Living in Christ places on our shoulders a heavy yoke. Do we have the shoulders of giants and the arms of heroes to carry this yoke? Are we willing to risk our lives so that the small branches may live and reach for the sky? There are two roads in life: one leads to heaven, and the other to hell. Which road are we willing to choose?

The Narrow Gate, the Wide Gate
In Matthew 7:13, 14, 19, 20, Christ said:

> Enter by the narrow gate; for the gate is wide and the way is easy that leads to destruction, and those who enter by it are many. For the gate is narrow, and the way is hard that leads to life, and those who find it are few.... Every tree that does not bear good fruit is cut down and thrown into the fire. Thus you will know them by their fruits.

The wide gate is easy, beautiful, well-paved, covered with roses and lilacs, but this gate leads to destruction. The narrow gate is ugly, dangerous, bloody, and full of skulls and bones. But this gate leads to life eternal. This gate leads you to Calvary, and the only joy which you experience in it is the joy of the Cross.

Did you experience this joy during the past year? I pray that some of you did. As for myself, I have experienced only moments of that joy. The rest of my days were full of anxiety, restlessness, and dissatisfaction. Some of you might ask: "Why are you dissatisfied? We have strong organizations, we are building churches and cultural centers, we are contributing our nickel per week to the archdiocese, and some Sundays we sell candy or we organize spaghetti dinners to help the poor." Yes, you do all these nice things, but I am *still* dissatisfied. I am the first among you to be condemned because of the lack of commitment on my part to the Cross of the Master. I am dissatisfied because the inner temple is nothing but ashes. I am dissatisfied because my nickel per week is too insignificant and not enough to support our seminarians and seminaries, provide for auxiliary bishops, open new missions, educate more seminarians, help the poor in this country and abroad, build a new archdiocesan headquarters, provide full-time directors for our thirteen departments, help our young people to find themselves in this turbulent time, and improve our religious education and sacred music materials.

The Holy Synod, Orthodoxy in America
I am dissatisfied because the Holy Synod of Antioch is still engaged in vain talk and fruitless debate; it has lost its sense of history and destiny. When sacred duty called us to cross the ocean last April for Lebanon to attend the meetings of the Holy Synod, we did it gladly because of our devotion to the Mother Church. But my friends, "we have labored all night long to no avail." After twenty-five days of meetings, we accomplished nothing except the reading of the minutes of the last synod meeting. We experienced much distress and frustration, and came back convinced beyond the shadow of a doubt that we must work hard for a united Orthodoxy in America, for our own sake and for the sake of the mother churches. We shall continue to support the See of Antioch both spiritually and financially, but we are not willing to waste time anymore on nothingness.

The only joy which we had during our trip was derived from our visit with the young seminarians at the Balamand School. The new Theological Academy which we are building there is almost completed, but we have no idea how this academy is going to be staffed or operated financially. Only the Almighty God knows.

I am also dissatisfied with the progress towards a united Orthodox Church in America. You know well that our archdiocese is not the stumbling block. As a matter of fact, we are the only archdiocese which is doing something concrete to achieve this goal. We have been using English in our churches for many years; we have opened the door of Orthodoxy for many converts, both clergy and laity alike; we have sponsored and encouraged pan-Orthodox parishes and missions throughout this land; we are the least nationalistic among the Orthodox jurisdictions in this country. But if we cannot convince the rest of our Orthodox brethren to rise above their ghetto mentalities and face the challenges of this cosmic era, I cannot see any Orthodox unity in the foreseeable future.

At our request last January, we met with some Orthodox hierarchs and theologians to discuss the prospects of one united Orthodox Church in America. The meeting was very fruitful, except that it was not followed up by more meetings, and when the executive secretary of our archdiocese called the hierarch who promised to host the second meeting to remind him of his promise, the answer was, "We have no time." So do not be deceived when you read in some Orthodox magazines that we Antiochians are taking the passive role in the process of Orthodox unity in America.

These were some of last year's disappointments, but disappointments and dissatisfaction do not mean despair and discouragement. We have a definite determination to go forward and upward in spite of all difficulties.

Some of the joy which I have experienced last year resulted from the following achievements:

Missions: If we want to find a description for the last year in the history of our archdiocese, we may say that it was a year of missions. I am happy to inform you that two of our missions graduated to the rank of parishes: St. Michael's of San Fernando Valley, California, and St. Mary's of Yonkers, New York. The rest of our missions in Pleasant Hills, California, Tucson, Arizona, Huntington, West Virginia, and Fort Lauderdale, Florida, are doing well. We are planning, in the near future, to start two more missions, one in San Diego, California, and one in Jacksonville, Florida. In order to achieve our missionary goal, we need more money and more priests. "The harvest is plentiful, but the laborers are few; *pray therefore the Lord of the harvest* to send out laborers into His harvest" (Matthew 9:37, 38).

We have reached a stage in our development when the divine command to "go therefore and make disciples of all nations" (Matthew 28:19) is once again meaningful. America is scattered with groups of Orthodox families of various national origins hungry for church life. Many have accepted substitutes for their children and many have been lost, but there is still a tremendous missionary potential among the unchurched Orthodox in this land. Every good-sized town has a nucleus, almost every city has a group unable to worship in the foreign parishes confined to a single language group.

Whenever Antiochians are among the unchurched and we can find a priest, we do not hesitate to encourage a mission. Our first concern, however, is with unchurched people of our own background. Antiochian Christians have never been nationalistic in their faith, thus, we welcome any who are not committed to another diocese. It is too late to create branch ghettos. Orthodox unity in America can grow from the grassroots as well as from the top. We cannot, like Byzantium, withdraw into our established centers—that is the road to defeat and organizational death.

When we reach out in our planning and thinking with our funds and energy, with our hopes and dreams, we shall find that many local problems will be forgotten as we focus on new goals. Our young people tell us that there is nothing deadlier than an establishment running in the same rut year after year. We say the Holy Spirit is creative, inspiring, life-giving, but we try to domesticate Him and keep Him caged and limited. We must communicate the Spirit, stir up the grace that is in us. Remember, we are the successors of the Apostles, the messengers of God, and mission is the channel for this life with the Spirit.

What are the goals of missions? First, we must provide for communities of our own people who have no church, but need one. This goal has priority because with each passing year the individuals in such groups drift farther and farther away from our orbit. Second, we must encourage pan-Orthodox groups to organize parishes to serve all Orthodox people, regardless of national origin. Lastly, we must continue the policy of this archdiocese that began in 1905 of providing for converts from the non-Orthodox world who have found the true faith.

We are guided by certain policies and principles in pursuing these goals. There must be reason to believe that a given group will eventually attain self-support with a worship center, a regular pastor, and a budget qualifying for parish status in the archdiocese. The field must be free; we would not, in the words of Saint Paul, "build on another man's foundation," especially in pan-Orthodox projects. We must have priests and lay leaders who are equal to the difficult task of missionary work. Of course, there must be money, but more important, there must be the love of God and the dedication of His faithful servants. Let mission be the theme of our church life as it was in apostolic times, and among the early Christians.

Our Young People: The outstanding reality which marked our conferences this year was the concern of our young people with the Church, society, and the world. Our young people are searching with anxiety and intellectual curiosity for new spiritual horizons and for a more meaningful life in Christ. I am very much encouraged by their search. It is this increasing intellectual ferment that is calling into birth once more the compelling Socratic questions: What is the purpose of life? The meaning of work? What is man? Plato gave the answer: "Man is that creature who is constantly in search of himself. A creature who at every moment of his existence must examine and scrutinize the conditions of his existence. He is a being in search of meaning."

Besides their healthy search for meaning, our youth this past year have conducted a successful charity drive to help unfortunate people in the Middle East. This was their second charity drive and it surpassed their first one. We thank God for the Christian zeal of these young people.

Drinking His Cup, Accepting His Baptism

My beloved friends, in conclusion let me remind you again that the gate is narrow and the road is difficult, and unless we become serious about this glorious faith it will be taken away from us. If we want to ascend to the peak of the mountain and bathe in the eternal light of the Transfiguration, we have to make a painful decision and commit ourselves totally to the agony of the Cross. Nicholas Berdyaev said, "No man who is divided can be free, and a man who cannot make the free act of choosing the object of his love is condemned to this division."

Can you then drink His cup? Can you accept His baptism of fire? Are you willing to go through hell in order to reach the gates of Paradise? If you are willing to do so, you will reach the peak, you will destroy all boundaries, you will overcome all limitations, and finally, you will gloriously shout with Nikos Kazantzakis: "Die every moment, but say, death does not exist."

Meditation on the Nativity of the Lord
1969

Lord,
> What shall I offer You on Your birthday in return for Your infinite love?
> I have neither gold nor silver, neither myrrh nor frankincense.
> My house is without a roof. I have no room for You; not even a manger.
> My soul is even darker than the clouds of my passion.
> My eyes are too dim to look beyond the horizon of myself.
> Help me behold Your bright star; "For in thy light shall we see light."

Lord,
> You have been knocking on my door for many years,
> But I never dared let You in because my garment is not white as snow.
> Forgive me if I do not invite You to my table,
>> for my table is full of everything You despise.
>
> I have denied You more than Peter.
> I have doubted You more than Thomas.
> I have betrayed You more than Judas.
> My hands are empty. My lips are not clean to sing Your praise.
> And my heart is wrinkled with sorrow like a withered leaf under autumn's wind.

Lord,
> The only thing I can offer You on Your birthday is myself.
> Drown me in the ocean of Your love.
> Feed me with Your heavenly bread, for the bread of this world will never satisfy my hunger.

Quench my thirst with Your divine fountain, for the water of this earth will never satisfy my thirst.
Give me Your eyes to see what You see, Your ears to hear what You hear and Your heart to love what You love.
Take me with You to Mount Tabor and let me bathe in Your eternal light.

Lord,
"Create a clean heart in me. Cast me not away from Thy face,
Restore unto me the joy of Thy salvation, and strengthen me with a perfect spirit."
Teach me how to pray in simple words, for only through prayers
I may overcome my loneliness.
Help me to care for the needy, the oppressed, the orphans, the sinners and the despised whom You love.
As I kneel before Your manger with love and humility I beseech You to listen to my prayers.

Editor's Endnotes:

1. *Other issues in the Miami address of 1969 with which the Metropolitan dealt for the future of the Church and his archdiocese are as follows:*

    A. *Regarding the **Clergy:** Philip emphasizes the need for those with Master's Degrees to pursue higher education, thus preparing specialists in various areas of theological and pastoral knowledge; summarizes new clergy accepted into the archdiocese, and new ordinations; mentions the release of clergy and those who requested a leave of absence; finally, remembers the clergy who fell asleep in Christ.*

    B. *Regarding the **archdiocese office:** Father Antoun Khoury, later consecrated Bishop Antoun, was to be transferred from Toronto to assume responsibility of managing the archdiocesan office with the assistance of a professional secretary.*

    C. *Regarding the **youth movement:** he reviews the self-examination that they undertook during the past year, the result being to make the annual youth conferences more spiritually and intellectually meaningful.*

2. *The reader should know that it was at this convention that the official name of the archdiocese was accepted: The Antiochian Orthodox Christian Archdiocese of New York and All North America. Dropping the word "Syrian," although it met with some resistance, was final.*

Chapter 5

THIS HOME IS YOUR HOME

> *When the Church loses her missionary dimension . . . when she fails to renew herself, she becomes complacent and stagnant; she becomes satisfied with the status quo.*
>
> Metropolitan Philip

- *This Home is your Home: The Charism to Build, 1970*
- *The Place of Women in the Church, 1970*
- *Paschal Meditation, 1970*

Our first address, given in 1970 at Montreal, was chosen for this collection because it represents the beginning of a certain trend. This trend well matched the charism of Metropolitan Philip to eventually become the dynamic builder he showed himself to be. The group he addresses is the Men's Club of Montreal, and the time is five years into his ministry. The charism, however, is developed at a cost: Philip begins an exhausting journey from Canada to Florida, from New York to California, knowing that a new phase must begin: raising substantial funds, as he says, for "the work of the Church and the proclamation of the Gospel." What exacerbates the cost of this trend, the reader should remember, is that this rigorous schedule so closely follows the heart attack he suffered two years earlier in 1968. His doctors recommended against this rigorous schedule.

*Relative to the address itself, Philip, as he will do throughout his ministry, appeals to the members: "Help me to help the Church." The appeal was issued at a time in history before he had auxiliary bishops and when the archdiocese was in transition from Brooklyn, New York, to Englewood, New Jersey. A new home, it was recognized, was needed for proper offices and chancery. Of course, as he has continually done since that day, he welcomes all his people to the headquarters: **"This home is your home."***

Also included in this chapter is a document which the young Metropolitan wrote as a response to the many questions which were being raised during his rigorous schedule of traversing the country. Many serious questions were being asked of him regarding the place of women in the Church. After noticing the radical positions which were being taken during his many parish discussions, he decides to write the commentary on "The Place of Women in the Church." One can see that this was the prelude to his thought and initiative in creating the Antiochian Orthodox Christian Women of North America (AOCWNA) three years later in 1973.

Finally, we include in this chapter Philip's "Paschal Meditation," written as a reflection of his own life and service in light of the Crucifixion and Resurrection of our Lord.

J. J. A.

This Home Is Your Home: The Charism to Build
1970

Reverend Fathers and leaders of our community in this city, I am most thankful to you for giving me this opportunity to talk to you this evening about the past five years in the life of our archdiocese.

Five years have elapsed since my consecration on August 14, 1966. I will reflect on those years, not in order to be a prisoner of the past or to dwell in the house of yesterday, nor to boast or to be proud of my personal achievements, but to rejoice with you in the work which we have done together for the glory of God and His Holy Church.

The Immediate Past: What Is Going to Happen Now?
At dawn of a wintry and gloomy day of February, 1966, Metropolitan Antony ended his lifelong struggle for the Church and departed from life temporal to life eternal. The news of his departure weighed heavily on our souls, and the entire archdiocese plunged into bitter sorrow and tears. During the sad days of Metropolitan Antony's funeral, we were overwhelmed by a sense of uncertainty and fear of the future. The main question which tormented our minds was: What is going to happen to this archdiocese after Archbishop Antony? I could hear his voice shouting from the grave, "Oh, ye of little faith." Little we knew that the Church is founded on Christ, and her survival does not depend on mortal beings such as Antony, Philip, Ilyas or any other person.

On March 16, 1966, our unity was magnificently demonstrated when orderly and peacefully, we nominated three clergy for the widowed archdiocese according to the Constitution of the Antiochian Patriarchate. After the nomination, we lived through six months of anxiety and frustration, not knowing what to expect from a divided Synod in the Church of Antioch. But despite the uncertainties of that period, we made it very clear to the Mother Church that this archdiocese is firmly established and strongly united and that no power in the world will be able to destroy its unity. Finally, on August 5, the Eve of the Transfiguration, the Holy Synod honored your wishes and elected my humble person to be your Shepherd in Christ, despite my weakness and unworthiness.

On August 14, 1966, in St. Elias Monastery, the same place where I began my life in the Church as a subdeacon in 1945, I was consecrated Archbishop of this great Archdiocese of New York and all North America. Immediately after my consecration, I flew to San Francisco to preside over the 1966 Archdiocesan Convention. During the convention, I had the pleasure, for the first time, of officially meeting with the Board of Trustees of this archdiocese. I found myself in complete harmony with a dedicated group of people who have given so much of their time, money and energy for the progress of this archdiocese.

Now we must ask ourselves the main question: "What have we done in the past five years?" In answering this question, I will focus on five points among the many others we have sought to accomplish.

The Building of the New Balamand Academy of Theology

In 1965, Metropolitan Antony decided to build a theological school for the Mother Church in order to create a spiritual renaissance in the entire Arab East. Thus, to accomplish this project, he pledged $250,000. Unfortunately, Metropolitan Antony fell asleep in Christ before the realizing of his dream. The Board of Trustees of our archdiocese was determined to fulfill Metropolitan Antony's pledge. On August 15, 1966, one day after my consecration, we broke ground for the new academy. Our $250,000 pledge was fulfilled in 1969. In May, 1970, the Board of Trustees of the new academy requested an additional $44,000 to finish the last phases of the building. Our

Board considered this request and $44,000 was sent to Balamand. To date, we have spent $301,000 on this school. I am happy to report to you that the school opened last October and that twenty students of theology were admitted.

The Arab Refugee Foundation

After the tragic war of June 1967, we initiated a drive for the relief of Arab refugees which netted $90,000. With interest and additional gifts, the total value of this fund is now $100,000. Preferring long-term results rather than quickly dissipated emergency measures, our Board of Trustees established a permanent foundation to educate the children of the refugees in the fields of science, medicine, business administration and technology. A Board of Trustees was appointed to administer this foundation and to devise fair and efficient methods of choosing qualified candidates for scholarships. Last year, our foundation paid fifty per cent of the tuition of sixty-five students who are studying in the Near East and Europe. Most of the recipients of our help were students from Kneitra, Syria. Kneitra is one of the communities overrun by the invaders during the June War of 1967.

Between the Balamand Academy, the Arab Refugee Foundation and our annual grant to the Mother Church, we have spent in the Near East in the past five years more than a half-million dollars.

The Clergy Insurance Plan

In 1967, I brought to the attention of our Board of Trustees the necessity of a group insurance plan for our clergy to give them some financial security and to safeguard our parishes from financial burdens, when and if their priests get sick or retire. The Board of Trustees was very receptive to this idea, and we started work immediately. A commission was appointed under the chairmanship of Father James Meena to present to the Board the best possible plan. After a year and a half of meeting and consultation with insurance brokers, underwriters and consultants,

a program was finally adopted on April 2, 1968, which provides the following benefits:
   a. Retirement benefits
   b. Death benefits
   c. Long-term disability
   d. Basic hospitalization

In order to make this plan possible for all the clergy, the Board of Trustees of the archdiocese agreed to pay up to forty percent of the cost of this plan—the balance to be paid equally between the priest and the parish. Last May the program was reviewed and updated. Information was sent to our priests and parishes in this regard. You might be interested to know that for the three-year period ending May 15, 1971, there were 134 claims paid to the clergy and their dependents for total disbursements of $46,488. These payments do not include life insurance payments made by the archdiocese to the families of deceased clergy. I have appointed Father John Badeen, of Detroit, Michigan, an expert in this field, to be the permanent chair of our Insurance Commission to constantly review and watch this plan and advise us accordingly.

New Parishes and Missions

Missionary work is the most important aspect in the life of the Church. Since her inception, the Church started as a mission. Our Lord commissioned His disciples to "go and teach all nations, baptizing them in the name of the Father and the Son and of the Holy Spirit." When the Church loses her missionary dimension, she becomes complacent and stagnant. Bearing this in mind, we have established in the past five years, the following parishes:

   St. George Church of Chicago, Illinois
   The Church of the Holy Resurrection, Tucson, Arizona
   St. Michael's Church, Van Nuys, California
   St. George's Church, San Diego, California
   The Church of the Holy Spirit, Huntington, West Virginia
   The Church of the Virgin Mary, Yonkers, New York

We now have five active missions, which are:
  The Mission of the Holy Nativity, Mt. Pleasant, California
  The Mission of St. John, Lake Charles, Louisiana
  St. Anne's Mission, Mt. Holly, New Jersey
  The Mission of St. Andrew the Apostle, Willingboro, New Jersey
  The Mission of St. Philip, Ft. Lauderdale, Florida
Our faithful in Fort Lauderdale this year purchased two and one-half acres of land with two homes on the property. All our new parishes and missions are pan-Orthodox in nature.

New Archdiocese Headquarters
For fifteen years, we have talked about a new chancery for our archdiocese. The present facilities are no longer adequate for our general operation. Last December 18, 1970, your Archdiocese Board, with the advice of the Building Committee, purchased a new home for the archdiocese. This new home is located at 358 Mountain Road, Englewood, New Jersey. This property, located in the beautiful East Hill area, consists of the following:
  a. Three and one-half acres of the finest residential area throughout Northern New Jersey. Land in that area presently sells for approximately $50,000 per acre.
  b. A home consisting of fourteen rooms, constructed of all brick, with slate roof and a detached two-car garage.
  c. A seven-room guest house which we hope to use as living quarters for our staff.
We have already added to the main house, three large offices. The present library in this house will be the archbishop's office. All offices, plus the chapel, living room, dining room, etc., are on the first floor. We have added a new entrance to the main house which will give it greater dignity and beauty. We plan to move to these new headquarters some time during this fall.

Conclusion: We Are Still Far From Perfect
Those are some of the highlights of the past five years. We have

done other things on which time does not permit us to elaborate, such as the creation of new departments, the organization of a national Teen SOYO, the reorganization of the Christian Education and Sacred Music Departments, the amending of our Archdiocese Constitution which made it possible for us to add more talent to the Board of Trustees. We have done all this, yet we are still far from being perfect. The Church must always renew herself; otherwise, she becomes lazy, stagnant and satisfied with the status quo.

My dear friends, we have been talking about our new chancery for the past fifteen years. Finally, our dream has come true. *This home is your home,* and you will be most welcome to visit us in the future and witness for yourselves the fruit of your labor.

The Place of Women in the Church
1970

In order to understand the role of women in the life of the Church, we must examine the history of salvation and find out what kind of role women played in this history. In the Book of Genesis, we notice that after God created man, He said: "It is not good for man to be alone on earth," so He created Eve to be his partner and his helpmate. Thus we see the very beginning of this history unfolding in Scripture. For our present purposes then, we rely solely on the Scripture—both the Old and New Testaments—before we note their implications for our contemporary world.

In the Old Testament
Whenever we glance through the pages of the Old Testament, we come across women who have served the divine purpose by their examples, their life and good deeds, such as Sarah, who was called the mother of nations, Rebecca, Rachel and Ruth. When Ruth's husband died, she was given a choice to go back to her tribe or stay with her mother-in-law. Ruth chose to stay with her mother-in-law, and said these famous words: "Entreat me not to leave thee, or to return from following thee: for whither thou goest, I will go and where thou lodgest, I will lodge: thy people shall be my people, and thy God my God. Where thou diest, will I die, and there will I be buried." What a great example of loyalty and devotion Ruth offers to all modern women.

In the Book of Proverbs, there is a perfect and living portrait for a good woman. "Who can find a virtuous woman?" the Book of the Proverbs said, "For her price is far above rubies. The heart of her husband doth safely trust in her, so that he shall have no need of spoil. She will give him good and not evil, all the days of his life. . . . Her husband is known in the gates when he sitteth among the elders of the land. . . . Strength and honor are her clothing and she shall rejoice in time to come.

She opens her mouth with wisdom and on her tongue is the law of kindness.... Beauty is deceitful and vain; but a woman that feareth the Lord, she shall be praised" (Proverbs 31:10–12, 23, 25, 26, 30).

In the New Testament
The New Testament gave women a greater role in the history of salvation; they became equal to men in their responsibilities to the Church. St. Paul said: "In Christ's Kingdom, there is no male or female, because all are one."

The most important personality among the New Testament women is the Theotokos, the Blessed Virgin Mary. She was given many titles, such as Second Eve, Queen of Heaven, and Blessed among women. She obediently and willingly accepted her role as the Mother of God. St. Luke tells well the story of her obedience to the divine will through the following words:

> And in the sixth month, the Angel Gabriel was sent from God unto a city of Galilee named Nazareth, to a virgin espoused to a man whose name was Joseph, of the House of David. And the virgin's name was Mary. And the angel came unto her and said: "Hail, thou art highly favored, the Lord is with thee, blessed art thou among women." And when she saw him, she was troubled at his saying, and cast in her mind what manner of salutation this should be. And the angel said to her, "Fear not, Mary, for thou hast found favor with God. And behold, thou shall conceive from thy womb and bring forth a Son and you shall call His name JESUS. He shall be great, and shall be called the Son of the Most High, and the Lord God shall give unto Him the throne of His father David, and He shall reign over the house of Jacob forever, and of His kingdom, there will be no end." Then said Mary unto the angel, 'How shall this be, since I know not a man?" And the angel answered and said to her: "The Holy Spirit shall come unto thee

and the power of the most High shall overshadow thee; . . . for with God, nothing shall be impossible." And Mary said, "Behold the handmaid of the Lord! Be it done to me according to thy word" (Luke 1:26–35, 37, 38).

How many of us today would accept with such obedience the divine challenge? God created us for a purpose. This purpose cannot be fulfilled unless we say to God what the Virgin Mary said: "Be it done to me according to thy word." By her willingness to accept the divine challenge, the Virgin Mary was saved. Salvation is complete cooperation between the human and the divine. Although the Virgin Mary does not say much in the Gospel, she speaks to us silently through her irresistible impact on the life of the Church.

We also read in the New Testament that many women followed Jesus; some of them were more faithful to Him than His own disciples. Remember that Peter denied Him, Judas betrayed Him and Thomas doubted Him. And during the darkest hour, on the Cross, all His disciples deserted Him except John and a few women who were there at Calvary, watching Him with torn hearts.

In the story of the Resurrection, we read that it was not the disciples who first saw the empty tomb, but rather a group of faithful women. St. Mark tells the story:

> And when the Sabbath was past, Mary Magdalene, and Mary the mother of James, and Salome brought sweet spices, that coming they might anoint Jesus. And very early in the morning, the first day of the week, they came to the sepulcher, the sun being now risen. And they said to one another, "Who shall roll us back the stone from the door of the sepulcher?" And looking they saw the stone rolled back. For it was very great. And entering into the sepulcher, they saw a young man sitting on the right side, clothed with a white robe, and they were

astonished. Who saith to them, "Be not affrighted; you seek Jesus of Nazareth who was crucified: He is risen, He is not here, behold the place where they laid Him. But go, tell His disciples and Peter that He goeth before you into Galilee; and there you shall see Him, as He told you" (Mark 16:1–7).

During the apostolic and patristic eras, many women ministered to the sick, the orphans, and the needy ones. A special order for women was established by the Church, such as the deaconesses to help in the work of charity and social relief. In spite of these various orders, the activities of women were restricted to a few areas such as the home first, and second, the Church.

We can now summarize what we have already found in the Scriptures: Before the industrial and technological revolutions, women had a defined role to play and a strong sense of belonging. They were deeply rooted in the family, which was in reality their kingdom. Does not the Church crown them during the marriage ceremony to play this role?

In the Contemporary World

Now, what about contemporary women? The industrial and technological revolutions definitely changed and enlarged the role of women in life and involved them deeply in many social affairs. Today, they are doctors, soldiers, businesswomen, scientists, pilots, cab drivers, ministers, detectives, politicians, etc. Modern women have acquired such new roles combined with their traditional and more limited role. But at the same time the scale of our values has been turned upside down. Men are dissatisfied, women are dissatisfied, children are dissatisfied and everyone is trying to be what he is not. God created the woman to be a queen, a mother, and not a man. Men and women are indeed equal, but they are also different; equality does not mean sameness. Without that discernment, life becomes less, falls into confusion, lacks completion.

Nikos Kazantzakis, in his book, *The Saviors of God*, said: "We are living in a critical violent moment of history. An entire world is crashing down. Our epoch is not a moment of equilibrium in which refinement, reconciliation, peace and love might be fruitful virtues." Dissatisfaction marks our age and disturbs our happiness. We have become detached from ourselves, from others, from nature and ultimately from God. We are, as Camus said, "strangers in the world." Our society is stricken by mental disorders, violence and crimes. We have lost our sense of destiny. We are nobody, from nowhere, going noplace. Alienation is the stigma of our age. This word *alienation* has been used by philosophers, psychologists and sociologists to refer to an extraordinary variety of psychosocial disorders, including self-anxiety, despair, ruthlessness, apathy, social disorganization, loneliness, meaninglessness, isolation, pessimism and the loss of beliefs and values. Some in the present age blame the women's movement for this state of affairs.

But could we honestly say that women alone are responsible for this state of affairs? Absolutely not! All of us are responsible, men and women, priests and laymen. We must reassess our values and give priority to what comes first. What is more important to us—a second television and a second car, or a mentally well-balanced child? Both men and women today are supposed to provide bread for the family, and both men and women are supposed to provide love: "for man shall not live by bread alone." Many children have left home and become hippies, not because of the lack of bread but because of the lack of love. But despite the equality of the sexes, do we not know the special place of the woman's love, the maternal love?

True Womanhood

Can you ever forget the warmth of your mother's kisses? The tenderness of her arms? And the sweetness of her smile? How wretched we would be if we never experienced this reality. My mother was not a philosopher or a soldier, but she was a poet in her own right. She opened my eyes to the beauty of life, to the holiness of the holy and above all, she taught me to serve and how to love others. She gave herself totally to us, expecting nothing in return. Does a nightingale expect anything in return for his singing? Does a rose expect anything in return for its fragrance? This is your mother and my mother—this is true womanhood.

I would like to conclude this talk with the following story: Four priests gathered together to discuss the various translations of the Bible. The first one said, "I like the King James translation because of its beauty." The second one said, "I like the Douay translation because it is accurate." The third one said, "I like the Revised translation because it is simple." The fourth one said, "I like my mother's translation." The rest of the priests said to him, "We didn't know your mother translated the Bible." He said, "Yes, she did. She translated the Bible into life."

There is definitely a place for women in the Church, and by God's grace, we shall work to properly establish it.

Paschal Meditation
1970

Lord, I am talking to You between airports, between flights, in the midst of rushing crowds and noisy engines. Please forgive me if my words are vain and empty.

The last time I talked to You, You were in a lonely manger. As I stared at You, I saw the wounds in Your tiny hands, the spear in Your tender side and the crown of thorns on Your bleeding head.

You have been slain for my sake since the foundation of the world.

Lord, every time I gaze at Your Crucifix I tremble with fear and ask myself, "Why did You love me so much?" I should be hanging there in Your stead. I rebelled against You in Paradise. I murdered my brother in the field. I betrayed You in Gethsemane. And when they crucified You I was the leader of the gang.

Lord, why do You love me so much? I do not deserve one drop of Your sweat, one drop of Your tears, and one drop of Your blood. Why did You wash my filthy feet? Why did You share Your body and blood with my unworthy lips?

Lord, why did You weep over my Jerusalem? The streets of the city which You loved are still stained with Your innocent blood, and the tears of Your little friends in Jerusalem have become rivers of suffering and agony. Your little friends in Your land, Lord, are drinking their mother's tears and eating their mother's flesh, but no one cares.

Lord, You called me "friend" but at the night of Your trial I cursed, I swore, and I said, "I know not that man." Instead of water, I gave You vinegar and when that heavy Cross was crushing Your shoulders I did not lift a finger to help.

Lord, You had reached the abyss of agony and despair when You cried with a mighty voice, "My God, My God, why hast Thou forsaken Me?" This was Your last cry in this world before You gave up the spirit, and it fell on deaf ears. After that You died. "And there was darkness all over the land."

Lord, beyond the innocence of Bethlehem, the tears of Gethsemane, and the agony of Calvary, there is the joy of the new wine, the brightness of the new dawn, the hope of the new creation and the eternal reality of the empty tomb.

"O Death, where is thy sting?"
"O Hell, where is thy victory?"

Lord, let the immortal light of Your Pascha penetrate the thickness of our dark nights. Roll away the heavy stones from the doors of our sepulchers. Liberate us by Your divine freedom. Wash away our iniquities, "O Lamb of God who takest away the sins of the world."

Editor's Endnotes:

1. *In the first address given in 1970 at Montreal, Philip, after reviewing the points which highlight his first five years, and reminding his audience that "the Church must always renew herself; otherwise she becomes lazy, stagnant and satisfied with the status quo," focuses his attention on a direct appeal to help in the building and renovation of the recently purchased headquarters in Englewood, New Jersey.*

2. *In that same address, he also shares with them the financial cost of the new headquarters building; the profit realized from the sale of the Brooklyn residence and the two acres which were previously purchased in Alpine, New Jersey; the need to appeal for funds to the entire archdiocese; and his gratitude to the two large Montreal parishes and philanthropic parishioners for their pledges.*

Chapter 6

CHANGED FROM GLORY TO GLORY

> *Despite the painful lessons of history, we continue to build towers and to turn our eyes away from the splendid glory of God. As a result, we find ourselves living, as T. S. Eliot said, "in a wasteland," i.e. in a spiritual vacuum. We have too much to live **on**, but nothing to live **for!** If bread alone is sufficient, why then all the frustration, anxiety, fear, boredom and despair?*
>
> Metropolitan Philip

- *Man: Despair or Hope, 1970*
- *Man as a Worshipping Being, 1971*
- *From Heart Attack to Heart Surgery, 1973*
- *On Unity in the Church, 1973*

It was after his first five years, i.e., beginning in the 1970s, that Metropolitan Philip began to deliver addresses which focused on themes. These themes, passing beyond—but certainly inclusive of—the practical and administrative issues in the Church, capture with more power the ecclesiology and theology of the man.

The following three addresses, given in Chicago (1970), Worcester, Massachusetts (1971), and Charleston, West Virginia (1973), as well as an article which was published in various journals in 1973, begin to show how Philip's orientation is to bring Orthodox theology into his, and the Church's, challenge of ministry.

The first of these three he entitles, "Man: Despair or Hope," and it is certainly relevant to the questions of identity and meaning marked by the Vietnam War, etc., which prevailed in America during that time. In a sense, it carries over from his Miami address of 1969, but the reader will note that in this talk, Philip reaches much deeper into the philosophy of the age. It is delivered to the Archdiocesan Convention.

In the second of this group, "Man as a Worshipping Being," Philip turns his attention to the theme of the Eucharistic Liturgy. In the pedagogical style which he often assumes when speaking in parish settings, Philip discusses the early roots of the Liturgy, up to the contemporary practice. As also became his style, he is interested in teaching his people **practically,** *rather than remaining in the esoteric realms which are reserved for the few academicians. Here, then, we truly see the bishop as father and teacher.*

The third piece of literature included here shows how Philip's understanding of his episcopacy is marked by his heart attack and subsequent surgery. In 1973, he pens an article which summarizes his life and ministry in light of those traumatic events, and the impact they have on his vision of the future.

The final presentation in this grouping is truly an historic event. We have chosen to include it here because it highlights how Philip uses Scripture to bring about practical results in the contemporary Church. And this time, the result, which for generations seemed impossible to achieve, was the unification of the Antiochian Church in North America. The reader will notice how he applies St. Paul's letter to a divided Corinthian Church, now to a divided Antiochian Church. Referring to the division which began generations earlier, a division which left relatives and parishes fighting each other, the Metropolitan, like the great Apostle, calls for a badly needed unity. But again, as is typical of Philip's practical approach, he does not remain in theory; he presents the way, the organization and the plan by which that unity can be realized. As history eventually attests, the unity of the Antiochian Church in North America is achieved, and begins heading for a blossoming nobody expected.

Thus, as the Metropolitan begins developing such themes, he calls the people of his archdiocese to follow the way of spiritual growth in which they can be **changed from glory to glory.**

J. J. A.

Man: Hope or Despair
Chicago, 1970

The theme of my message to you this year is taken from Psalm 8:

> What is man that Thou art mindful of him, and the son of man that Thou dost care for him? Yet Thou hast made him little less than the angels, and dost crown him with glory and honor. Thou hast given him dominion over the works of Thy hands, Thou hast put all things under his feet. All sheep and oxen, and also the beasts of the field, the birds of the air and the fish of the sea; whatsoever passeth along the paths of the sea.

The various conferences I have attended this year throughout the country proved to me beyond a doubt that we are not a Church of immigrants any longer. On the contrary, I feel we are deeply rooted in this land; thus the religious, social and intellectual trends which affect this entire society definitely leave their marks on our souls.

Last January, I had the honor of meeting here in Chicago with the spiritual and lay leaders of our youth movement to determine whether this archdiocese has become another institution in our Church existing by the dead letter or whether it is still the dynamic movement which was born to answer a spiritual challenge. After two days of meditation and deliberation, we all agreed to add to our basic principles two words: *Awareness* and *Commitment.* The question which we may ask now is: awareness of what and commitment to what? If we can answer this question clearly and profoundly, we may discover the roots of our problem and decide on our course for the future.

The Towers We Build
We must be fully aware that our Church and our entire world

are faced with the most serious and most dangerous problems in history. Let us migrate from the world for a while to our inner selves and examine whether my statement means anything. Self-awareness means full cognizance of our place in this world vis-à-vis God, man and nature. According to the biblical view, man was created in the "image of God and His likeness." The poet David, in Psalm 8, tells us that man was made little less than the angels. He was crowned with honor and glory and all things were put under his feet. By his own actions and free will, however, man refused that divine freedom, thus alienating himself from God, his fellow man and nature.

The towers which he built ended in utter confusion, despair and destruction. Despite the painful lessons of history, we continue to build towers and to turn our eyes away from the splendid glory of God. As a result of all this, we find ourselves living, as T. S. Eliot said, in a "wasteland," in a spiritual vacuum. We have too much to live *on* but nothing to live *for*! If bread alone is sufficient, why then all our frustration, anxiety, fear, boredom and despair?

A modern sociologist described our time as follows:

> Our age is marked by multitudes of factory and white collar workers who find their jobs monotonous and degrading; the voters and nonvoters who feel hopeless and don't care; the juveniles who commit senseless actions of violence; the growing army of idle and lonely people; the stupefied audiences of mass media; the people who reject the prevailing values of our culture, but cannot or may not find any alternatives; the escapists, the retreatists; the nihilists and the desperate citizens who would solve all major political problems by moving our society underground and blowing up the planet.

Such words reflect clearly the sickness of man in our age, his lack of identity and purpose. This sickness is evident in all mechanized societies because science and technology give us control only over a fraction of our world. During the past two centuries, we have witnessed the reduction of man into small entities such as science, technology, sex and economics. Today, the Western man has become "mechanized, routinized, made comfortable as an object."

A French poet recently said:

> Why are the times dark?
> Men know each other not at all,
> Governments clearly change from bad to worse,
> Days dead and gone were more worthwhile,
> Now what holds sway? Deep gloom and boredom
> Justice and law nowhere to be found
> I know no more where I belong.

Is not this cry of this poet our own cry? Do we belong anywhere? Do we belong to the Church in the true sense of belonging? Do we represent any view at all concerning man and his destiny? Do we encounter God in our worship, meditation and tragedy? Man truly knows himself when he is confronted by God. Read the Bible and you will find that all those who have had a profound encounter with God became radically changed. We may know the human only when we are confronted by the divine, we may know the temporal only when we ponder the eternal, and we may know the depth of the valley only when we look at it from the peak of the mountain. We are sick and paralyzed by fear and will never be healed without a true encounter with Christ. What is the Church doing about that?

In the past sixty-five years, we have built beautiful churches, cultural centers and have become very well organized both on the national and local levels. We have become experts in raising money, in business, in canon law, in constitutions and cookies, bake sales, raffles and lately, bingo. Is this the true mission of the Church? When the Church becomes one more institution, one more bureaucracy, will she say anything worthwhile? Can we enrich our spiritual poverty by cookies and bake sales? Can we cover our spiritual nakedness with bricks and stones?

The Church in the Face of the Crisis
Most of our Orthodox people in this land are still on the boundary, arguing whether God understands English or not. How can we reach the heart of this nation if we continue to chew the past and speak to our youth a language which they do not understand?

How can we stop the cruelty of man to man and of man to nature if we continue to accuse our young people of immorality every time they genuinely disagree with our distorted principles and values? We have already had two barbaric wars during the first half of this century and we continue to wage a senseless war in Vietnam. How can we explain to our young people the morality of seventy-three senators who want to stop a war in Vietnam and start another in the Middle East? How can we stop the cry of our young people for peace when our world is madly dancing on the edge of the abyss? All it takes is a madman to push the button and the entire earth would be incinerated. It is indeed sad to see the Church both in the East and in the West enslaved to political ideologies which view man as a mere object which must be utilized for the well-being of society or the ruling bureaucracy. I am fully aware that convinced Christians have become a minority in the world and perhaps a small remnant, but let me ask: How many Christians did we have on Pentecost Day?

In the past two years, we have talked much about pollution of our air, our rivers, our lakes and our oceans; but nobody said a word about our inner pollution. We have breathed our inner poison in the air, we have dumped our inner garbage in the water, and unless we clean the garbage from within, that garbage from without will definitely suffocate us. The late Paul Tillich said,

> Many of us have lost the ability to live with nature. We fill it with the noise of empty talk instead of listening to

its many voices, and through them, to the voiceless music of the universe. Separated from the soil by a machine, we speed through nature catching glimpses of it but never comprehending its greatness or feeling its power.

What I have already said clearly indicates that we are faced with a spiritual crisis. Have we then reached the dead end? The "no exit" of Jean Paul Sartre? Shall we surrender to despair, or is there hope for a better world? I am not a pessimist, nor shall I ever surrender to despair, because my Church is a Church of hope. Despite the thickness of the clouds, the sun can still brightly shine. If you study the life of Christ, you will find in it moments of sadness, moments of tears, moments of tragedy and moments of joy. This is how I understand history. The Church never promised us a paradise on earth; therefore, we must reject all social Utopian thinking and accept both the blind and bright moments in history with faith, hope, dignity and courage.

My hope for a better world lies in the uniqueness of the Orthodox Church and her strong emphasis on the following aspects: the doctrine of man, the theology of hope, the relevancy of our liturgical life. Let us briefly turn to each.

1. *The doctrine of man* in our theology is based on the biblical view which was fully defined by our Church Fathers. Man has all the potentialities for perfection, simply because he was created in the image of God. St. Maximus the Confessor states:

> Those who have followed Christ in action and contemplation will be changed into an even better condition, and there is no time to tell of all the ascents and revelations of the saints who are *being changed from glory to glory*, until each one in order receives deification.

Man was not created to be a slave, neither to society nor to history, neither to science nor to technology, neither to communism nor to capitalism. Even though nature has limitations, these limitations can be overcome by the sacramental life of the Church. Each and every one of us can become Christlike through prayer, contemplation, and action. St. Maximus further says:

> While remaining in his soul and body entirely man by nature, he becomes in his soul and body entirely God by grace. Deification involves the whole human being.

All the ancient Greek dichotomy between body and soul disappears in St. Maximus. When God created man, he created him as a whole being, and when man collapsed, he collapsed not partially but as a whole being. Likewise, when man was redeemed, he was redeemed totally, body and soul. Through the sacrament of the Holy Eucharist, God enters into union with the whole man. How long, then, can we continue to reduce man into small entities? One of my favorite poets is St. Simeon the New Theologian. Listen to him describe his encounter with God:

> I have often seen the light. Sometimes it has appeared to me within my self, when my soul possessed peace and silence. Sometimes it has appeared only at a distance, and at times it was even hidden completely. Then I experienced great affliction believing that I will never see it again. But from the moment when I began to shed tears, when I bore witness to a complete detachment from everything and to an absolute humility and obedience, the light appeared once again like the sun which penetrates the thickness of the clouds.

2. The second aspect is the ***theology of hope.*** While other Christians have focused their eyes on Calvary, we have focused ours on the empty tomb. Do we not experience this reality every year on Easter morning when we shout, "Christ is risen from the dead"? In 1 Corinthians 15:14, 22 St. Paul said:

> If Christ has not been raised, then our preaching is in vain and your faith is in vain. For as in Adam all die, so also in Christ shall all be made alive.

On Great Friday, there were tears, pain, agony and death, but on the third day, the darkness of Great Friday was dissipated by the bright light of the empty tomb. The new Pascha inaugurated the new age, the new being, and the new man. The Orthodox Church celebrates this joyful event every Sunday. The following are some of the hymns which we chant on the morning of the Holy Resurrection which reveal to us this joy and this new being:

> Let us cleanse our senses that we may behold Christ shining like lightning with the unapproachable light of Resurrection, that we may hear Him say openly "rejoice," while we sing to Him the hymn of triumph and victory.
> Verily this day which is called Holy is the first day among Sabbaths, it is their King and Lord, it is the feast of feasts, and the season of seasons.

Where are those like Sartre or Camus who say there is "no exit"? Let them gaze at the empty tomb. Our hope then is genuine because it is rooted in the reality of the Resurrection. It is not an empty utopian hope which ends in false security. It is the hope of the realization of God's kingdom first within us, and ultimately, beyond the veils of temporal existence.

3. The third aspect is the ***relevancy of our liturgical life.*** During the dark ages of Orthodox theology, our Church survived because of the richness of her liturgical life. If you understand our various liturgical services, you will understand the whole theology of the Orthodox Church. While others talk about liturgical poverty and liturgical renewal, as Orthodox, we must concentrate our efforts on liturgical understanding. In the past two years I have talked to our young people about the many aspects of our Church life, especially the Divine Liturgy. Ninety-five per cent of them have expressed deep satisfaction with the liturgy and were against any drastic liturgical changes. Some of them, however, have asked for more understanding of our Liturgy, and I believe that this request is very much justified.

Any Liturgy which does not permeate the faithful with a strong feeling of the holy is a meaningless service. If you have a living priest, a living choir and a living congregation, then you will find yourself involved in a wonderful mystical experience. We cannot acquire a mystical experience in the Church if the Liturgy is nothing but a business meeting or another lecture. A few years ago I talked to a group of non-Orthodox students about the nature of our worship. One of them asked: "Why don't you preach in the Orthodox Church?" I said, we do preach in the Orthodox Church, but we do more than that. We do not tell the faithful only what Christ said, but what He in reality did through the Sacrament of the Holy Eucharist. In the Liturgy of St. John Chrysostom, the priest reads during the Anaphora the following:

> Thou it was who didst bring us from nonexistence into being, and when we had fallen away didst raise us up again, and didst not cease to do all things until Thou hast brought us back to heaven.

And from the same Liturgy, just before the Lord's Prayer, we read the following:

> Unto Thee we commend our whole life and our hope, O Master, who lovest mankind, and we beseech Thee and pray Thee and supplicate Thee: make us worthy to partake of the heavenly and terrible mysteries of this sacred and spiritual table with a pure conscience; unto remission of sins, unto forgiveness of transgressions, unto communion of the Holy Spirit and unto inheritance of the Kingdom of Heaven.

In the Orthodox Liturgy, one can see God, man and nature in their proper perspective. Our Eucharist answers the central questions: Who are we? Where are we going? What is the meaning of life and who is God? The emphasis in the Orthodox Liturgy is first on *being,* then on *doing.* If your personality is disintegrated and if the image of God in you is distorted, then your actions will undoubtedly reflect this disintegration and that distortion.

During the past ten years, we have noticed a definite reaction among the American youth against rationalism and pragmatism. This proves that our youth are searching for the mystical experience which will take them beyond the cruel and cold realities of this world. The young feel that the rational, technological and social society in which we live will inevitably lead to the mechanization of man and hence to his destruction. Some of these young people have found an alternative in LSD, marijuana and other kinds of narcotics and destructive drugs. Such aspects of our new youth culture are indeed very frightening. Therefore, it is extremely important to make our youth aware of the richness of the liturgical and mystical life of the Orthodox Church. If anyone is searching for a mystical experience, let him go to church during Holy Week. Let him kneel in the shadow of the Cross on Holy Thursday. Let him walk in the procession of Great Friday. Let him feel the joy of Pascha on Sunday morning.

The Challenge of the Future
The uniqueness of Orthodoxy as expressed in the three aforementioned categories cannot be covered in this one message. However, these were some leading thoughts which I wanted to share with you as we begin a new decade in our spiritual pilgrimage. Sooner or later the cruel steps of history will march over our graves, so let us not waste time in vain talk and vainglory. Let us lay a firm foundation for an Orthodox spirituality in this land. In Matthew 7:24, 25, Christ said:

> Everyone then who hears these words of Mine and does them will be like a wise man who built his house upon the rock; and the rain fell and the floods came, and the winds blew and beat upon the house, but it did not fall because it had been founded on the rock.

The floods are about us and the storms of our time are blowing very hard. If we have the strong faith of our forefathers, we can walk on the water and silence the howling wind. But if our convictions are weak, the floods and the winds will sweep us away to the ocean of oblivion.

I appeal to you in the name of everything which we represent to join me in a glorious venture for an Orthodox future of hope, joy and fulfillment. We have tarried long enough on the shore. It is time that we sail and plunge into the depth. If you totally commit yourselves to these goals in the 1970s, God will bless you, and once again, He will say to you:

> Be fruitful and multiply, and fill the earth and subdue it; and have dominion over the fish of the sea and over the birds of the air, and over every living thing that moves upon the earth (Genesis 1:28, 29).

Man as a Worshipping Being
Worcester, 1971

In this presentation, I will attempt to discuss the origin of Christian worship with a special emphasis on the Holy Eucharist, to which we often refer as the Divine Liturgy.

In her book entitled *Worship*, Evelyn Underhill wrote: "Worship, in all its grades and kinds, is the response of the creature to the eternal." If we examine the archeological remains of the primitive human, we find that he always knew that there was a power greater than himself. The human's concept of that power depended on his intellectual and spiritual capacities. Man's primitive worship was polytheistic (the belief in many gods). He found his gods in the natural forces such as rivers, mountain, stars, etc. Monotheism (the belief in one God) appeared in a later stage of human spiritual development. From all this we can gather that the human being was always a worshipping being. At this time, however, I shall not concern myself with pagan worship but rather with Christian worship.

Distinguishing Christian Liturgy

It should first be said that Christian worship is deeply rooted in Jewish worship, in form but not in spirit. The Passover which the Jews celebrate is not the same Passover which is celebrated by Christians. The primitive history of the Church proves beyond doubt that the Church began as a worshipping community. Our Lord Himself went many times to the Temple to pray. In the fourth chapter of St. John's Gospel, there is a recorded conversation between Christ and a Samaritan woman at the Well of Jacob. The Samaritan woman posed a question to Jesus: Do we have to worship in Jerusalem or in Gariszim? Note how our Lord answered her: "A time is coming, in fact, it is now here, when true worshippers will worship the Father in spirit and in truth. Such are the worshippers the Father demands. God is spirit and His worshippers must worship Him in spirit and in truth" (John 4:21–24). It is evident, therefore, from our Lord's own words that the new worship is of a different kind, and according to St. Paul, it is defined by one's offering of himself to the Almighty God as a living sacrifice.

Despite persecution, the early Christians met at a definite hour for the celebration of the Holy Eucharist. St. Ignatius of Antioch emphasized this reality very strongly in his letters to the faithful. He told the Ephesians: "Come together in common, one and all without exception in charity, in one faith, and in Jesus Christ, to break together the one bread of immortality, with your bishop and the presbyters." And to the Christians of Smyrna, he wrote the following: "Let that Eucharist be held valid which is offered by the bishop or by one to whom the bishop has committed this charge. Wherever the bishop appears, there let the people be, as where Jesus Christ is, there is the Church."

The early Christians of Jerusalem continued to go to the Temple to pray. However, for the celebration of the Eucharist, they gathered secretly at different places. The pagan authorities considered these gatherings crimes against the state. The main accusation against the Christians was this: They met in darkness to eat the flesh and drink the blood of somebody. In the eyes of the pagan state, this was considered atheistic cannibalism. However, the Christians held fast to their assemblies, even though they could have prayed individually at home. It was precisely because of the Eucharist that the Church survived.

The primitive Church did not have large cathedrals for the celebration of the Eucharist. To the early Christians the place of worship was of no importance, for God does not dwell in buildings made of stones and clay. "Ye are the temple of the living God," said St. Paul. A large hall, a table, a few chalices, bread and wine—that was all they needed to celebrate the Eucharist.

From the Book of Acts, we learn that the first Christians selected Sunday as their Holy Day, since on Sunday Christ had risen from the dead and had appeared to the disciples gathered together for a meal. The early Christian documents testify that Sunday was called "the Day of the Lord," and a little later the *Didache* said, "Meet on the Lord's Day, break the bread and celebrate the Eucharist." In the Book of Genesis, the Sabbath was the day of rest, but Christianity—as the new reality—looked beyond the Sabbath to Sunday, the eighth day which the Christians considered the beginning and the end. In the early Church, Sunday and Easter were the only two main feasts. Easter was to the course of the year, what Sunday was to the course of the week; it still is.

The Eucharistic Meal
According to St. Paul, the celebration of the Eucharist was connected with a meal. This is evident from the Apostle's first letter to the Corinthians. This meal was in essence the continuation of the sacred Jewish meal, and we find that to the majority of the Near Eastern people, every meal was sacred and was very significant. Our Lord compared the kingdom of heaven to a great supper.

What did this meal look like? In his book, *The Shape of the Liturgy*, Gregory Dix describes this meal as follows:

> Our Lord first took bread; second, gave thanks over it; third, broke it; fourth, distributed it saying these words: "Take ye, eat, this is my body which is broken for you for the remission of sins." Later, He took a cup, gave thanks over it, handed it to His disciples, saying these words: "Drink ye, all of this, this is my blood of the New Testament which is shed for you and for many for the remission of sins."

It is evident from this that our Lord departed from the old Jewish tradition of merely blessing the meal by giving the Last Supper a new meaning and a new content, now related to the death and resurrection of Christ.

At the end of the first century, the Eucharist acquired a definite shape as follows:
first, the Liturgy of the Word;
second, the Liturgy of Thanksgiving, or the Liturgy of the Faithful;
third, the fraction and communion.

Although the Eucharistic Liturgy takes place in time and space, its purpose is to transform man and lead him beyond time and space to the heavenly altar. The Orthodox liturgical scholar, Father Alexander Schmemann, describes the Eucharist as a journey:

> The journey begins when Christians leave their homes and beds. They live indeed in this present and concrete world and whether they have to drive fifteen miles or walk a few blocks, a sacramental act is already taking place. For they are now on their way to constitute the Church, or to be more exact, to be transformed into the Church of God. They have been individuals—some white, some black, some poor, some rich. They have been the natural world and a natural community and now they have been collected to come together in one place to bring their lives, their very world with them and to be more than what they are—a new community with a new life. We are already far beyond the categories of common worship and prayer.

Our Lord continued His presence in the Church through the eucharistic gathering. No wonder, then, that the early Church, even under the most difficult circumstances, met together to celebrate the Eucharist. There were no outstanding ceremonies to attract people to such gatherings. What brought the early Christians together was their strong faith that their Lord would be in their midst through the breaking of the bread and the blessing of the cup.

The Liturgy of Chrysostom

Now let us analyze briefly the Liturgy of St. John Chrysostom, with which the Orthodox are most familiar. This Liturgy begins with the solemn doxology, "Blessed is the Kingdom of the Father, the Son and the Holy Spirit now and ever and unto ages of ages." From the beginning the destination of the journey is announced. It is the heavenly kingdom. This journey begins with a prayer for peace, but what kind of peace? It is not the peace of the Versailles Treaty. It is not the peace treaty which was signed after the Second World War. It is also not the kind of peace which the Americans and the North Vietnamese are negotiating in Paris. It is that heavenly peace. It is that peace from above, one which St. Paul describes as "that peace which surpasses all understanding."

The next act of the Liturgy is the Entrance with the Gospel, the coming of the celebrant to the altar. This entrance is the passage of the Church from the old world to the new world, to the new reality, to the new being, to the kingdom. As the celebrant approaches the altar, the Church intones the hymn which the angels eternally sing at the throne of God: "Holy God, Holy Mighty, Holy Immortal." After the singing of this hymn, the Epistle and Gospel are read, followed by the homily, which explains the Word of God. All this constitutes the Liturgy of the Word. It is instructive to note that the Epistle is traditionally read by a layman to indicate that the laity have their definite role in the Liturgy and that they were baptized to perform a definite ministry in the life of the Church.

After the Liturgy of the Word, the choir sings the Cherubic Hymn and the gifts—bread and wine—are transferred from the table of oblation to the altar. After we place the gifts on the altar, we begin the Liturgy of Thanksgiving or the Offertory. The highlights of this part of the Liturgy are the Kiss of Peace, which today only the clergy exchange. In the early Church the entire community shared this kiss, and someday I hope we will return to this ancient and meaningful gesture.

After the kiss of peace comes the Creed. The entire Church

confesses the same creed initiated in Nicea (A.D. 325) and completed at Constantinople (A.D. 381), and which became the frame of our faith. At the conclusion of the creed, the celebrant asks the people to lift up their hearts and the people respond: "We lift them up unto the Lord." This lifting up of our hearts is the ascension of the Church to heaven. "But what do I care about heaven," says St. John Chrysostom, "when I myself have *become* heaven."

And now as we stand before the heavenly altar, we sing, "Holy, Holy, Holy, Lord God of Sabbaoth, heaven and earth are full of Thy glory. Hosanna in the highest. Blessed is He that cometh in the name of the Lord." This hymn, rooted in the prophecy of Isaiah, is followed by the words of the institution, the oblation and the consecration of the Last Supper, together properly called the Mystical Supper. "Again we offer unto Thee this reasonable and unbloody service, and beseech Thee and pray Thee and supplicate Thee, send down Thy Holy Spirit upon us and upon these gifts here spread forth." In the liturgical sense, the whole Church is present in the particles which are placed on the paten (tray), the Church militant and the Church triumphant. This is described as follows: "All those who in faith have gone before us to their rest, patriarchs, prophets, apostles, preachers, evangelists, martyrs, confessors, ascetics and every righteous spirit made perfect in faith."

After the consecration we remember the place of the Theotokos, the Virgin Mary, noting her special place among these special names of saints and persons. As these are commemorated within the Eucharist, we remember that "God is marvelous in His saints." Finally, after this remembrance, we recite the Lord's Prayer, the perfect prayer as our Lord taught us. Thus, our journey reaches the eucharistic table itself, where the community partakes of the heavenly food, the Body and Blood of Christ; we become one in Christ.

Finally, to remind us that we have arrived at our destination, we sing, "We have seen the true light, we have received the heavenly spirit, we have found the true faith." We are ready to return to our world from which we left in the first place: "Let us go forth in peace."

The accomplishment of our liturgical worship, the remembrance that man is, indeed, a worshipping being, only inspires us to practice the liturgy after the Liturgy. We leave the gathering of believers, but the gathering never leaves us; we carry it within us into our world where we begin the liturgy of mission.

From Heart Attack to Heart Surgery
1973

*"For I will restore health to you,
and your wounds I will heal" (Jeremiah 30:17)*

By mid-September, 1972, our Archdiocesan Convention and youth conferences were over. A deep sense of satisfaction permeated my heart because of the beautiful and successful encounters which I had with our youth and faithful of the archdiocese. Between May and September, the pain in my chest had increased and I became convinced that I must undergo open heart surgery. After intense consultation with some of the great doctors throughout the country, I decided that the Miami Heart Institute was the place which may satisfy the cry of my heart for more blood.

Putting Things in Order
It has been my practice that before I make a long trip, I usually answer all my mail and leave my office in good order. Wednesday, September 13, everything was ready: my desk was clear, my suitcase was packed, and a room was reserved at the hospital for this major surgery. A short conference was held with my office personnel and it was time for departure. The old and majestic oak trees which lovingly and watchfully surround my home were still green and as beautiful as ever.

The last thing I did before I left home was my visit with God at St. John Chrysostom's Chapel. If there are pieces of heaven on earth, the chapel of St. John is one of them. As I was leaving the chapel, my eyes caught a glimpse of the words inscribed above the door: "Dedicated to Teen SOYO, June 3, 1972."

I thought of our little children, Teen SOYO, the youth, our archdiocese, and all the beautiful things that we can live for, then suddenly a feeling of indescribable joy permeated my soul and, as I left home, I was certain more than ever that I will be coming back to continue God's work with a healthier heart and much hope for a very promising future for our youth and our Church in the New World.

From Helplessness to Hopefulness

My friends and all the companions of my youth were utterly shocked by the news of my heart attack, January 5, 1968. Why did that happen? The answer to this difficult question remains nothing but speculation. Not one doctor has been able to pinpoint the real factors which have contributed directly to my heart condition.

After the Arab-Israeli War of June 1967, I became involved in a humanitarian campaign to help alleviate some of the suffering of the Arab refugees. January 5, 1968, I went to Washington, D.C. to meet with the Arab ambassadors at the Lebanese Embassy in order to exchange views on the Middle East crisis and offer my help to formulate a public relations program which would give the American people the objective story on the Middle East, and help improve the Arab image in North America, which was distorted by the news media and most vicious political propaganda. I was shocked beyond measure when one of the Arab ambassadors, whose country is floating on a sea of oil, said to me, "You have a fine program, Your Eminence, start the work and we will help you." Needless to say, my conference with their excellencies ended in utter disappointment and despair. I could not understand what these ambassadors were doing in this country, a country which has been playing many roles in all Middle Eastern events since the end of the Second World War.

At 3:00 P.M., January 5, I felt extremely weak and asked to be rushed to the hospital. Three days later my doctor informed me that I suffered a heart attack. When I heard the news I laughed, and for ten days I refused to believe it. I come from a healthy family and I always felt that I was in good physical condition. When I finally realized that I really suffered a heart attack, I went for a few days through a horrible psychological depression. I saw my ideals, dreams and plans for a better archdiocese and a better Antiochian Church suddenly reduced to ashes. How often did I look through the windows of my room to the outside world wondering whether I was still a part of it? How often did I wonder whether I will be able to walk, to work, to dream and plan for the future? When one gets sick, one loses touch with the world of reality. One's world becomes a world of sorrow and tears. After twenty days in the hospital, I began to regain some of my strength and my psychological depression was overcome by a great measure of renewed hope.

This psychological change from hopelessness to hopefulness was the greatest thing which happened to me in the hospital. The state of despair which encompassed my soul resulted from personal pride and some misunderstanding of the problem of suffering. I refused to accept the reality of my illness because I was young, strong, proud of my youth, and wherever I traveled I often heard, "Isn't he young? Isn't he strong? Isn't he dynamic?" I really believed that I was young, strong and immune from all illness.

I also believed that I could change history. I had my plans for the archdiocese, for Orthodoxy in America, for the Mother Church, for the Arab refugees and for the complicated political situation in the Middle East. In other words, I was trying to build my own Babylonian tower and not the kingdom of God. Was the sin of pride not the cause of our alienation from God?

After this leap into darkness, I began to see the light. I began to identify my suffering with the Cross. I began to feel that I was united with all those who suffer on this earth. "For if one member suffers all suffer together" (1 Corinthians 12:26). Moreover, I began to understand Christ's compassion on the sick, the blind, the paralyzed, the widow who lost her only son, the sinful woman and all sinners. Suffering can be extremely destructive if it is not understood in the light of the empty tomb. Goethe once said, "He who does not eat his bread with sorrow, he who does not spend the midnight hours weeping and waiting for the dawn, does not know you, ye heavenly powers."

Through creative suffering, I completely surrendered my life to God. Without faith in Him and without His sustaining power, we are nothing but dust and ashes. "Even though I walk through the valley of the shadow of death, I fear no evil; for Thou art with me; Thy rod and Thy staff, they comfort me" (Psalm 23:4). Surrendering to God made me feel, for the first time, at peace with myself, with others and with the world. Henceforth, I said to God, "my life belongs to You. You can do with it whatever You want. If You feel that my life has a purpose in Your world, then let me become an instrument of Your Divine plan; and if You feel otherwise, let me fade away in the darkness of the grave; for a little flower in Your field still has its fragrance and beauty."

Possible Factors

After four weeks in the hospital I was discharged and continued to recuperate well. The question which kept haunting my mind was, "Why the heart attack?" If doctors do not exactly know, how could I know? But if doctors can speculate, then I can speculate, too. Thus, after a great deal of speculation, I reached the following conclusion: since I do not have a family history of heart attacks, and since I have always been in good physical condition, then my illness must be the result of emotional stress. The years 1966, 1967 and 1968 were years of many emotional explosions in my life. Among many possible causes, I came to best understand four:

1. *The Death of Metropolitan Antony*

The last time I heard his distinct voice was two days before he went to the hospital in Boston, Massachusetts. When I asked him how he felt, for the first time I heard Metropolitan Antony say, "I do not feel well." He was a man full of confidence in his physical and mental health, and death was the most distant thing from his mind. His death in Boston was a tremendous emotional shock to me because I loved the man and admired him for his many excellent qualities.

I grew up in a country where the bishop is the master, and others are slaves. I grew up in a country where the bishop is untouchable, always frowning, always living in an ivory tower above the people and especially above the lower rank of the clergy. When I first met Metropolitan Antony, I felt completely at ease with him. I said to myself, "Thank God, at last I met a bishop who celebrates the feast of life, who smiles, jokes, laughs, tells funny stories, weeps, works hard, and above all, cares for ordinary people." Although he was not a perfect man by any means, no one can deny his tremendous contribution to the growth of our Church in North America between 1936 and 1966. On a gloomy and cold day of February, 1966, with much tears and sorrow, we buried Antony on a hill overlooking the city of Brooklyn where he spent most of his years.

2. *Nomination and Frustration*

In accordance with our constitution, a special Archdiocesan Convention was called in March, one month after the death of Archbishop Antony, for the purpose of nominating three clergymen so that their names might be submitted to the Holy Synod of Antioch to elect one of them for the widowed archdiocese. To my complete surprise, I received the majority vote of the clergy and laity of our archdiocese. But while the wishes of our archdiocese were made crystal clear on this continent, there was on another continent a great measure of synodical confusion, intrigues, conspiracies, and uncertainties. Dismayed and frustrated by the inaction of the Mother Church, our clergy and laity were most determined to preserve the sacred unity of our archdiocese at all costs. Messages and messengers were sent to Antioch warning the Synod not to play with fire. Some of my friends during this period urged me to make a trip to the Old Country and meet informally with the Synod, but I refused to make the trip for the sake of my dignity and personal integrity.

Finally, on the Eve of the great Feast of the Transfiguration, the Holy Synod of Antioch honored the wishes of our archdiocese and elected me to succeed Metropolitan Antony in this holy ministry. Thus, on August 14, 1966, I was elevated to the rank of the episcopate amongst family members, relatives, friends, and hundreds of curious people who came to St. Elias Monastery to catch a glimpse of the controversial American archbishop. Needless to say that August 14 was one of the most emotional days of my life.

After the consecration, I had to rush back to San Francisco via the Far East in order to preside over the Annual Convention of the archdiocese. When I reached San Francisco, I was so emotionally drained and physically exhausted that until now I do not know how I survived that convention. From San Francisco I returned to Lebanon to participate in the meeting of the Holy Synod which was still in session. The meetings of the Holy Synod lacked order, discipline, seriousness and future visions to such a degree that at one point I left the meeting very disappointed, went to my room and wept bitterly.

3. *A Year of Difficulties and Loneliness*

In the autumn of 1966, I returned from Lebanon to the United States to begin my work in the archdiocese. I will never forget that horrible October day when I entered the archdiocese home in Bay Ridge alone. Tired from traveling and the events of the past months, I was desperately in need of help. There was the *Archbishop of New York and all North America* in an old house without a cook, a secretary, a priest or even a custodian, which most parishes provide for their priests.

The Archdiocese of New York and all North America was one man: Metropolitan Antony Bashir, and when he died there was no organization. It is ironic that the closest members of the Board of Trustees to the late archbishop did not know much about the spiritual and financial conditions of the archdiocese. Metropolitan Antony did not leave any files to speak of, because his mind was his file and he grew up with the archdiocese. Our financial system and our annual budget were too inadequate to answer the future needs of the archdiocese. Some of our priests were neither liturgically nor psychologically fit to serve an Eastern Orthodox Church.

There was an awesome task ahead of me, and the difficult thing was to discern where to begin. My main concern was to know my flock and my clergy first. Thus I embarked on a visitation program which took me to almost every parish within the archdiocese. I found our people warm, hospitable, receptive to new ideas and very eager to join hands with me to work for a brighter future of our Church on this continent. I was determined to leap out of Antony's shadow, to make my own footsteps, and to write my chapters in the history of this archdiocese. The members of the Archdiocesan Board did not really know me well and were watching me with some caution. When they got to know me and realized what I was trying to do, they joined hands with me and became very much involved in the spiritual and financial affairs of the archdiocese.

These were some of the problems which caused me many sleepless nights. Thus the first year of my episcopate was the most difficult year of my life. The progress which we made in the subsequent years was the result of agonizing decisions, careful planning, and above all, excellent cooperation between our clergy and laity. But progress does not come easily; it is expensive, and someone has to pay the price.

4. *The 1967 Arab-Israeli War*

Since my early youth, I have always been proud of my people, their glorious history and tremendous contribution to world civilization. I believe that their heroic struggle to establish themselves in North America is one of the greatest human dramas ever written. Our people lack neither intelligence nor ambition. However, since the disintegration of the Arab Empire they have been plagued by dissension and disunity. And despite their unique strategic place on the global map and the tremendous natural resources which they possess, they have never been able to use all these advantages to influence world opinion in their fight for an honorable and just peace in the Middle East. The three military defeats which they have suffered in 1948, 1956 and 1967 were the ugliest and darkest chapters in the entire Arab history. It was hard to believe that the June War was decided in favor of Israel within a few hours, and it was heartbreaking to see the defeated Egyptian army wandering in Sinai aimlessly. But the most tragic and disgusting thing was to see how the Arab diplomats were begging the United Nations for a cease-fire. I will never forget how Dr. Charles Malek, who was visiting me that day, and I wept while watching the proceedings of the United Nations General Assembly. After a few tearful moments, Dr. Malek turned to me and said, "The Middle East will never be the same."

The news media and the news commentators made a mockery of the Arab nations. Even the weathermen laughed and made sarcastic remarks against the Arabs. Those of us who have pride in our heritage and national background were subjected, especially in New York City, to the most pathetic and humiliating experience. Subsequent to the June War, I started a national campaign to raise money for the Arab refugees—a campaign which took me to many cities all over the United States and Canada.

I believe that the aforementioned emotional events, as well as many others, have contributed directly and indirectly to my heart collapse in Washington, D.C. in January, 1968.

A Decision Made, an Action Taken

In September, 1968, a friend of mine at Cleveland Clinic convinced me to have a coronary arteriogram test to determine exactly the extent of damage caused to the heart arteries. The result of the test was discouraging, and I was told that if I did not undergo heart surgery immediately, I would die within six months. I had a strong feeling that I would not die within six months and after consultation with my personal doctor, Eugene Sayfie of the Miami Heart Institute, I decided against the operation.

From 1968 to 1972 I traveled extensively and followed my

normal schedule of work without any difficulties. In the late spring and summer of 1972, I began to experience some chest pressure and some shortness of breath. I underwent another coronary arteriogram test in San Francisco and found out that the disease had progressed. At that point I had no doubt in my mind that the operation was a must, regardless of the outcome. I recalled my conversation with God in 1968 and again I felt very much at peace with myself.

After the Los Angeles Convention, I returned home and immediately called Dr. Eugene Sayfie and told him to proceed with the necessary arrangements for the operation. After spending a few days in Hillsboro, Florida, with a good friend, Dr. Sayfie informed me that I needed another coronary arteriogram test. Needless to say, I was depressed to hear that because I hated to be subjected to another one of those tests. Upon examining the results of the test, Dr. Sayfie informed me that I would be operated on on Monday morning, September 18.

On Sunday, September 17, Fr. Antoun Khouri, my brother Najib and his wife Elaine arrived at the hospital; we spent a pleasant day recalling many beautiful past memories. Sunday afternoon, Fr. Michael Husson was kind enough to give me communion. Sunday evening, Dr. Trad, a member of the surgical team, explained to me the nature of the operation. The complexity of the surgery was beyond my comprehension and when Dr. Trad asked me whether I had any questions, I simply said "no." At 10:00 P.M., I asked Fr. Antoun to recite Psalm 50 to me in Arabic: "Have mercy upon me, O God, according to Thy great mercy. And according to the multitude of Thy tender mercies blot out my iniquities...."

When Fr. Antoun finished, I asked him to recite it once more and he did. Then it was time for him, Najib and Elaine to depart. After they left, a nurse came to give me a sleeping pill; I kindly thanked her and refused to take anything. I slept well until 7:00 A.M., when a nurse woke me up and gave me a shot to prepare me for the big operation. The last people I saw while leaving the room were Fr. Antoun, Najib and Elaine. I waved good-bye to them and slowly slipped into the realm of unconsciousness.

Monday, September 18, was a lost day of my life. I remained unconscious until 9:00 P.M. When I opened my eyes I saw nothing around my bed except doctors and nurses. They told me it was 9:00 P.M. and the operation was a success. I looked at them gratefully for a few moments and went back into a deep sleep. Tuesday morning I woke and began to be aware of myself and the world around me.

For a while I thought I was a spaceman because of the number of tubes and wires connected to my body. I looked through the window at the green trees and felt as if I were looking at the world for the first time. We were six in the intensive care unit; two had to be reoperated on because of internal bleeding, and I heard later that both survived. When Dr. Trad told me that the operation took six hours, I was amazed, thanked him for his skill, and thanked God for His infinite goodness and mercy. After four days in the intensive care unit I was transferred to a private room and began to feel stronger every day. Needless to say, the days and nights at the hospital were very long. The hospital world is a world of sorrow and tears, and a priest will never fully appreciate his ministry to the sick unless he suffers.

A Renewed Hope
The archdiocese response to my illness was most comforting. Hundreds of letters and cards were received from children and young people. About ten cards were received from different dogs in the archdiocese. Beautiful bouquets of flowers filled the room to the extent that one morning I woke up and thought I was in a funeral home. Such acts of human love made me realize more than ever how beautiful our people are and that my struggle on their behalf will never be in vain. I left the Miami Heart Institute with a renewed hope, renewed vigor and many visions for the future. A good friend offered me his beautiful apartment at Ft. Lauderdale's beach for my convalescence period. That place was indeed a piece of heaven. It was there where I spent some

of my happiest and most serene days. The first time I walked on that beach I felt like kissing every grain of sand, hugging every wave and embracing the whole world.

A few days before Thanksgiving, I returned home and went straight to the altar of St. John's Chapel and prayed from the depths of my heart. The trees around the house were naked, the leaves were wrinkled and the flowers were dead. Thus, with much lust for life, I began to dream, with the naked trees, the wrinkled leaves and the dead flowers, of another spring, another youth conference and another summer.

On Unity in the Church
Charleston, 1973

*"This is the day that the Lord has made;
let us rejoice and be glad therein."*

I would like to open my remarks this evening from the First Letter of St. Paul to the Corinthians, Chapter 1:1–13.

> I appeal to you, brethren, by the name of our Lord Jesus Christ, that all of you agree and that there be no dissensions among you, but that you be united in the same mind and the same judgment. For it has been reported to me that there is quarreling among you, my brethren. What I mean is that each one of you says, I belong to Paul or I belong to Apollos, or I belong to Cephas or I belong to Christ. Is Christ divided? Was Paul crucified for you? Or were you baptized in the name of Paul?

These words were written by St. Paul to the Christians living in Corinth almost two thousand years ago. If St. Paul, who was one of the founders of the Patriarchate of Antioch, would write a letter today to the Antiochian Orthodox people of North America, I believe he would put it this way:

> For it has been reported to me that there is quarreling among you, my brethren. What I mean is that each one of you says, I belong to Archbishop Philip, or I belong to the Orthodox Church in America, or I belong to Christ. Is Christ divided? Was Archbishop Philip crucified for you? Or were you baptized in the name of Archbishop Michael?

The Church is a divine institution founded on the firm foundation, the cornerstone which is Jesus Christ.

Thirty-seven years ago, our Antiochian people in North America were sadly divided by a deceitful telegram—and the senior Orthodox among us remember this very well. Thus, this tragic division was caused neither by the people of New York nor the people of Toledo. But unfortunately since then, in some of our cities, as a result of this misunderstanding, we see two Antiochian parishes belonging to different jurisdictions; we see neighbors fighting neighbors, relatives fighting relatives, parishes fighting parishes. I dare say, this has been a long dark night in the history of our people in North America.

In the past, we have had some encounters to find a solution to our North American problem. Regretfully, these encounters have failed because both of us, deep in our hearts, were relying on the Holy Synod of Antioch, which is 7,000 miles away from us, to resolve our problem and bring unity to our divided people in North America.

Little did we know that the Holy Synod of Antioch was not really interested in settling any problem in North America. And if we examine the contradictory decisions recorded in the minutes of the Holy Synod since the inception of this problem, we discover that these decisions constitute the darkest chapters in the history of the Holy Synod of Antioch. Just think how much time, how much effort, how much energy, we have expended and wasted in the attempts to move Antioch to solve our problem—but to no avail!

We are not here to dig graves or to continue chewing the past; we are not here to point fingers at anyone, or to sit in the judgment seat. God forbid! We are here to submit ourselves humbly to God and to ask His forgiveness for our false pride and the past iniquities. Our division in North America reflects exactly the sickness of the Arab world today. More than a hundred million people, despite all their human and natural resources, were more than once crushed by a little state because of their division and dissension.

How can we dream of a united Arab world, or how can we dream of a united Orthodox Church in North America, if our own family is divided? Therefore, our first priority must be to put our own house in order! Archbishop David is dead. Archbishop Antony is dead. Archbishop Philip will die and Archbishop Michael will one day die. But the Church will never die. For Christ said, "I will build my Church and the gates of hell will not prevail against her."

Being practical and realistic, just think of how strong we will be if we unite in one archdiocese: one Christian Education Department, one Sacred Music Department, one Theological Education Department, one Department of Finance, one Public Relations Department, one youth movement, etc.

Our destiny as Antiochian Orthodox people in this country is a prelude to uniting all Orthodox people on this continent. But this task can be achieved only if we Antiochians are first united.

Last winter, while in Florida recovering from heart surgery, I resolved that this division between us should no longer continue. Thus I decided to take the initiative to visit my brother in Christ, Archbishop Michael, and to discuss with him frankly and sincerely certain practical steps which would ultimately lead us to this most desired unity.

This past June, while in Toledo, I visited Archbishop Michael at his headquarters. Subsequent to this meeting I prepared for this personal visit by appointing two of my priests to visit him with specific instructions that needed to be settled. Finally, last month these representatives submitted to Archbishop Michael, on my behalf, the following proposal:

1. There shall be *one* archdiocese in North America, to be called The Antiochian Orthodox Christian Archdiocese of North America. We would sacrifice the words "New York," and you would sacrifice the words "Toledo, Ohio."
2. The primate of this united archdiocese will have the title, His Eminence, the Most Reverend Metropolitan. The archbishop of this united archdiocese will have the title, His Eminence, the Most Reverend Archbishop. This

does not leave out the possibility of having other auxiliary archbishops or bishops. However, there would be only one metropolitan.
3. This united archdiocese would have one vote in the Holy Synod of Antioch, that of the metropolitan or whomever he designates. This will ensure our united archdiocese a united front in the affairs of the patriarchate and will be the source of our unity and strength.
4. The metropolitan would reside at the headquarters in Englewood, New Jersey, using the mother Cathedral of St. Nicholas in Brooklyn, New York. The archbishop would reside at the headquarters in Toledo, Ohio, using the Cathedral of St. George in Toledo.
5. The cathedrals of the united archdiocese would be as follows: (a) Eastern Cathedral—St. Nicholas of Brooklyn; (b) Midwestern Cathedral of St. George of Toledo; (c) Western Cathedral—St. Nicholas of Los Angeles; (d) Southern Cathedral—St. George of Coral Gables of Miami; and (e) New England Cathedral—St. George of Worcester.
6. This united archdiocese in North America would have one treasury, one Board of Trustees, one youth movement, one religious education and sacred music program, the same discipline for clergy, laity and parishes; the same insurance program for the clergy; and the same annual youth and archdiocesan conferences and conventions, etc. In short, we will be one in every respect in reference to the Antiochian faithful in North America.
7. The hierarchs of this united archdiocese will receive their stipends from the general treasury of the united archdiocese. All hierarchs will be permitted free access to all parishes of the united archdiocese.
8. All parishes of the united archdiocese would be expected to joyfully fulfill all spiritual and financial obligations to the united archdiocese as defined in the canons, constitution and bylaws of the united archdiocese.

9. In all matters pertaining to discipline, protocol and spirituality, the canons of the Ecumenical Orthodox Church will be observed as well as the customs and the traditions of the Antiochian Church.
10. Upon agreement on the above and/or any other terms set forth by the two hierarchs, and upon ratification of the faithful as represented by the two Boards of Trustees, all terms shall then be submitted to the Patriarch and the Holy Synod of Antioch before final implementation can occur in North America.

This is our proposal which we hope you will consider with open minds and open hearts. I wish to conclude with these words from the First Letter of St. John:

> This then is the message which we have heard of Him, and declare unto you, that God is light, and in Him is no darkness at all. If we say that we have fellowship with Him, and walk in darkness, we lie, and do not speak the truth. But if we walk in the light, as He is in the light, we have fellowship one with another and the blood of Jesus Christ cleanses us from all sin.

Editor's Endnotes:

1. The reader should know that the address to the archdiocese in Chicago in 1970 is on the occasion of the 65th Anniversary of the establishment of the Antiochian Archdiocese, and the 25th Anniversary of the Annual Convention.

2. In September of 1970, shortly after the address given in Chicago, Patriarch Theodosius fell asleep in the Lord; one day later Patriarch Elias IV was elected to the Throne of Antioch and All the East.

3. In December of 1971, the new headquarters and residence was purchased in Englewood, New Jersey.

4. In September of 1972, Metropolitan Philip successfully underwent open-heart bypass surgery.

5. In 1973, Metropolitan Philip issued an edict establishing the Evening Divine Liturgy for the great feast days.

6. In July, 1973, His Eminence established the Antiochian Orthodox Christian Women of North America (AOCWNA).

7. With regard to the Charleston address presented in our collection, the unity for which His Eminence called in his 1973 address was ratified by the Holy Synod of Antioch in 1975. Thereafter, Archbishop Michael appeared with Metropolitan Philip at all archdiocesan meetings.

8. In 1975, His Eminence established the Order of St. Ignatius of Antioch, the philanthropic arm of the archdiocese. This organization, which began with 34 members, has grown to over 2,500 at the time of this publication.

Chapter 7

IS LIFE NOT MORE THAN FOOD?

In the past ten years, we can say that we have reached many goals. However, we will never reach our final goal "until we all attain to the unity of faith, to the knowledge of the Son of God, to mature manhood, to the measure of the fullness of Christ" (Ephesians 4:13). You have heard me say, therefore, that every time we climb to a summit, we discover more summits to be climbed. Nikos Kazantzakis put it this way: "There is no summit; there is only height. There is no rest." The Church teaches us that man is always becoming. Our future, therefore, is to continue struggling, to continue climbing.

Metropolitan Philip

- *What I Promised,* 1976
- *Blessed is the Nation Whose God is the Lord,* 1976
- *Orthodoxy and Contemporary Iconoclasm,* 1976

AND HE LEADS THEM

In 1976, the tenth anniversary of Metropolitan Philip's episcopate, His Eminence delivered the following three addresses. They were chosen for this collection because they both reflect his accomplishments over that first decade, and pose some new areas of challenge for the next decade.

The first is his tenth anniversary message to the thirty-first Archdiocesan Convention gathered in San Francisco. It was ten years earlier that Metropolitan Philip attended his first convention as Archbishop of North America, in the very same city. This speech is a summation of his episcopacy's first decade. We will present that address in its complete form; it speaks for itself.

The second address was delivered at that same convention in 1976. It is truly a unique presentation. In preparation for the two-hundredth anniversary of American independence, Philip decided that he would speak a second time at the convention about the various dimensions of freedom with which Americans are blessed. He addressed both the potential and the dangers of that freedom. The profundity of his exposition on the Christian understanding of freedom astonished not only the Orthodox, but also the non-Orthodox that were present.

This chapter's third address is his 1976 sermon on the Sunday of Orthodoxy in Pittsburgh, Pennsylvania. In this homily, Philip not only comments on aspects of contemporary iconoclasm, but also addresses an issue which hereafter is often the focus of his attention: a united Orthodox Church in North America. As the Bicentennial of the United States coincided with that year's celebration of the Sunday of Orthodoxy, the Metropolitan questioned: "What can Orthodoxy offer America?"

Taken together, these three addresses from 1976 are labeled with our present title because each is clearly subsumed under it: **"Is Not Life More Than Food?"** *This is a quote from Matthew's Gospel which Philip uses in the first of these addresses. It is most appropriate for the words he speaks in all the talks given during his tenth anniversary as Metropolitan of North America.*

J. J. A.

What I Promised
San Francisco, 1976

"For a thousand years in Thy sight are but as yesterday when it is past, or as a watch in the night" (Psalm 90:4).

These words from Psalm 90 come to mind as we immerse ourselves in the memories of a decade passed. It seems like yesterday when the Pan-American jet landed in San Francisco, after a thirty-six hour flight around the world. I still vividly remember the joy and curiosity which I read on your faces, as you welcomed me back from a triumphant, yet difficult and emotional trip to the Middle East.

A Decade of Struggle and Glory

On August 14, 1966, before the Holy Synod of Antioch and the Church, I made the following confession of faith:

> In this, my confession of the Holy Faith, I promise to observe the canons of the Holy Apostles, and the Seven Ecumenical Councils and of the pious Provincial Councils, the traditions of the Church, and the decrees, orders and regulations of the Holy Fathers. And all things whatsoever they have accepted, I also accept; and whatsoever things they have rejected, those will I also reject. I promise also to preserve the peace of the Church, and firmly to hold and zealously to teach the people entrusted to me. And I promise to rule the flock committed unto me, in fear of God and in devoutness of life.... I promise to visit and watch over the flock now confided to me, after the manner of the Apostles—whether or not they remain true to the faith, and in the exercise of good works—most especially the priests.

As far as I know, with the help of the grace divine, I have

lived up to my promise. I made this solemn pledge during a turbulent time in the history of the Patriarchate of Antioch and this archdiocese. When I promised God and His people to preserve the peace of the Church, I had first and foremost in my mind the division among our Antiochian people in North America. As you well know, after the death of Bishop Raphael Hawaweeny in 1915, our people became divided between "Russi and Antaki." In 1936, with the consecration of Archbishop Antony and Archbishop Samuel, the division continued, but now between Toledo and New York.

This unfortunate division lasted for sixty years, from 1915 to 1975. It created much misunderstanding among our people. Brothers were not talking to brothers; cousins were not talking to cousins; relatives were not talking to relatives; friends were not talking to friends; priests were not talking to priests and even bishops were not talking to bishops. When I came to America in 1956, invited by the late Archbishop Samuel David, it was difficult for me to understand the absurdity of this situation. Our people are so rich in beautiful traditions and deeply rooted in a great culture, yet it is very difficult to unite them in one heart and one mind. What is going on in Lebanon today is a living witness to this sad reality.

When my episcopate began in 1966, I was determined more than ever to "preserve the peace of the Church," and to unite our people in a strong Antiochian Archdiocese of North America. In Ephesians, St. Paul said:

> I, therefore, a prisoner for the Lord, beg you to lead a life worthy of the calling to which you have been called, with all lowliness and meekness, with patience, forbearing one another in love, eager to maintain the unity of the spirit in the bond of peace. There is one body and one spirit, just as you were called to the one hope that belongs to your call, one Lord, one Father, one Baptism, one God and Father of us all, who is above all and through all and in all (Ephesians 4:1–6).

Seeking Unity for Antioch in America

Three years ago in June, I was presiding over a Parish Life Conference in Toledo, Ohio. Sunday, after the Divine Liturgy, a few priests came to my suite to say good-bye. I asked one of them to call Archbishop Michael and ask him when he could receive me at his home. The priest looked at me as if I were crazy and said, "Do you really mean it?" I said, "Absolutely, I do."

The priest called and the appointment was immediately set. Archbishop Michael graciously received us in his home and I found him very receptive to the idea of unity and as eager for it as I was. We decided to begin a serious dialogue which lasted for two years and resulted in the agreement which we signed in Pittsburgh, Pennsylvania, June 24, 1975, and which subsequently was accepted by our people convened in Lake George and Louisville, Kentucky, and finally ratified by the Holy Synod of Antioch on August 19, 1975.

I believe that this unity is the greatest event which has taken place in the life of the Antiochian Patriarchate and perhaps in the life of Orthodoxy in this hemisphere. And I want to make it clear that, without the cooperation and courage of His Eminence, Archbishop Michael, this unity would never have been possible. Just think for a moment how much time, money and effort was expended in this direction throughout the years, but to no avail. This unity, my friends, is indeed a gift from God. "For every good and perfect gift is from above, and cometh down from Thee, the Father of Lights."

Let us, therefore, not lose sight of the fact that our Antiochian unity is not an end by itself. Let us not forget that Orthodoxy on this continent is administratively divided by ethnic barriers. Such division is nothing but a judgment on all of us. Let us pray that our Antiochian unity will inspire other Orthodox ethnic jurisdictions to emulate our example and unite among themselves as a first step toward total Orthodox unity. Orthodox unity, to us Antiochians, is not mere rhetoric. We know exactly what we are doing, and where we are going. When other Orthodox groups on this continent were wallowing in their ethnic cocoons, we were teaching, preaching, and translating books into English, establishing English church schools and organizing English choirs. The unity of six million Orthodox in this hemisphere remains one of our ultimate goals and we shall never rest until this goal is achieved.

The Antiochian Women
Although this movement is still in its formative years, in such a short time it has already left an impact on the life of this archdiocese. I have noticed last year and this year that the best attended meetings at our regional conferences were the women's meetings. Their devotion, dedication and efforts on behalf of their organization are an inspiration to all of us. As you well know, their national project last year and this year has been continuing pastoral education, a field which is almost neglected by our seminaries.

The purpose of pastoral education is to enlighten our priests about how to deal with serious problems and many others. Unfortunately, scholastic theology does not deal with these problems. We are living in a sick and constantly changing society. The problems which the Church faced in A.D. 325 are quite different from the problems which we are facing in the last half of the twentieth century. Through this program of continuing pastoral education, we are encouraging our priests to take a new look at these problems which are affecting our parishes, like everybody else, because we are no longer an ethnic island.

The Stewardship Program
One of the most important departments we have established is the Department of Stewardship. The main purpose of this department is to help you put your house in order on the local level. I do not know how many times you have asked me, "What should we do with people who are not active and do not support the Church?" We have provided the answer to this agonizing question through our stewardship program.

All we ask from you, especially our parish councils, is to

participate in our regional conferences and see for yourself how much we have to offer in this field. If you implement this program properly in your parish, it will solve ninety-nine percent of your spiritual and financial problems.

I would like to caution you, however, that the primary purpose of this program is not to increase your income instantly; it is rather to bring people "to the love of God the Father, and the communion of the Holy Spirit." Bring people to church first, and money will come. Our Lord said: "Seek first His kingdom and His righteousness, and all things will be yours as well" (Matthew 6:33).

The Order of St. Ignatius of Antioch
In the Gospel of St. Mark, our Lord said:

> You know that those who are supposed to rule over the Gentiles lord it over them, and their great men exercise authority over them. But it shall not be so among you; but whoever would be great among you must be your servant, and whoever would be first among you must be slave of all (Mark 10:42–44).

An excellent brochure entitled "A Call to Greatness through Service" was printed and this brochure will reach every family within the archdiocese shortly. It describes through simple words, figures and fine art the various departments of the archdiocese and demonstrates clearly what we have and what we lack. If you read this brochure, you will find that some of our departments have no budgets at all, and whatever others budgeted for other departments is far from being adequate; we cannot serve you properly without the necessary funds.

The purpose of this order, therefore, is not to create a super organization which will "exercise authority and lord it over you," but rather to serve you. It is a call to greatness through service. Only through service can greatness be attained and there is no other way. If you are among those who ask, "What is the archdiocese and what does it do?" you will find part of the answer in this brochure. It is time that we stop to think and plunge into the depth of our being, asking ourselves: "*Is not life more than food*, and the body more than clothing?" (Matthew 6:25).

Without your commitment to Christ, we cannot provide for your spiritual needs. We invite you to become members of this order and to help us create a greater spiritual renaissance in this archdiocese for the sake of your children, grandchildren and future Orthodox generations.

Theological Education

It is obvious that without theological education, Orthodoxy will have no future. We have tried hard in the past ten years to increase the number of theological students and to support our theological schools. I am pleased to tell you that during the past year, we enrolled eighteen students of theology at different seminaries. Five of our seminarians this year were ordained priests and assigned to parishes.

As you well know, through your continued support and generosity our seminarians receive from the archdiocese full scholarships plus spending money on a monthly basis. In addition, our seminarians are assigned to help in our New York–New Jersey area parishes, where they also receive some financial assistance and experience the complexity of parish life in a practical way.

Four months ago, the Very Reverend Alexander Schmemann, Dean of St. Vladimir's Seminary, appealed to us for financial help in their proposed building program. We were delighted to learn that more and more young men and women have been accepting the challenge of the Gospel, hence the need for more space at the seminary. Instead of burdening you with another drive, I brought this matter to the attention of the archdiocesan trustees at our annual spring meeting. I am delighted to report to you that the trustees voted unanimously to grant St. Vladimir's Seminary $50,000 from Metropolitan Antony Bashir's memorial fund. On July 15, during a luncheon at the archdiocese headquarters, I presented Dean Schmemann and members of the faculty a check in your name: fifty thousand dollars for the building fund.

The Civil War in Lebanon
The war in Lebanon is now in its sixteenth month. We are very much concerned with this tragedy because many of us have families and relatives there. Moreover, whether we are from Arab descent or not, our spiritual roots lie deep in that beautiful soil which has been stained by the blood of innocent men, women and children. Words are inadequate to describe to you the depth of this tragedy. You ask about friends and relatives in Lebanon and these are some of the answers which you receive: this one was killed by a rocket while at home; this one was killed by a sniper's bullet while going to buy bread for his children; that family was burned to death by fire, etc. On July 12, I received the following telegram:

> Drastic development in Koura district, North Lebanon, left a great number dead and wounded. Physical damage is huge. Mass enforced immigration to Tripoli is taking place and over 35,000 displaced persons are now in Tripoli. We need your immediate help. Wire any amount of money in the name of Archbishop Kurban, care of Banque Francaise, Tripoli, via Homs, Syria c/o French American Banking Corporation, 120 Broadway, New York, New York. Signed—Archbishop Ilyas Kurban.

Last October, I was instrumental in forming the Standing Conference of Middle-Eastern Christian and Moslem Religious Leaders. We met at our headquarters in New Jersey and issued an appeal in the name of all Arabic-speaking people in North America to the people of Lebanon, urging them in the name of the spiritual values which they represent to stop this bloodbath at once and solve their problem through negotiation rather than confrontation. Our appeal went unheeded. Subsequently, we appealed again and again to both sides to stop this madness, but to no avail.

On April 15, we visited the President of the United States, Gerald Ford, and urged him to use his good offices to bring this war to an end. The president had already dispatched Dean Brown to Lebanon to mediate the crisis. His efforts were for naught. The president seemed genuinely concerned with Lebanon and its reconstruction, but unfortunately, the war persists.

Who is to blame for this tragedy? There is no simple answer to this question. However, I believe that the leaders of the Lebanese right and the leaders of the Lebanese left are to be blamed. I believe that the Palestinians are also to be blamed, for instead of dedicating all their efforts and energy to liberating their land, they are dying in Lebanon for nothing. But above all, I believe that the Arab countries who have demonstrated their complete impotence vis-à-vis this tragedy are to be blamed. It is time that the Arabs should stop blaming others for their tragedies and liberate themselves from their childish bickering and contradictions.

You have already heard the heartbreaking telegram of Archbishop Kurban. We have initiated a drive to help the victims of this war. Many of you have not responded. The need for help is beyond measure and we are still waiting to hear from you.

1977 Antiochian Holy Year

Shortly after his enthronement, our Father in Christ, His Beatitude Elias IV, Patriarch of Antioch and all the East, expressed his desire to visit his spiritual children in North America. I kindly asked His Beatitude to postpone his visit until the reunification of our people. As soon as the Holy Synod of Antioch ratified our agreement last August 19, 1975, I extended a tentative invitation to His Beatitude to visit us in 1977. Last November, at the fall meeting of the archdiocese Board of Trustees held in Montreal, Canada, the visit of the patriarch was thoroughly discussed and the Board voted unanimously on the following:

(a) to extend an official invitation to His Beatitude to visit North America in 1977. The invitation was extended and accepted by the patriarch; (b) to proclaim 1977 as the Antiochian Holy Year in North America; (c) to establish, in appreciation of the patriarch's visit, a half-million-dollar foundation for the Balamand Theological Academy; (d) to invest this money in North America and forward the interest from this investment to His Beatitude for the Balamand Academy.

Some of you might ask: "Why the foundation?" The answer is simple and clear. The Balamand Academy is the only Orthodox theological school left in the entire Middle East. The Patriarchates of Constantinople, Jerusalem and Alexandria have no theological schools. Thus, without the Balamand Seminary, Orthodoxy will have no future whatsoever in the Middle East.

I am sure you remember that one year before his death, Metropolitan Antony promised to build this academy. He passed away in February 1966. On August 15, 1966, one day after my consecration, we broke ground for the academy because our Board of Trustees was determined to build this greatly needed institution. In the fall of 1971, I and a delegation from the archdiocese were delighted to participate in the solemn dedication of this new and beautiful academy.

Unfortunately, because of security reasons and the complete collapse of the Lebanese economy, this school has been closed for the current academic year. We want to make sure that as soon as peace again reigns in Lebanon, this academy will reopen. Without your financial help, the reopening of this school will be just impossible. Patriarchs, bishops and hundreds of priests, some of them serving in this archdiocese, have studied at the old Balamand Seminary. The Balamand Academy is a beacon of light in a world of darkness and an anchor of hope in a sea of despair.

This is the first time in our history that we are going to welcome our patriarch to this continent. Patriarch Elias IV is the successor to Saints Peter, Paul and Ignatius of Antioch. He represents two thousand years of spirituality and a multitude of saints, martyrs, confessors and ascetics who "were made perfect in faith."

As We Look to the Future

Ten years have swiftly gone like a flickering of a wing or a twinkling of an eye, yet in such a short span of time, you have done almost the impossible. You have reorganized the archdiocese. You have built the Balamand Theological Academy. You have established a foundation to help needy Palestinian students. You have established the clergy insurance plan. You have founded new parishes and missions. You have increased the number of our theological students. You have purchased and renovated the new archdiocese headquarters. You have helped the victims of the October War in Syria. You have continued to improve and publish Christian education and sacred music materials. You have published new liturgical books for the Vesperal Divine Liturgy. You have built many new churches and cultural centers. You have continued to fight on behalf of the oppressed in the Middle East and everywhere. You have supported seminarians in this country and abroad. You have focused your attention on the problem of Christian stewardship. You have established the Order of St. Ignatius of Antioch. You have participated to a great extent in the sacramental life of the Church and you have reunited the Antiochian people after sixty years of division. These are some of the highlights of the past ten years. After all this struggle, have we made any spiritual progress? Only God knows. How can you measure the depth of the human spirit?

In the past ten years we can say that we have reached many goals. However, we will never reach our final goal "until we all attain to the unity of the faith and of the knowledge of the Son of God, to mature manhood, to the measure of the stature of the fullness of Christ" (Ephesians 4:13).

Twenty-five years ago, writing about life, I said, "Every time we climb a summit, we discover more summits to be climbed." Nikos Kazantzakis put it this way: "There is no summit, there is only height. There is no rest." The Church teaches us that man is always becoming. Our vision of the future, therefore, is to continue struggling and to continue climbing.

In conclusion, I would like to leave you with these words from St. Paul to the Philippians:

> Finally, brethren, whatever is true, whatever is honorable, whatever is just, whatever is pure, whatever is lovely, whatever is gracious, if there is any excellence, if there is anything worthy of praise, think about these things. What you have learned and received and heard and seen in me, do: and the God of peace will be with you (Philippians 4:8, 9).

Blessed Is the Nation Whose God Is the Lord
(Psalm 33:12)
San Francisco, 1976

As the United States of America embarks on its third century of proclaiming liberty and justice to—and for—all mankind, I would like to share a few brief thoughts with you before we conclude this convention and disperse to our communities throughout North America.

In the Book of Deuteronomy, chapter eight, verse seven, we read:

> For the Lord your God is bringing you into a good land, a land of brooks of water, of fountains and springs, flowing valleys and hills, a land of wheat and barley, of vines and fig trees and pomegranates, a land of olive trees and honey, a land in which you will eat bread without scarcity, in which you will lack nothing, a land whose stones are iron, and out of whose hills, you can dig copper. And you shall eat and be full, and you shall bless the Lord, your God, for the good land He has given you.

On November 19, 1620, after a perilous journey, during which the Mayflower encountered a number of dangerous storms, the pilgrims woke to the shout of "Land!" One of them, William Button, died during the journey and was buried at sea. Another, John Howland, was carried overboard by a wave, but was rescued; and Steven and Elizabeth Hopkins became parents of a son, named Oceanus for his birthplace. Thus, led by the star of freedom, about one hundred pilgrims dropped anchor off Provincetown, Massachusetts.

It was this love of freedom which motivated the early pioneers to take such risks and suffer hardships. They did not want riches or fame; it was their ambition only to build themselves homes, to educate their children in the traditions of the motherland, and to worship God as their conscience dictated. They decided that in all the world, America was the one place that offered them these opportunities. It is evident, therefore, that the first era of our early history was marked by fierce struggle for mere existence.

The second and most brilliant era of our national life was marked by a tremendous struggle for freedom and independence. The search for liberty—religious, civil or personal—brought thousands of early settlers to these shores and peopled the young America with a race of men to whom liberty was more precious than life. We are most indebted to these courageous individuals who were ready at any moment to sacrifice their lives so that the future American generations may enjoy freedom, justice, prosperity and human dignity. If we examine carefully the Declaration of Independence, we find that the authors of this declaration had a strong faith in God, who created all men equal with inalienable rights to live freely, happily, and to worship God according to the dictates of their consciences. Thus, from the very beginning of our national life, there was a strong emphasis on the right of the individual. Such emphasis is deeply rooted in our religious heritage. In the Book of Psalms, we read the following:

> What is man that Thou art mindful of him, and the Son of man that Thou dost care for him? Yet Thou hast made him little less than the angels, and dost crown him with glory and honor. Thou hast given him dominion over the works of Thy hands. Thou hast put all things under his feet (Psalm 8:4–6).

Based on this divine revelation, the right of the individual to seek freedom, justice and equality, regardless of creed, race or color is very sacred. We must thank Almighty God that we Americans are enjoying a great measure of freedom, justice and equality. Because of our human weakness, however, we have a tendency to use our freedom to the detriment of others. My freedom ends where your freedom begins. Freedom must not become a license to deprive others of their God-given rights. Freedom does not give us the right to suppress others and monopolize the wealth of the world at the expense of the poor.

If there is a starving child in America, this means that all Americans are starving. And if there is a starving child in this world, this means that the entire world is starving. St. Paul said, "Who is weak, and I am not weak? Who is made to fall, and I am not indignant?" (2 Corinthians 11:29). Man has never been an island unto himself. The shores of his concern have expanded from his neighborhood to his nation, and from his nation to his world. Free men have always known the necessity for responsibility. This responsibility should weigh heavily upon the hearts of all free men. Dostoevsky realized this when he wrote:

> I tell you man has no more agonizing anxiety than to find someone to whom he can hand over the gift of freedom with which the unhappy creature is born.

Freedom without responsibility is chaos. Only responsible freedom is a divine gift which we must preserve and cherish, and responsibly pass on to the next generation. In October 1973, Alexander Solzhenitsyn wrote:

> The most important part of our freedom, inner freedom, is always subject to our will. If we surrender it to corruption, we do not deserve to be called human.

During the past two hundred years, we have made the greatest contributions to mankind in the fields of science, technology, medicine, economics and social concerns; and we Orthodox can be justly proud of our important role in these developments. We must be cautious, however, lest we become arrogant and self-sufficient. Arrogance and self-sufficiency bear the seeds of our own destruction as individuals and, ultimately, as a nation. Many nations and empires have risen, flourished and collapsed because of arrogance and moral decadence. Edward Gibbon in his famous work, *The Decline and Fall of the Roman Empire*, cited five reasons why the great Roman Empire withered and died. Here are the factors he cited:

1. The undermining of the dignity and sanctity of the home—the very basis of human society.
2. Higher and higher taxes; the spending of public money for free bread and circuses for the populace.
3. The mad craze for pleasure; sports and other entertainment becoming every year more and more exciting, more brutal and more immoral.
4. The building of great armaments when the real enemy was within . . . the decay of individual responsibility.
5. The decline of religion—faith fading into mere form; losing touch with life, losing power to guide the people.

Can we read in America, today, some of these signs which Edward Gibbon painted hundreds of years ago about the collapse of the Roman Empire? Let us pray that our great republic will never have the same fate. As we plunge into a new century, let us resolve that the greatness of America lies within you and me, within the individual. America cannot grow taller and stronger than the individual who makes America. Walt Whitman, the poet of America, summed up this reality as follows:

> It is not the earth, it is not America, who is so great; it is I who am great, or to be great—it is you up there or anyone. It is to walk rapidly through civilizations, governments, theories, through poems, pageants, shows, to form great individuals.

Let us affirm our deep faith in God, the Lord of History, who controls with His mighty hand the destiny of nations and empires. Without God, everything which we have built throughout the years will be consumed by fire and turn into dust and ashes. Let us never forget God's words in Deuteronomy:

> You shall remember the Lord your God, for it is He who gives you power to get wealth; that He may confirm His covenant which He swore to your fathers, as at this day. And if you forget the Lord your God and go after other gods and serve them and worship them, I solemnly warn you this day that you will surely perish (Deuteronomy 8:18–20).

Orthodoxy and Contemporary Iconoclasm
1976

Every year, on the first Sunday of the Great Lent, the Church celebrates her triumph over the iconoclastic heresy. Some church historians believe that this heresy was deeply rooted in political and social reasons. However, I believe that the theological reason was the most predominant. Emperors Leo III and Constantine V waged a savage war against the icons, a war which resulted in much suffering, destruction and bloodshed.

Iconoclasm in History
The Church was accused by the iconoclasts of worshipping idols. It was inevitable that the war against images would lead to a tremendous Christological controversy. The iconoclasts stated that:

> The form of the Servant assumed by Christ was no longer in the realm of realities. He undoubtedly assumed it, but in order to transform it into a divine reality; it is important, therefore, that the Christians, if they desire to anticipate the glory that is His, and to which they also aspire, should contemplate God in the purity of their hearts and not in artificial images of an historical past that is now over.

The iconoclasts further stated that material images are "barriers" which hinder the soul from returning to the immaterial prototype.

The Church of the eighth century was indeed fortunate to have brilliant, valiant and articulate people like St. John of Damascus, St. Theodore the Studite, Patriarch Germanus and Patriarch Nicephorus who courageously defended her position vis-à-vis iconoclasm. Even before the iconoclastic decrees, Patriarch Germanus of Constantinople emphatically stated that it is possible to make an image of Christ because He "deigned to become man." According to St. John's Gospel, "the Word was made flesh, and dwelt among us and we beheld His glory, the glory as of the only Begotten of the Father, full of grace and truth" (John 1:14). Thus, since Christ became man and was seen, heard and touched by people, the Christian iconographer can represent His human character because He became like one of us in all things except sin, by assuming our total human nature.

The representation of Christ's divine and incomprehensible nature, however, is beyond the realm of iconography and art. St. John of Damascus profoundly stated this reality as follows:

> If we made an image of the invisible God, we would certainly be in error, but we do nothing of the sort; for we are not in error if we make the image of the Incarnate God, who appeared on earth in the flesh, and who in His ineffable goodness lived with human beings and assumed the nature, the thickness, the shape and the color of the flesh.

When we venerate the icon of Christ, we do not venerate wood and color, but the Creator of the universe who became matter for our salvation.

We owe a great measure of gratitude to the Church of the iconoclastic era for defending the Orthodox faith, thus preserving for us the beautiful icons which adorn our Orthodox Church and continue to instill in us a deep sense of the holy. When we worship and look at the holy icons, we feel that the Church of the Old Testament, the Church of the New Testament, and the Church throughout history is praying with us and interceding for us. A church without icons is a church without windows to heaven.

Later Forms of Iconoclasm

Despite the doctrinal victory which the Church scored against the iconoclastic heresy of the eighth century, iconoclasm continued to challenge the Church relentlessly through many socioeconomic, philosophical and political ideologies. Such ideological challenges were no longer aimed at Church icons but rather at the human, the real and living icon of God.

From the beginning, according to the Book of Genesis, "God created man in His own image, in the image of God created He him; male and female created He them" (Genesis 1:27). Both the Old and the New Testaments reveal to us that man is God's most precious creation. God made him a steward over the natural world. He gave him "dominion over the fish of the sea, and over the birds of the air, and over the cattle and over all the earth, and over every creeping thing that creepeth upon the earth" (Genesis 1:26). Surely the Incarnation has a cosmic dimension, but the primary purpose of God's marvelous and decisive intervention in human history was to embrace man and restore to him that divine sonship and that divine image which was distorted by sin. "When the fullness of the time was come, God sent forth His Son, made of a woman, made under the law, to redeem them that were under the law, that we might receive the adoption of sons" (Galatians 4:4–6).

The European Renaissance inaugurated a new era of iconoclastic heresies, one which led to forms such as godless humanism, godless Marxism and godless nationalism. These ideologies, under the influence of power politics in both capitalist and communist countries, tried to enslave man, to reduce him to a mere tool of production, and to make him feel self-sufficient by divorcing him from God, and consequently, from a total Christian view of himself and history. The Russian author Evgeny Barabanov, in a recent essay entitled "Schism Between Church and the World," said:

> It is impossible for man to settle in the world completely without God. Although proud of its successes and

attainments, the world sees every day more clearly the provisional and insufficient nature of its civilization. On the verge of having its foundations shaken to the core, it thirsts as never before for the true light.

Unfortunately, only a few prophets such as Barabanov and Solzhenitsyn understand the tragedy of man under both capitalism and communism. We read in the Psalms that God made man "a little lower than the angels and has crowned him with glory and honor" (Psalm 8:5). Yet our economic systems, philosophical concepts and modern technology have dehumanized man and reduced him to an object of psychological and natural categories.

New Forms of Iconoclasm
The Church today is beset by all kinds of contemporary iconoclasm, many more than can be included here. However, let me mention the most serious one that, in a sense, represents the many others: world hunger.

The most serious problem born out of a modern iconoclasm with which our world is faced today is no longer a nuclear confrontation. It is rather mass starvation. We Americans have made an "icon" out of power; we want to hoard the goods of the earth. An American agronomist warned against the evils of this iconoclasm by stating that "unless mankind is wise enough and compassionate enough to design a better food security system, we may be seeing the beginning of the end of our civilization."

Let us look at the facts. According to the latest United Nations statistics, world population is increasing at the rate of ninety-five million people a year. Five hundred million people in Asia, Africa and Latin America are threatened with starvation. In certain provinces of northern India, famished Indians have stripped the trees of all edible leaves, and newspapers carry nightmarish reports of entire families who have committed suicide to end the agony of slow death by starvation.

We Americans comprise six percent of the world's population, yet we consume between thirty-five and forty percent of the earth's goods. How long can America survive as a little, wealthy island in an ocean of poverty? The money we give in foreign aid is too insignificant in comparison with the billions of dollars we derive from exporting destructive weapons and other commodities to poor nations. An editorial published in the *New York Times*, February 24, 1976, stated, "The shameful expansion of American arms sales abroad from less than one billion dollars in 1970 to an estimated twelve billion dollars in the fiscal year ending next June raises political and moral issues that neither the administration nor the Congress can ignore."

Connected with this, there is a new theological trend sweeping the Christian world today, called "theology of liberation." We have been asked to define our Orthodox position vis-à-vis this theology. Can the Church remain passive and silent in a world of hunger, racism, totalitarianism, economic exploitation and social injustice? And if not, can the Church advocate armed resistance and encourage social revolutions as ways and means to liberate oppressed nations? We need answers to this and to other new iconoclasms. We also have to speak in a prophetic way against other trends which are destroying God's image in man, such as sex and violence on television and movie screens, pornography, the disintegration of the family, the spread of nuclear power and corruption in our government, especially during this election year. Each and every one of our candidates for the highest office in the land is sacrificing his human dignity and moral principles in order to win votes.

What Orthodoxy Can Offer America

It is a beautiful thing that this year our Sunday of Orthodoxy celebration coincides with the Bicentennial of our nation. What can Orthodoxy offer America for her birthday? We have much to offer to America. We can offer America two thousand years of spirituality in a language America understands. Instead of Transcendental Meditation and Hari Krishna, we can offer America St. Simeon the New Theologian, St. John Chrysostom and St. Basil the Great. We have been on this continent for more than a century, selfishly enjoying our ethnic traditions and talking to America in languages America does not understand. No wonder, then, that despite the depth of our spirituality, which this pragmatic culture badly needs, we have not been able to leave any spiritual impact on the life of this nation. Our presence in the media, for example, is so insignificant that it does not extend beyond a statement on the Middle East, or a statement on why women cannot attend an All-American Sobor, or a plunge into some river to retrieve a cross. Who is to blame for this apathy and lack of leadership? All of us, clergy, laity, and above all, the Standing Conference of Orthodox Bishops in America, which did not do much in the past sixteen years to enhance Orthodox unity in this hemisphere.

It is another coincidence that we are gathered here on the eve of the sixteenth anniversary of the Standing Conference. The memorandum which the late Metropolitan Antony Bashir sent to the American hierarchs inviting them to a meeting at the Greek Archdiocese, March 15, 1960, included among many items the following: "Standardized liturgical texts." As of this date we still do not have one common translation, even for our Creed or Lord's Prayer.

Forgive me if I indulge in self-criticism. We Orthodox have a tendency, especially on the Sunday of Orthodoxy, to glorify the past and feel proud of ourselves. There is no doubt that the Church of the Ecumenical Councils was glorious and courageous because she responded to the challenges of her time. Have we responded to the challenges of our time? As individual jurisdictions, I believe that we have succeeded in building new churches, in educating young priests and in organizing choirs and church schools; but collectively, we have done absolutely nothing. Where is our common witness in the ecumenical settings? Where is our influence on our national and local politics? Where is our common position vis-à-vis abortion, euthanasia, homosexuality, social injustice and world hunger? In short, where is our common response to contemporary iconoclasm? After our celebration this evening, we will return to our ethnic islands and I wonder if we will see each other before next Sunday of Orthodoxy.

We Are Here to Stay
We must make a firm decision that we are here in America to stay. I say this because some of us, clergy and laity, at least psychologically, are still in the Old Country. Orthodoxy on this continent will remain insignificant and ineffective as long as we continue to live in our ethnic ghettos. Consequently, if we do not express our inner unity in concrete, external action, we will continue this insignificant presence for many years to come. The most important question we must ask ourselves honestly and earnestly is, how can we achieve Orthodox unity in America? There is no simple answer to this question. We would be most naïve to think that Orthodox unity can be achieved through an edict from some patriarch in some Old Country, or through a directive from the Standing Conference of Orthodox Bishops in America. I believe, however, that despite the complexity of our problem, we can take certain steps which will ultimately lead to that blessed day.

First, each ethnic jurisdiction must unite and put its own house in order. How can Arabs unite with Serbs if Arabs cannot unite with each other? "The Arabs agree to disagree." This is a famous saying among the Antiochians; yet despite sixty years of division and misunderstanding, last year, Archbishop Michael of Toledo and I met in this city and laid a firm foundation for a united Antiochian Archdiocese in North America. If we Antiochians can unite, there is no reason why Russians, Serbians, Romanians, Albanians, Ukrainians, etc. cannot unite. Thus, on this Sunday of Orthodoxy I challenge you, fellow Orthodox, to put your houses in order as a first step toward Orthodox unity.

The second and most effective step toward Orthodox unity is inter-Orthodox cooperation on a grassroots level. I wish that in every city in America we could have an Orthodox Clergy Association like yours of Greater Pittsburgh. Your hierarchs cannot impose unity on you if you are not ready for it on the local level. Moreover, I honestly feel that you on the local level are more responsive to the question of Orthodox unity than your hierarchs, who are overburdened by administrative and jurisdictional work.

Beloved in Christ, the greatest gift we can offer America on her bicentennial is a strong resolve that Orthodox unity will be a reality before this century fades away and sinks in the ocean of eternity. Twentieth-century iconoclasm is more dangerous, more subtle and more challenging than that of the eighth century. The only way we can respond effectively to this challenge is through Orthodox unity.

Editor's Endnotes:

1. *During the Archdiocesan Convention of 1976, and within the first address of this chapter, Metropolitan Philip announces the invitation to Patriarch Elias IV to travel to America; that an Antiochian Holy Year is declared for 1977; that the Foundation for Balamand University will begin in the parishes in September of that year, ending in April.*

2. *In his sermon in Pittsburgh, "Orthodoxy and Contemporary Iconoclasm," Philip also comments on other various iconoclastic forms such as mercy killing and the accepted scriptural basis of sexual relations.*

3. *In 1976, Philip meets with President Gerald Ford to discuss the Middle East in general, and in particular, the civil war raging in Lebanon.*

Chapter 8

MAKE DISCIPLES OF ALL NATIONS:
A Struggle Not to Be Abandoned

> *We often remain in the eyes of our fellow Americans some kind of oriental cult or museum for ancient relics. We have a tremendous opportunity to preach Orthodoxy in this land. America is thirsty for our spirituality and theological stability, but how can America understand us if we continue talking to her in languages which she does not understand? I am not against ethnic cultures; I simply believe that we can achieve Orthodox unity despite our cultural diversity . . . we have always championed Orthodox unity in this land, and we shall in no way abandon this struggle.*
> Metropolitan Philip

- *Blessed Is He Who Comes in the Name of the Lord, 1977*
- *In Anticipation of the 'Great Synod': Orthodox Unity and Cultural Diversity, 1977*
- *Seeing Visions, Dreaming Dreams: Mission to America, 1978*
- *Fight the Good Fight of Faith: The Priestly Office, 1978*

AND HE LEADS THEM

The following four addresses were delivered by Metropolitan Philip in 1977 and 1978. Each addresses a special topic of interest in his ministry as a Church leader in North America: the mission of the old Church in the New World.

The first address in our grouping is his 1977 presentation in Washington, D.C., where he summarizes the Antiochian Holy Year. It is delivered in the presence of—and often directed to—Elias IV, the first Antiochian Patriarch to visit America. This becomes the cause for Philip to reflect upon Orthodoxy in the New World, now as a response to Orthodox perceptions held in the Old World.

The contrast which Philip has always seen, however, does not preclude his great admiration for the roots of Orthodoxy in history. This is only made more evident as he summarizes his recent visit to Russia, where the Church was still living under the heavy heel of communism. Philip shows how greatly he is impressed by what he saw, and believes that the hope which is inherent in the faith of the Russian people will allow "the bells of the Kremlin to ring again in the name of God." This call was prophetic, as we now have seen.

Indeed, one will find a connection between this first address and the other three precisely in this area of concern: the Old and New Worlds. The second of this grouping, given in 1977 at the Greek Orthodox Cathedral in New York, and in the presence of the members of the Standing Conference of Orthodox Bishops in the Americas (SCOBA), raises the issue of a Great Synod, one which should truly consider Orthodox unity in the diaspora. It is delivered in the form of a sermon on the Sunday of Orthodoxy during the Hierarchical Liturgy. It "stirred up the spirit" in many Church leaders of both the Old and New Worlds!

*The third address, delivered in 1978 in Houston, Texas, focuses upon mission and missions. It paints an even stronger contrast between a status quo Church, which merely rests in its connection with the Old World, and a dynamic Church, which must go out into the New World and **"make disciples of all nations"** (Matthew 28:19).*

The fourth and final address in this group is Philip's unique presentation to his clergy, gathered in 1978 in Houston, Texas. In this truly fatherly talk, the Metropolitan speaks of priesthood and its spirituality. It is reflects what a priest in the New World must hear.

Taken as a whole, this group of addresses well reflects Philip's call throughout his episcopacy: to raise the consciousness of the Orthodox Patriarchates and Synods in the various "mother churches" regarding the life which Orthodox Christians live in America, Western Europe and Australia, i.e. in the diaspora. After these addresses, and in subsequent developments along this line, the Metropolitan becomes known on both sides of the Old/New issue as one who does not fear to raise the objective and necessary points. Everyone knew the insecurities, anxiety and disputes it would raise. As he addresses Patriarch Elias, he says, "We shall not in any way abandon this struggle!"

J. J. A.

Blessed Is He That Comes in the Name of the Lord
Washington, D.C., 1977

It seems like yesterday when we met in San Francisco, California, to celebrate the bicentennial of this great nation, the tenth anniversary of a new era in the life of this archdiocese, and the much cherished unity of our Antiochian family in North America. The most welcome presence, this year, of our Father in Christ, Patriarch Elias IV, has added to this convention a new dimension and a tremendous significance which we have never experienced since the foundation of this archdiocese. Thus, Your Beatitude, we greet you today with these words from our matins service: "Rejoice with gladness, O Chief Shepherd, as thou beholdest thy children's children round about thy table offering branches of good deeds."

It has been customary that I report at these assemblies on the state of the archdiocese since the last convention. Undoubtedly, the highlight of this Antiochian Holy Year is the historic visit of our Father in Christ, Patriarch Elias IV, to this North American continent. Before I elaborate on his visit, I would like to report to you about certain significant events which have marked the life of our archdiocese during the past year.

Visit to Russia
Invited by the Moscow Patriarchate last September, 1976, I and a group of our clergy flew from New York City to Moscow. The cordiality and hospitality of the Moscow Patriarchate was indeed outstanding from the moment of our arrival to the moment of our departure. My visit to Russia was one of the most significant experiences of my entire life. You may hear stories or read books about the Church in Russia, but unless you go there and experience for yourself the spiritual depth of the Russian people, your knowledge of the Russian spirituality remains purely

academic. Despite the limited freedom which the Church enjoys under an atheistic government, it is not unusual in Russia to celebrate vespers and Divine Liturgies with five, ten or twenty-five thousand faithful. The Russians have no pews in their churches, yet they stand and pray with eyes fixed on heaven, pouring out their hearts with soft tears before the Almighty God.

While in Russia, we visited some of the most beautiful churches in the world, in Moscow, Leningrad and Zagorsk. Every icon in Russia is a window to heaven and every church in Russia is a little piece of heaven. If you look at Moscow or Leningrad from the air, you see nothing but church cupolas piercing the sky. At every turn of the road there is a church; a constant reminder that Christ, and not Marx, is the Lord of history. It is one of the contradictions of life that the most spiritual people on earth have to live under the most godless and materialistic system.

I told my hosts, almost on every occasion, that Russian history without the Church is meaningless, and that the land which gave the world spiritual and intellectual giants such as Seraphim of Sorov, Nil of Sorsk, Tolstoy, Dostoevsky, Tchaikovsky, Rachmaninoff, Nicholas Berdyaev, George Florovsky and Alexander Solzhenitsyn will never be crucified forever. Beyond Calvary there is the empty tomb. On this hope the Russian people live and wait for the heavy stone to be rolled away from the door of the sepulcher.

In a new book entitled, *Our Hope*, by Father Dmitrii Dudko, a contemporary Russian priest, Father Dudko was asked: "Where do people believe better, in Russia or the West?" Father Dmitrii answered:

> Everyone wants people to believe better where he, himself, lives. I am Russian and I would like to think the best of Russia. I know there are more believers in the West, but remembering Christ's words about the little flock upon which He leans, I would say that if you want

to believe in Russia, you have got to stand there next to Christ as He is nailed to the cross. In Russia, today, that is the only way you can believe. Therefore, I think that people believe better in Russia, just like the first Christian martyrs.

Before we flew back to America, I told my hosts at the farewell dinner the following: "I hope that when I return to Russia, the bells of the Kremlin will be ringing again and the name of God will be praised in all the churches which were forced to close; otherwise, the soft tears which we saw in the eyes of the Russian people will become mighty rivers which will sweep away all indifference to God in your beautiful land."

Archdiocese Activities
If I told you that we have had a very busy year, it would be an understatement. Despite our total involvement in planning the visit of His Beatitude and the events of the Antiochian Holy Year, we have devoted time to certain issues which are of concern to all of us.

On March 14, 1977, your archdiocese hosted a meeting for the Standing Conference of American Middle Eastern Christian and Moslem leaders. The members of the Standing Conference were joined by the leaders of cultural, social and political bodies in an extraordinary session and unanimously endorsed the following statement:

1. We call for unity among all persons and organizations of Arabic-speaking background in the United States.
2. We are for the unity and independence of Lebanon. Our position is nonpartisan, with deep concern for all the people of Lebanon, and for the continued independence, unity and integrity of a sovereign Lebanon. We support the efforts of the new President, Elias Sarkis, as he works to bring complete peace to Lebanon.
3. We call upon the United States Government to take a

prominent role in the humanitarian and reconstruction aid for Lebanon. A fully restored and independent Lebanon is in the interest of the United States, the Middle East and all the world.
4. We applaud President Carter's moral stand on human rights, and we look forward to his application of that moral creed to all the peoples of the Middle East—Jews, Christians and Moslems.
5. Recognizing that the root cause of the conflict in the Middle East has been the injustice done to the Palestinian Christian and Moslem people and that the Palestinian people as primary parties to the conflict should participate in any peace negotiations in fulfillment of their right to self-determination, we call upon our government to support all efforts toward that desired end.

This statement was adopted by the Orthodox, the Melkites, the Maronites, the Muslims, the Druse, the Palestinians, the Armenians, the Syriacs, the National Association of Arab Americans, the American Lebanese League, the American Ramallah Federation and the World Lebanese Cultural Union. Senator James Abourezk was kind enough to attend this meeting. The significance of this conference lies in the fact that for the first time the leadership of our people, regardless of religious and political affiliations, have met and agreed on something. It was not easy to bring all these people together, but if you have the will, nothing is impossible. I do hope, however, that our people in Lebanon will emulate our good example and start talking to each other in order to rebuild and bring lasting peace to their beautiful country.

An Historic Visit

The highlight of the Antiochian Holy Year is the visit of our Father in Christ, His Beatitude, Elias IV, Patriarch of Antioch and all the East. For the first time in history, an Antiochian Patriarch sets foot on this North American soil. We have been dreaming of this apostolic visit for many years. However, it could never have been possible before the reunification of the Antiochian family in North America. We thank God, Your Beatitude, that after sixty years of division and misunderstanding, our people are reunited, and there is no power on earth which will divide us again, because our unity is sealed in Christ. We also thank God that this reunification happened during the reign of our Holy Father, Patriarch Elias IV.

For the past two years, the theme of our gatherings and conventions has been, *"Blessed is he that cometh in the name of the Lord."* Before the arrival of His Beatitude, this theme was somehow an abstraction, but now, "he that cometh in the name of the Lord" is here. He is real. We have seen him, kissed his hand, embraced him and touched him. Although we have always been united with him in the same chalice and in the same bread, his presence among us makes our unity with him very real, despite the oceans and mountains which separate us. Surely, love transcends all barriers.

Patriarch Elias IV represents two thousand years of spirituality. He comes to us as the successor of Saints Peter and Paul, St. Ignatius of Antioch, St. John Chrysostom, St. John of Damascus and a "cloud of witnesses" of martyrs and ascetics. I have read lately that after the famous TV series, *Roots*, many Americans have been trying to rediscover their ancestral and cultural origins. In our case, we do not have to try hard. Our spiritual roots are deeply planted in Bethlehem, Nazareth, Galilee, Jerusalem, Beirut, Damascus and Antioch.

Patriarch Elias IV represents all this glory, yet he represents much suffering. History has not been very kind to us. From Ignatius to Elias IV, the history of Antioch has been written in blood. Antioch knows very well the meaning of martyrdom, persecution, oppression, controversy and even heresy. Strange is the Antiochian mind! Many times while trying to focus on the transcendent God, it went beyond its limits and fell into heresy. Yes, we have suffered much throughout history from so-called Christians and non-Christians alike.

Your Beatitude and beloved father, when you accepted our invitation to visit this North American continent, we rejoiced and decided to initiate a project in order to express to you our thanks and gratitude. Sixteen years ago, while returning from a frustrating trip to the Holy Synod of Antioch, the late Metropolitan Antony said to me, "The only way to create a spiritual renaissance in the Patriarchate of Antioch is to build a theological academy for the entire Middle East." I could not agree with him more because the Patriarchates of Jerusalem, Alexandria and even Constantinople all are without theological academies. Unfortunately, Metropolitan Antony died in February, 1966, before the realization of his dream. This archdiocese, with its Board of Trustees and all its faithful, was determined to accomplish this task without any hesitation or delay. We expended the money, broke ground for the new school in August, 1966, and in 1971, Patriarch Elias IV dedicated this beautiful academy, which will always stand as an expression of our love for our Mother Church.

As you well know, due to the Civil War in Lebanon, and because of security reasons and the total collapse of the Lebanese economy, this school has been closed for the past two years. I know beyond doubt that the most precious institution to the heart of Patriarch Elias is the Balamand Academy. On many occasions, His Beatitude emphatically told me that without the Balamand Academy, Orthodoxy in the Middle East will have no future.

Your Beatitude: Being fully cognizant of the importance of theological education and knowing how much hope you have invested in the Balamand Academy, and realizing that without an annual fixed income, this school cannot survive, we have tried our best to help you keep this school open. Ladies and gentlemen, I joyfully announce to you the establishment of the Patriarch Elias IV Foundation for the Balamand Academy, in the amount of a half-million dollars. You did it! We have reached our goal. You did not disappoint me. You never did. I pray that under the leadership of Patriarch Elias and with the full cooperation of the members of the Holy Synod of Antioch, this school will open soon and will never be closed again. Your Beatitude, we have just one humble request. Please make the Balamand Academy truly an Antiochian school which will answer our particular needs and reflect our Antiochian history and spirituality.

Beloved Father in Christ, for the past two and one-half months your presence has transfigured this archdiocese from glory to glory. You have traveled to Canada and throughout the United States and presided over our meetings and conventions. Thousands of our people have had the opportunity to kiss your hand and receive your blessings, an experience which they will never forget. You have made a tremendous impression on the Orthodox hierarchs of this land.

I am sure that Your Beatitude agrees that Orthodoxy in the New World has a vigor, a vitality and a dynamism which is missing in the Old World. Individually, the various Orthodox jurisdictions in this country have done well for themselves. But unfortunately, we have not done much collectively to spread the Orthodox message in this hemisphere. According to unofficial statistics, we have between eight and ten million Orthodox in North America, yet we have not made any serious impact on the spiritual and moral life of this nation because of our ethnic division. The multiplicity of jurisdictions in one given territory fundamentally contradicts the canonical and ecclesiological teachings of our Church. Orthodoxy in its essence transcends ethnicism and nationalism. Thus, if we do not destroy these ethnic barriers and feel at home in America, we will remain, in the eyes of our fellow Americans, some kind of an oriental cult or a museum for ancient relics.

We have a tremendous opportunity to preach Orthodoxy in this land. America is thirsty for our spirituality and theological stability, but how can America understand us if we continue talking to her in languages which she does not understand? I am not against ethnic cultures at all. I believe that we can achieve Orthodox unity despite our cultural diversity.

Antioch and the Future of Orthodoxy

Last November we heard that a Great Orthodox Synod is in the making and one of the topics which will be discussed is the Orthodox diaspora. The last Ecumenical Council took place in 787. Thank God that after 1,190 years, a Great Synod will convene to hopefully respond to the many spiritual and moral challenges of our time.

Your Beatitude, regarding the diaspora, your people in North America have always championed the cause of Orthodox unity and *we shall not in any way abandon this struggle.* In one of your past epistles to our people, you said:

> As Antiochians, our hope for Orthodox unity in North America is that it be realized with the blessings of the mother churches which have branches on the North American continent. A unity achieved in this fashion will be solid, strong and productive. This is our conviction and we shall continue to work for its actualization . . . we should never forget that Antioch must play a great role in peace, love and good will.

This is a great statement, Your Beatitude. This is our conviction, too. Now we must work together to translate our convictions into realities. We agree with you wholeheartedly that Antioch must play a great role in world Orthodoxy, especially in the forthcoming Great Synod. Among all the Orthodox patriarchates in the world, Antioch is the only patriarchate which can act freely, positively and effectively. We Antiochians have never fixed our eyes on any particular piece of land, nor have we ever become slaves to any particular culture. We always believed in one Holy Catholic and Apostolic Church, a catholicity which transcends all frontiers and all cultures. Orthodoxy in the diaspora and otherwise has long been victimized by an historical tension between Moscow and Constantinople. It is time, Your Beatitude, to put an end to this cold war. It is time, Your Beatitude, to rise above historical considerations which no longer exist either in Moscow or Constantinople. Only a strong Antioch can play this positive role. The Patriarch of Antioch cannot be stronger than the people of Antioch; therefore, this archdiocese which loves you and respects you puts all its potentialities in your hands as you struggle to bring Orthodox unity to this continent and Orthodox cooperation through the world.

Your Beatitude, your visit to this archdiocese will linger in our memories for many, many years to come. Rest assured that wherever you go, our thoughts and love will constantly surround you, and our fervent prayer shall always be: "Among the first be mindful, O Lord, of our Father, Patriarch Elias, whom do Thou grant unto Thy holy churches in peace, safety, honor, health and length of days and rightly dividing the word of Thy truth."

In Anticipation of the Great Synod: Orthodox Unity and Cultural Diversity
New York, 1977

At the last annual meeting of the Standing Conference of Orthodox Bishops in the Americas, it was unanimously decided that all members of SCOBA concelebrate the Divine Liturgy on the Sunday of Orthodoxy. Thus, we are gathered in this beautiful cathedral to commemorate the triumph of Orthodoxy over the iconoclastic heresy, to express our oneness in the Holy Orthodox Faith and to discover together new horizons and new visions for the future.

We owe a deep sense of gratitude to the Church of the iconoclastic era for her responsiveness and courage in defending the "faith which was once for all delivered to the saints" (Jude 3). Names such as John of Damascus, Theodore the Studite, Patriarch Germanos and Patriarch Nicephorus will always shine in the history of the Church, like the stars of heaven. I do not intend today to elaborate on the historical circumstances which led to the iconoclastic heresy, nor will I attempt to present a new theology in defense of the holy icons. The Holy Fathers have written extensively on this subject, and I doubt if any of us can add much to their brilliant thoughts. I hope you do not get the impression that I am minimizing the past. Those who have no past have no present and will have no future. We Orthodox, however, have a strong tendency to always glorify the past and bask in its glory. We seem to know so much about the past, but so little about the present, while the future is constantly pressing upon us.

I was delighted last November to read about the proposed Great Orthodox Synod. The last Ecumenical Council was convened in 787. This means that 1,190 years have elapsed since the last Ecumenical Council, which dealt mainly with the problem of iconoclasm. Many religious, moral, political and socioeconomic events have taken place since 787 and deeply affected the life of the Church. One might ask, "Why did the Church not meet since 787 to respond courageously and effectively to these challenges? Has the Church lost that dynamism and responsiveness which distinguished her life during the first ten centuries?"

There is no doubt that the Church has experienced very difficult times since the last Ecumenical Council. However, this does not excuse the stagnation which has marked her life for the past 1,190 years. It is indeed strange that while we are active in the ecumenical movement, attending World Council of Churches meetings in America, Europe, Asia and Africa, we have had very insignificant inter-Orthodox activities, both on the national and international levels. When we heard of the pending Great Orthodox Synod, we thanked God that at long last and after many centuries of silence, a Great Synod will convene to respond to the many challenges of our time.

American Participation

At the last meeting of SCOBA, we unanimously authorized the Chairman of the Standing Conference, His Eminence, Archbishop Iakovos, to contact His Eminence, Meliton, Metropolitan of Chalcedon and chairman of the first pre-Synod pan-Orthodox consultation, for the purpose of inviting our conference to participate in some capacity in all future pre-Synod pan-Orthodox consultations. Our request was well received, and in a communiqué addressed to His Eminence, Archbishop Iakovos, dated December 4, 1976, Metropolitan Meliton wrote: "In reply, I wish to inform you and through you the Standing Conference that your petition, being of special significance, will be conveyed to the Church, so that she may define the way by which the participation of our Orthodox brethren in America in the next pan-Orthodox consultations may be effected and their voice may be clearly heard."

Subsequent to the pan-Orthodox consultations in Switzerland, in which thirteen patriarchates and churches were represented, a proposed agenda of ten points was approved for the Great Synod. To be honest, I was not much impressed with the agenda, especially after 1,190 years of expectation, because some of its topics were outdated and irrelevant. Missing from the agenda, for example, are important contemporary issues such as abortion, homosexuality, euthanasia, the ordination of women and lesbians to the priesthood, etc. Although the teachings of our Church are clear vis-à-vis such issues, yet the Church must again and again reaffirm her position and constantly proclaim the truth in order to eliminate any possible confusion in the minds of the faithful.

One of the topics, however, which concerns us very much as Orthodox in this hemisphere is the situation of the Orthodox diaspora (believers living in areas which are not traditionally Orthodox). This development occurred as a result of different waves of migration from Eastern Europe, Russia, Greece and the Middle East, who settled this hemisphere, Western Europe and Australia. These exist in many geographically overlapping, largely ethnic jurisdictions, a situation considered canonically and theologically indefensible as a lasting arrangement. I am indeed delighted that our Orthodox situation in America will be discussed at the Great Synod, which I pray will convene!

I wonder, however, how much the venerable hierarchs of the Church in the Old World truly understand our Orthodox situation in America. It is therefore our sacred responsibility to provide our Orthodox brethren across the ocean with a true and clear picture about our successes and failures, especially during the current century. Our brethren in the Old World must realize that Orthodoxy on this continent is no longer a child. In his book, *The Individual and His Orthodox Church*, Father Nicon Patrinacos states:

> The American Orthodox of today, having come of age as regards his personal religious experience and that of the group within which he moves, seeks a more definite

and convincing articulation of his faith, and a way of practicing it, to which he could fully subscribe without hesitation or reservations and without fear of being severed on account of it from his American environment.

Deeply Rooted in America
The first pan-Orthodox encyclical in the United States, which was released to the press last December, stated: "The Divine Liturgy was first sung on this continent three decades before the American Revolution by Orthodox pioneers who were swiftly followed by Russian missionaries bringing the faith of Jerusalem, Antioch and Byzantium to the native Americans who still cherish it."

There is no doubt whatsoever that our faith is deeply rooted in the American soil. We will be forever indebted to our fathers and forefathers who have planted and nurtured the seeds of Orthodoxy in America, but our mother churches must realize once and for all that we are no longer a Church of immigrants. Our Orthodox children have died on the battlefields of many wars defending American principles and ideals. Our Orthodox people have contributed generously to the realization of the American dream in business, education, art, entertainment, science, medicine, law and government. The crime rate among our people is almost nonexistent.

Our various Orthodox jurisdictions have done much to preserve Orthodoxy in this land. The *Orthodox Observer* published by the Greek Archdiocese on January 5, 1977, carried the following news item entitled, "Greek Leader Praises Church," which I would like to share with you. "I will become a Greek and fervent supporter of all I saw in the Greek Orthodox Church in America." This statement was made here by Chrysostom Karapiperis, the former Minister of Education in Greece, prior to his departure for Athens on December 28.

Karapiperis, a well-known Greek political figure, was in America for more than one month and visited, with his wife, many Greek Orthodox parishes. Speaking of the archdiocese, he referred with enthusiasm to the Greek Orthodox faithful in the Americas. He expressed his great admiration for the organized life of the Church here. He expressed also the hope that the Orthodox Church in Greece—disorganized today and confused, not even having a Church constitution at present—having as a prototype the organization of the Greek Orthodox Archdiocese in the Americas, will proceed to its own reorganization. Karapiperis attributed the progress and organization of the American Archdiocese primarily to the person and leadership of Archbishop Iakovos, and the ability of the Church here to organize itself without political influence.

What Mr. Karapiperis said about the progress and organization of the Greek Archdiocese of North and South America can also be said about the Orthodox Church in America, the Antiochian Archdiocese of North America and the rest of our respective jurisdictions. I have traveled in the Middle East and walked in the footsteps of the early missionaries; I have visited Greece and seen the glory of the past centuries; I have visited Russia and been overwhelmed by the piety of the Russian people. But I can honestly say that despite the glory of the past, and the spiritual depth of the suffering Church in Russia, Orthodoxy in the New World stands unique in its vigor, vitality and dynamism.

If the mother churches are not aware of these special characteristics which distinguish the life of the Church in this hemisphere, we say to them, "Come and see." Yes, come and see our organizations, our institutions, our liturgical and theological publications, our theological schools, our dedicated clergy, our faithful laity and our youth movements. Where in the whole world today can you find six million free Orthodox except in North America?

I am not suggesting that all is perfect with Orthodoxy in

this hemisphere. Despite our rootedness in the American soil, despite the success which we have achieved during this century, and despite the unity of faith which we enjoy as brothers and sisters in Holy Orthodoxy, we are still living in our ethnic ghettos and we very seldom see each other except on the Sunday of Orthodoxy. Individually we have done much for our respective jurisdictions, but collectively we have not yet begun to explore the tremendous potentialities that could be ours were we administratively united under one jurisdiction.

For example, how much can we contribute to the ecumenical movement if we don't first put our house in order? We Orthodox are fortunate that we represent two thousand years of theology and spirituality. But where is our spiritual impact on the life of this nation? Who is articulating our Orthodox theology for the benefit of our Christian brethren who have been victimized and confused by all kinds of theological innovations? Where is our presence in the media? Where is our moral influence on our national and international politics? We used to delight in seeing His Eminence, Archbishop Iakovos, taking part in the inauguration of presidents. This year we were even denied this simple right.

Orthodoxy, despite her past glory, remains the best-kept secret in this land because of our failure to understand the missionary dimensions of the Church. America does not understand us because we are still talking to her in languages which she does not understand. We are still talking to America as Greeks, Russians, Serbians, Ukrainians, Romanians, etc. No wonder, then, that six million Orthodox have no presence on the American scene. Is it difficult for six million Orthodox to establish a television and radio foundation in order to preach Orthodoxy to this nation? The answer is yes, as long as we remain divided, moving in our own ethnic orbits.

Unity Despite Diversity

Please do not misunderstand me. I am not advocating here a revolution against our ethnic cultures. I am proud of my heritage and I am sure that you are proud of yours. I am just trying to share with you a vision for the future, especially in anticipation of the Great Synod. If we will be invited to participate in the pre-Synod pan-Orthodox consultation according to Metropolitan Meliton's letter, what are we going to say to the mother churches? I believe that the problem of the diaspora, this tremendous exodus of millions of Orthodox Christians from their native countries, constitutes a major and unprecedented experience in the history of the Church. The multiplicity of jurisdictions in one given territory fundamentally contradicts our canonical and ecclesiological teachings.

No one can deny that we are dealing here with a very complex problem. This multiplicity of jurisdictions is deeply connected with the self-evident reality of our various ethnic cultures. Such cultures cannot be eliminated by a statement from SCOBA or by an edict from some patriarch somewhere. Only time can take care of this problem. Despite this reality, however, we cannot consider this present Orthodox situation in America as final because, by so doing, we will betray Orthodoxy and her basic principles.

I believe that we can achieve administrative unity despite our cultural diversity. The first step toward this goal would be the elevation of the Standing Conference—which has already served its purpose—to the rank of a Synod with the blessings of the mother churches. Such a Synod will be able to speak to America and the world with one voice and one accord. This Synod, which will truly represent six million free Orthodox, will be able to respond effectively to the moral and social challenges of our time. Why should we issue, for example, ten Orthodox statements vis-à-vis abortion? The most important task for this Synod, however, will be the preparation for the establishment of a future Orthodox patriarchate in America which will reflect both our organic unity and the richness and diversity of our ethnic cultures. I want to make it clear here that this patriarchate can only be established by a common decision of all Orthodox Churches.

In conclusion, I would like to thank the Chairman of SCOBA, my beloved brother in Christ, Archbishop Iakovos, for giving us the opportunity to worship with you on this Sunday of Orthodoxy, hoping and praying that he will respond courageously to the many challenges facing Orthodoxy in this hemisphere because he represents the most powerful Orthodox archdiocese on this continent. It is not enough to romanticize the past and bask in the glory of yesterday, "for yesterday is already a dream, and tomorrow is only a vision, but today well lived, makes every yesterday a dream of happiness and every tomorrow a vision of hope."

Seeing Visions, Dreaming Dreams: Mission to America
Houston, 1978

"These men who have turned the world upside down have come here also" (Acts 17:6).

This year, 1978, was proclaimed by our archdiocese as a Year of Mission. The activities of our regional conferences have revolved to a certain extent around the theme, "Go Preach the Gospel." The theme of our Archdiocesan Convention, "Go, therefore, and make disciples of all nations" (Matthew 28:19), is very much related to the theme of our Parish Life Conferences. Therefore, all our efforts this year have been directed toward this missionary goal.

Why Missions?
Some may ask: Why this sudden emphasis on mission? Is this some kind of innovation or a new fad in the life of the Church? The answer to such questions can be found in the Scripture, which is our most authentic and authoritative point of reference. From reading the Gospels, we learn that our Lord was the perfect missionary. Was He not sent to us by the Father on a redemptive mission and did not His earthly ministry clearly reflect this reality? In the New Testament, we read that "He went about all Galilee, teaching in the synagogues and preaching the gospel of the kingdom, and healing every disease and every infirmity among the people" (Matthew 4:23).

Before His Ascension to heaven, our Lord left us a very serious commandment, which is recorded at the conclusion of two of the synoptic Gospels. In Matthew 28:16–20, we read,

> Now the eleven disciples went to Galilee, to the mountain to which Jesus had directed them. And when they

saw Him they worshipped Him; but some doubted. And Jesus came and said to them, "All authority in heaven and on earth has been given to me. Go therefore and make disciples of all nations, baptizing them in the name of the Father and the Son and of the Holy Spirit, teaching them to observe all that I have commanded you; and lo, I am with you always, even unto the end of the world."

In Luke 24:45–49, we read,

> Then He opened their minds to understand the Scriptures, and said to them, "Thus it is written, that the Christ should suffer and on the third day rise from the dead, and that repentance and forgiveness of sins should be preached in His name to all nations, beginning from Jerusalem. You are witnesses to all these things. And behold, I send the promise of My Father upon you; but stay in the city until you are clothed with power from on high."

In the Book of Acts 1:8, Christ told His disciples,

> But you shall receive power when the Holy Spirit has come upon you; and you shall be my witnesses in Jerusalem and in all Judea and Samaria and to the end of the earth.

One can see from these texts that our Lord commanded His disciples to be His witnesses after they received "power from on high." In the second chapter of the same book, we read:

> When the day of Pentecost had come, they were all together in one place. And suddenly a sound came from heaven like the rush of a mighty wind, and it filled all the house where they were sitting. And there appeared tongues as of fire, distributed and resting on each one of

them. And they were all filled with the Holy Spirit and began to speak in other tongues as the Spirit gave them utterance.

Thus on Pentecost Day, the following prophecy of the Prophet Joel was fulfilled: "And in the last days it shall be, God declares, that I will pour out My Spirit upon all flesh, and your sons and your daughters shall prophesy, and your young men *shall see visions,* and your *old men shall dream dreams*" (Acts 2:17).

I have mentioned these biblical references to show that the missionary spirit in the Church is not a fad. On the contrary, it is deeply rooted in the eternal Christian message. We all know that the Church was born on Pentecost Day as a missionary movement which changed history. The Book of Acts is the best reference we have on the early mission of the Church. Preaching, repentance and baptism were very common events in the life of the early Church. After the famous sermon of Peter on Pentecost, "Those who received His word were baptized, and there were added that day about three thousand souls" (Acts 2:41), and those converts to the new religion "devoted themselves to the apostles' teaching and fellowship, to the breaking of the bread and the prayers" (Acts 2:42). In a very short time many "heard the word and believed, and the number of the men came to about five thousand" (Acts 4:4). "And walking in the fear of the Lord and in the comfort of the Holy Spirit, the church multiplied" (Acts 9:31).

Christ's commandment to "go and make disciples of all nations" is true today as it was yesterday and it shall be until the end of history. Those of us who neglect this commandment betray the essence of the Christian message. Unfortunately, many people in our archdiocese are very parochial in their concept of the Church. They cannot distinguish between the parish and the Church universal. They imagine that the Church, the whole Church, is the four walls where they worship on Sunday, and everything else is none of their business. Unless we study the Scripture and understand the true nature of the Body of Christ, we cannot overcome this narrow and distorted concept of the Church.

The proclamation of 1978 as a Year of Mission is more than empty words or a superficial slogan. It is a tremendous challenge to all of us, especially in the following three main areas.

1. Self-Evangelization

Self-evangelization means bringing the gospel of Jesus Christ to yourself first. If we are not converted on a personal basis, how can we convert others to Christ? Conversion to Christ is a lifelong process. Striving for perfection is a constant struggle. It begins with baptism, chrismation, communion, prayer, fasting and almsgiving. St. Seraphim of Sarov said, "Save yourself and thousands around you will be saved." Self-evangelization is not an easy task. It takes a great deal of discipline, soul-searching, restlessness, inner struggle and pain. It is easier to invade outer space than to invade our inner being.

Very often people ask me, "What can I do to become religious?" This is a common question in a push-button and deodorized culture. We do not have pills which can make you religious. Read the Scripture, read the Lives of the Fathers, get involved in the sacramental life of the Church, and God will illumine your heart and show you the way. The whole aim of the Christian life is *theosis,* or deification. It is that ultimate union and free communion with God. St. Irenaeus said, "The Word of God, Jesus Christ, on account of His great love for mankind, became what we are in order to make us what He Himself is."

In his second Epistle, St. Peter said: "His Divine power has granted to us all things that pertain to life and godliness, through the knowledge of Him who called us to His own glory and excellence, by which He has granted to us His precious and very great promises, that through these you may escape from the corruption that is in the world because of passion, and become partakers of the divine nature" (2 Peter 1:3–5).

2. Parish Revitalization

It is not enough to build beautiful and adequate facilities for the church to meet and glorify God. Revitalizing our communities means bringing each and everyone in the parish to the fellowship of Christ. In the Book of Acts, St. Paul said, "And He commanded us to preach to the people, and to testify that He is the one ordained by God to be judge of the living and the dead" (Acts 10:42). During the apostolic time, Antioch and Jerusalem were headquarters for the early missionaries. Peter and Paul and the rest of the disciples were not satisfied with establishing churches and leaving them on their own. On the contrary, they revisited these churches, and when they could not visit, they sent letters admonishing the people to remain steadfast in the faith. Many times the disciples were beaten, many times they were imprisoned and many times they almost drowned in the sea. And, ultimately, most of them bore witness to Christ by their own blood.

We have not yet asked you to accept beating, imprisonment and martyrdom for Christ's sake. We are asking you, beloved children, to be missionaries in your own parishes and to your own people. We are asking you to go after the lost sheep. It is most unfortunate indeed that to many of us the lost sheep is just a number. Instead of doing some missionary work in the parish, we waste so much time in trying to determine who is a member in good standing and who is not. I asked one of my priests once: "Father, why don't you go after these seventy-five families and bring them back to Christ?" He said, "Saidna, they are no good." I said, "This is precisely why you should minister to them. If they are no good, it is our duty to make them good." Our Lord said, "Those who are well have no need of a physician, but those who are sick; I came not to call the righteous but sinners" (Mark 2:17).

In the end, how can we "go and make disciples of all nations," if we can't bring back our own Orthodox people to the fellowship of the Church?

3. New Community Development

The third phase of our missionary program is to explore new areas where no Orthodox witness exists and establish new parishes for Orthodox and non-Orthodox alike. According to statistics, there are eighty million unchurched people in this land. A Gallup poll on the unchurched which was released lately came as a severe indictment of organized religion. Among the criticisms of religion shared by both the churched and unchurched is that most churches "have lost the real spiritual part of religion." "They are too concerned with organizational as opposed to theological or spiritual issues." "They are not effective in helping people find meaning in life," and "they are not concerned enough with social justice." One can see that the harvest is indeed plentiful. Millions of people in this country and otherwise are thirsty for the living water and the heavenly bread, which is treasured in the Orthodox Church.

There is so much confusion today on the American religious scene. Some of the so-called evangelists in this country are making a mockery of religion, and yet they are very popular. They preach what the people *want* to hear, not what the people *should* hear. A few weeks ago, I watched "Sixty Minutes," a CBS television program. A segment of the program was dedicated to some new evangelical trends: mainly, preach Americanism, capitalism, and the pursuit of happiness; in other words, make people feel good and you will have a large audience and you become a successful preacher. Sweeten Christ, package Him nicely, advertise Him well and surely, you will become a multimillionaire. Did Peter, Paul, Barnabas, Steven and Ignatius of Antioch preach that way? Did our Lord, Himself, preach the gospel to make people feel good? Not at all! Listen carefully to the Gospels of the first three evenings of Holy Week. I have mentioned these facts to show the tremendous missionary task which lies ahead of us.

In the past twelve years, we have established twelve new parishes despite our limitation in funds and personnel. We now have twelve missions; some of them are receiving monthly financial assistance from the archdiocese, namely: St. Ignatius Mission of Windsor, Ontario, Canada; St. Elias Mission of LaCrosse, Wisconsin; St. Basil's Mission of New Orleans and St. John the Evangelist Mission of Oakland, California. The newest mission in the archdiocese is St. Philip's Mission in Edmonton, Alberta, Canada. All missions receive from the archdiocese, free of charge, their Christian education materials, sacred music materials and liturgical books.

The harvest is indeed plentiful, but the workers are few. We do not have enough missionary priests to accomplish our missionary goals. I, therefore, challenge our clergy, during this Year of Missions, to dedicate their lives to the missionary goals of the Church. I cannot promise you much money or much luxury, because a missionary priest will have neither. I challenge our young people to go to the seminary and prepare themselves for missionary work. "For what does it profit a man if he gains the whole world and loses his own soul" (Mark 8:36).

At the end of the liturgy, we sing this moving hymn. "We have seen the true light, we have received the heavenly spirit. We have found the true faith." Then the priest says, "Let us go forth in peace." Through the priest, Christ is inviting you to go forth, transform the world and bring it back to God.

Antiochian Village as a Source of Mission

Isaiah the Prophet said, "Come, let us go up to the mountain of the Lord, and to the house of the God of Jacob and He will teach us His ways and we will walk in His paths" (Isaiah 2:3).

In my message to the twenty-eighth Archdiocesan Convention held in Atlanta, Georgia, in 1973, I spoke about the reserve funds of the archdiocese. I said: "These funds give your archdiocese some financial security. In the future, when we reach a certain financial plateau, your Board of Trustees will seriously consider spending some of our savings on youth programs and various projects which will enhance the spiritual life of this archdiocese." For the past five years, I have been searching for a place where we can escape the noise of this world and spend time rediscovering ourselves through prayers, retreats, meditation and meaningful human encounters, all of which are part of our missionary goals. After some negotiation with the Pittsburgh Presbytery, on March 31, 1978, we purchased Camp Fairfield (now known as Antiochian Village) for the amount of $350,000 from the reserve funds of your archdiocese.

Briefly, the Village consists of 280 acres of beautiful wooded and open ground in the Laurel Mountains of Western Pennsylvania. There is something mysterious about a mountain which is difficult to describe. In the Old Testament, Moses received the commandments on a mountain. St. Elias the Prophet witnessed the living God on a mountain. In the New Testament, our Lord preached the most beautiful sermon ever preached on a mountain. And when He wanted to reveal His glory to His disciples, He was transfigured on a mountain. On Ascension Day, He ascended to heaven with our human nature from a mountain. Thus, my friends, when you become weary, depressed, tired of life, empty, laden with heavy burdens, when you lose direction in life and communication with God, go to the mountain, to the Antiochian Village, and you will find rest.

The Antiochian Village will add a new spiritual dimension to our life and inaugurate a new era of mission and religious maturity in this archdiocese. Study the history of our Church in this country and you will distinguish three main eras: the era of immigration, the era of organization and the era of mission and spiritual maturation symbolized by the Antiochian Village. St. Paul said, "When I was a child, I spoke like a child, I thought like a child, I reasoned like a child; when I became a man, I gave up childish ways" (2 Corinthians 13:11).

Our possibilities in the Antiochian Village are unlimited. Besides the tremendous facilities which we now have, I envision a conference and retreat center, a rich library for theological research, a monastery, an old-age home for our clergy and laity, a farm and who knows, perhaps a seminary to satisfy the needs of the Church in South America and the Middle East if the Balamand does not open.

Beloved in Christ, I would like to conclude my message, during this missionary year, with a story from the seventeenth chapter of the Book of Acts:

> Paul and Silas went to Thessalonica to preach the gospel. Many Greeks, men and women, embraced the new faith. "But the Jews were jealous, and taking some wicked fellows of the rabble, they gathered a crowd, set the city in an uproar, and attacked the house of Jason, seeking to bring them out to the people. And when they could not find them, they dragged Jason and some of the brethren before the city authorities crying, these men who have turned the world upside down have come here also" (Acts 17:5, 6).

Ladies and gentlemen, you, too, can turn the world upside down, if you have faith.

Fight the Good Fight of Faith: The Priestly Identity
Houston, 1978

Dear Fathers and coworkers in Christ: I welcome you to this Thirty-third Annual Archdiocesan Convention. In the past few years, the agenda of such meetings was planned by the Department of Theological and Pastoral Education, which has been running clergy workshops throughout our archdiocese. Because of these pastoral workshops, which are very necessary, I have not been able to talk to you in a formal way as your bishop and father in Christ.

During the past twelve years we have enjoyed a very good relationship. I have tried to make myself accessible to you and your families as much as possible. I told you more than once that the bishop is no longer a picture on the wall or living in some ivory tower. On the contrary, the bishop must be very much involved in the life of his sheep. Otherwise, the word "shepherd" becomes completely meaningless.

The complexity of modern life, the many serious problems which we encounter in ministering to our people, the loneliness, cynicism and even despair which some of us experience from time to time raise a very important question concerning our priestly image, or our *priestly identity*. Who are we? And what are we doing? Are we a bunch of professionals trying to satisfy certain needs of the people? Or are we a "royal priesthood and a chosen generation," called by God to realize His divine purposes in history? Do we know where we are going? Do we have a sense of purpose, a sense of direction?

I once heard a story about a man who was on a horse galloping swiftly along the road. An old farmer, standing in the fields, seeing him pass by, called out, "Hey, rider, where are you going?" The rider turned around and shouted back, "Don't ask me, ask my horse!"

We lose our identity as priests, as servants of our people, when we fail to know where our horses are going. I believe that, when we feel that we are losing our direction, it is spiritually refreshing to take refuge in the Scripture and the writings of the Fathers.

What is the priestly office? St. John Chrysostom described it as follows:

> The priestly office is indeed discharged on earth, but it ranks amongst heavenly ordinances; and very naturally so; for neither man, nor angels, nor archangels, nor any other created power, but the Paraclete ... the Holy Spirit ... Himself instituted this vocation, and persuaded men to represent the ministry of angels.

I am sure you have noticed that Chrysostom describes the priestly office as a "vocation," not a "profession." A vocation is a divine calling, specifically a "voice" which calls us. A profession, on the other hand, is to engage in a job for gain or livelihood. One can see that there is a fundamental difference between priesthood as a vocation and priesthood as a profession. All of us are tempted to become professionals, that is, to administer the affairs of the parish without concern for the spiritual dimension of our vocation. A professional priest knows the law very well, but nothing beyond the law. A professional priest goes through the motion of prayer but does not pray. A professional priest preaches about love without the experience of what is love. A professional priest visits the sick but does not care whether they live or die. He presents a façade without the content.

Self-Evangelization and Self-Control

In our archdiocese, 1978 is a missionary year. One—and perhaps the most important—aspect of our missionary program is "self-evangelization." How can a priest evangelize his community and the whole world if he does not first bring the gospel to himself? Every sermon has meaning and value only when it is the result of personal spiritual experience and knowledge. Every sermon pronounced only with our lips is dead and false, and those who listen will unmistakably feel it. In his First Epistle to Timothy, St. Paul said:

> But as for you, man of God . . . aim at righteousness, godliness, faith, love, steadfastness, gentleness. *Fight the good fight of the faith*; take hold of the eternal life to which you were called when you made the good confession in the presence of many witnesses (1 Timothy 6:11, 12).

Without self-evangelization we cannot expect community revitalization, and by extension, world conversion. St. Seraphim of Sarov said, "Save yourself, and thousands around you will be saved." When we speak about community revitalization, we expect the clergy to be the agents of change in this important process. Your work within the community reflects your devotion and dedication to the cause of Christ. I expect you to behave in a manner befitting your priestly dignity: "An athlete is not crowned unless he competes according to the rules" (2 Timothy 2:5). Add to that: "For God did not give us a spirit of timidity, but a spirit of power and love and self-control" (2 Timothy 1:7).

Self-control is extremely important in exercising your ministry. I regret to inform you that it has come to my attention that some of you act inappropriately at parish parties, at weddings and some other social functions. For example, some of your parishioners who compliment you as "marvelous" dancers, laugh at you in secret. This has been reported to me, and it saddens me. Do not forget that you are a priest and have a special image, a very special ministry, in the life of your community. Always remember that you are not "one of the boys"! Your are *not* the insurance man, *not* the plumber, *not* the undertaker—you are the priest and leader of the community, and you are expected to behave like a priest and leader of the community.

You have been sent to save souls and not to be stumbling blocks to the proclamation of the gospel.

Another wish I have is that when you are in the parish fulfilling your ministry, you dress like a priest. Our official dress code in the Antiochian Archdiocese is a black suit, black shoes, a black shirt and the collar. I expect you, therefore, to dress as such, except when you are on vacation when you may dress as you please.

In the Model Constitution and in the Priest's Guide, the priest is the official representative of the bishop in the parish. To represent someone is to be his image. To represent the bishop is to make the bishop present in your community. In the past twelve years, I have supported you before the laity even when you were dead wrong. My priest is always right except when he is alone with me. I want you to reciprocate this action, not for my own sake, because I get my strength from God, but for the sake of our Orthodox ecclesiology and this great archdiocese in which we serve together.

Therefore, when I send you a directive or when I initiate a policy, I expect you to abide by such directives and to execute my policy, again, for the sake of order in the archdiocese. When and if you disagree with me, keep your disagreement to yourself, unless I commit a heresy, God forbid. Although we may live thousands of miles apart, I still know very well what goes on in every parish; I keep a very close watch over this vineyard which was entrusted to me by God.

Administering Clergy in the Archdiocese

I would like you to know that one of the most painful experiences in my life as your bishop is transferring priests from one parish to another. Why do we transfer priests? Because of three main reasons: (1) sometimes the priest himself asks to be transferred; (2) sometimes the parish requests that the priest be transferred; (3) sometimes the bishop transfers priests for the well-being of the archdiocese. In all cases, transferring priests is an agonizing process. I am sure that many of you have been transferred more than once from one parish to another. This year more than ten priests will be transferred for the welfare of the archdiocese. The acquisition of the Antiochian Village placed on my shoulders heavy burdens regarding transfers. I expect you, therefore, to cooperate with me and not to put obstacles in our way.

A priest is a soldier in the army of Christ, and he is expected to fight on the front to which he is assigned. Disobedience does not benefit anyone. Moreover, the priest who disobeys his bishop loses the respect not only of his bishop, but of his community, and ultimately he brings disaster upon himself. What would happen to the discipline of this archdiocese if we violated the rules and disobeyed the laws? I assure you that my decisions in transferring priests are not made haphazardly. On the contrary, I make my decisions after a great deal of thinking, and such decisions are never influenced by those who love the priest or those who dislike him. The only thing which matters to me is the welfare of the Church and the archdiocese to which God has assigned me.

My dear friends, in the *Diary of a Russian Priest*, Father Alexander Elchaninov wrote, "What a joy to be a priest. Yesterday I heard the confessions of an entire family. The children were most lovable . . . two boys of about seven or eight. All the evening I was almost rapt in ecstasy." Yes, what a joy to be a priest! Despite its tears, hardships and loneliness the priesthood is still, in my opinion, the most joyful vocation. It is that joy which the world does not comprehend. It is the joy of laying down your life for others. That sounds crazy, but did not our Lord Himself say, "For whosoever will save his life shall lose it; but whosoever shall lose his life for My sake and the gospel's, the same shall save it."

We have labored together for the past twelve years to make this archdiocese a model to be emulated by the Orthodox world. A critical part of this model is the health of our various organizations. Thus, we must all remember that our archdiocesan organizations—i.e. our youth and women's organizations, as well as the Order of St. Ignatius of Antioch—deserve our utmost and undivided attention. If you do not have chapters for these organizations in your parishes, please delay no longer and begin that work immediately. History waits for nobody!

Finally, dear Fathers: I want you to know that I thank God for all the efforts which you have expended on behalf of His vineyard. The disappointments which we have had cannot in any way be compared with the joys which we have shared. I pray God to continue guiding us, "until we all attain the unity of the faith and the knowledge of the Son of God, to mature manhood, to the measure of the stature of the fullness of Christ" (Ephesians 4:13).

As we leave this evening, let the words of this beautiful prayer, which the bishop reads during the ordination of a new priest, ring in our ears, penetrate our minds and hearts, and therefore remind us, once again, of our priestly identity:

> O God, great in might and inscrutable in wisdom, marvelous in counsel above the sons of men: Do Thou, the same Lord, fill with the gift of Thy Holy Spirit this man whom it hath pleased Thee to advance to the degree of priest; that he may be worthy to stand in innocence before Thine altar; to proclaim the Gospel of Thy kingdom; to minister the word of Thy truth; to offer unto Thee spiritual gifts and sacrifices; to renew Thy people through the laver of regeneration. That when he shall go to meet Thee, at the Second Coming of our great God and Savior, Jesus Christ, Thine Only-Begotten Son, he may receive the reward of a good steward in the degree committed unto him, through the plenitude of Thy goodness.

Editor's Endnotes:

1. *During the address to the Archdiocesan Convention of 1977, the first entry in this chapter, Philip thanks those who were responsible for the foundation dinners on behalf of the Patriarch Elias IV Foundation for the Balamand Academy; notes that the SCOBA meeting which he hosted on March 24, 1977, was the first meeting between the hierarchs and the Orthodox Christian Education Commission (OCEC) since he became Metropolitan eleven years earlier; announces the establishment of a Radio and Television Foundation to teach the Orthodox Faith in the media; and announces the establishment of three new missions and the consecration of three new churches.*

2. *Philip meets with President Jimmy Carter in 1977 to discuss the situation of the Middle East in light of the hostage crisis which is occurring in Iran.*

3. *In his 1978 address to the convention at Houston, the third entry in this chapter, Philip also announces that the Antiochian Village will be dedicated on Sunday, October 1, 1978; announces that the Archdiocesan Conventions will be held biennially, that is, every other year on the odd-numbered years, beginning 1979; the even-numbered years being the Clergy Symposium, beginning 1980; and announces the mailing of* **The WORD** *magazine to every home in the archdiocese as a result of the increase in parish assessments.*

Chapter 9

BE DOERS OF THE WORD

There is a deafening noise in the media about God, yet nobody sees Him. We no longer want to hear about Jesus of Nazareth. We want to meet Him face to face and talk with Him. We Orthodox represent two thousand years of history. History can be a blessing if we penetrate its depths, or it can be a curse if we permit ourselves to be crushed by its weight. Modern Orthodox history leaves much to be desired; we have been chewing the past, imitating and reiterating. We are so afraid of writing a new song, seeing new vision and creating a new day. As "doers of the Word" we must not imprison Christ in our temples, in our libraries and in our rituals.

Metropolitan Philip

- *Theological Reflections on the Forthcoming Great Council: The International Conference of Orthodox Theologians, 1978*
- *In Memoriam: Patriarch Elias IV, 1979*
- *Doing God's Word and Caring for the Children, 1979*

In 1978, Philip was invited to address the Third International Conference of Orthodox Theologians on behalf of the Standing Conference of Orthodox Bishops in the Americas (SCOBA). It was sponsored by the Orthodox Theological Society of America (OTSA) and held in August at the Holy Cross School of Theology in Brookline, Massachusetts. In light of his Sunday of Orthodoxy sermon given the previous year (1977) at the Greek Orthodox Cathedral in New York, the Metropolitan was asked to further develop and refine his thoughts for this particular international gathering of theologians. The words of the previous year which he spoke in that sermon had indeed "stirred up the spirit" and remained "in the air." Now SCOBA wanted it further crafted for those who would return to their various countries and churches. How else would their awareness be lifted? Thus Philip is requested, as he says, "at the eleventh hour," to address this august body. In editing this address, we have tried to minimize the redundancies from that sermon of 1977, although some, of course, had to remain to do justice to the integrity of the presentation, as well as preserving the context in which it is delivered.

The second piece of literature which is included in this chapter is the short, but profound, reflection which Philip writes **In Memoriam** *for Patriarch Elias IV. There is simply no hiding Philip's deep love for this man, a man characterized by "spontaneity and simplicity." He also calls him one "who was influenced in all his theological thinking" by the Fathers of the Church. Seldom are such gentle words projected with such intensity.*

We close out the era of the late 1960s and '70s with the Metropolitan's address in 1979 to the Archdiocesan Convention gathered in Florida. It is a most appropriate topic with which to end this first section: a combined focus on "doing God's word" and "caring for the children." This latter focus is included because 1979 is the International Year of the Child, and, as the reader will discover, Philip's heart turns tender when it is softened by the thought of the children. This is especially seen as he interjects humor into the most serious concern regarding the life and well-being of the child.

The reader will note that in this last address, Philip truly seems to be summarizing the decade of the seventies. For example, he does this in terms of the revitalization of the youth movement, in which the old regional conventions would become **Parish Life Conferences,** *where entire families and parish organizations would be gathered precisely "to do God's work." It is most appropriate for him to emphasize this new form, since 1979 would be the last annual Archdiocesan Convention, and, since this Convention would henceforth be meeting every two years, the Parish Life Conferences would begin to serve the important linkage between the archdiocese and the local parish.*

In perfect line with this, Philip presents his vision for the **Antiochian Village,** *a vision which so well speaks of the dynamism which His Eminence always proposed for the Church, and which the reader will so clearly note in his quoting of Paul Evdokimov: "As soon as Orthodoxy hinders the future movement of tradition, it degenerates into an immobile traditionalism and betrays its vocation." As the 1970s come to an end, then, Philip encourages the Orthodox Church precisely not to "betray its vocation."*

J.J.A.

Theological Reflections on the Forthcoming Great Council
1978

It gives me great joy to address this assembly and to welcome, on behalf of the Standing Conference of the Canonical Orthodox Bishops in the Americas, our distinguished brothers in Christ from throughout the world to this Third International Conference of Orthodox Theologians hosted by the Orthodox Theological Society of America, during its tenth anniversary year.

The topic of your deliberations, "Theological Reflections on the Forthcoming Great Council," is of paramount interest to the American Orthodox community. In my remarks to you this evening, I will not presume to theologize to theologians, but neither will I speak in trite platitudes. My message, solicited at the eleventh hour, will be a personal assessment of the possibilities offered by such a Great Council. It will also attempt to offer you candid insights into the contemporary American Orthodox scene, to provide you with some small measure of practical knowledge of the Church's situation in the New World and to familiarize you with the aspirations of its faithful.

In November of 1975 I was delighted to learn of the proposed Great Council of Orthodoxy. The last Ecumenical Council was convened in 787—1,191 years ago—to deal with the problem of iconoclasm. In the nearly twelve centuries which have elapsed since the last Council, many religious, moral, political and socioeconomic events have taken place which have deeply affected the life of the Church. One might ask: Why didn't the Church meet in council since 787 to courageously respond to these challenges? Has the Church lost that dynamism and responsiveness which characterized her life during the first eight centuries? There is no doubt that the Church has experienced very difficult times since the last Council. However, this does not excuse the stagnation which has marked her life for the past 1,191 years. It is indeed strange that while we are active in the ecumenical movement, attending WCC meetings in America, Europe, Asia and Africa, we have had a most insignificant inter-Orthodox contact on either the national or international levels. When we learned of the forthcoming Great Council we thanked God that at long last and after many centuries of silence, a Council would convene to respond to the many challenges of our times.

At a 1976 meeting of the Standing Conference of the Canonical Orthodox Bishops in the Americas (SCOBA), we hierarchs unanimously authorized the chairman, His Eminence Archbishop Iakovos, to contact His Eminence Metropolitan Meliton of Chalcedon, the chairman of the pre-synodal consultations, for the purpose of inviting our conference to participate, in some capacity, in future pre-Synodal consultations. Our request was well received and in a communiqué addressed to Archbishop Iakovos, dated December 4, 1976, Metropolitan Meliton wrote:

> In reply, I wish to inform you and, through you, the Standing Conference, that your petition, being of special significance, will be conveyed to the Church, so that she may define the way by which the participation of our Orthodox brethren in America, in the next pan-Orthodox consultations may be effected, and their voice may be clearly heard.

At the first pre-Synodal Consultation, attended by representatives of thirteen patriarchates and churches, a proposed agenda of ten points was approved for the Great Council. I was not very much impressed with this agenda, because, after twelve centuries of expectation, some of the topics were outdated and irrelevant. Missing from the agenda, for example, are topics of contemporary concern such as abortion, homosexuality, euthanasia, the ordination of women and lesbians to the priesthood, cloning, procreation through artificial insemination, test-tube babies, etc. Although the teachings of the Church are clear vis-à-vis some of these issues, the Church must again and again reaffirm her position, and constantly proclaim the Truth in order to eliminate any possible confusion or misdirection on the part of the faithful. To demonstrate the urgent need for facing these issues, I will briefly mention the current situation in North America.

Abortion: In January, 1973, the Supreme Court of the United States legalized abortion. Such a decision was a tremendous blow to our Christian ethic and has caused the murder of millions of innocent, unborn children—over 1 million in 1977 alone. Dr. R. A. Gallop wrote:

> Once you permit the killing of the unborn child, there will be no stopping. There will be no age limit. You are setting off a chain reaction that will eventually make you the victim. Your children will kill you because you permitted the killing of their brothers and sisters. Your children will kill you because they will not want to support you in your old age. Your children will kill you for your homes and estates. If a doctor will take money for killing the innocent child in the womb, he will kill you with a needle when paid by your children. This is a terrible nightmare you are creating for the future.

Should not such a "nightmare" be addressed on the agenda of the Great Council?

Euthanasia: I am not surprised at all by the heated debate which is going on all over the world concerning the legalization of euthanasia. The legalization of abortion in an ever-increasing number of countries, "Christian" countries, will necessarily lead to the legalization of "mercy killing"; for what is the difference between terminating an unwanted life in the womb and an unwanted life in the hospital? Both cases are indicative of the world's growing lack of reverence for life. Russell Chandler, religious editor of the *Los Angeles Times*, in an article entitled "The Option of Death: Who May Choose?" wrote:

> The sophisticated and thorny ethical problems of abortions, euthanasia, genetic engineering, organ transplantation and test tube babies were remote—if not unreal—to most clergymen, let alone to the average person. According to experts in the field, the number of persons advocating an individual's right to terminate his or her own life is growing. Others, although not going that far, feel comfortable about passive euthanasia, allowing death to occur by removing medical life supporting systems.

We know that no one has the right to terminate life except the giver of Life, but we must articulate this belief to a wandering world. Man's creative energy is continuously leading to new discoveries. In other words, what was impossible to medical science in the past, is possible today. Open-heart surgery, for example, was unthinkable twenty-five years ago. Now it is a daily practice, and I would venture to say that in the past ten years millions of lives were saved through this operation. Clearly this, and other bioethical issues which I believe will be rapidly arising, belongs on the agenda.

Homosexual Practice: When a society loses its moral fiber, it falls prey to immorality and all kinds of perversions. Homosexual practice today is openly and widely publicized in the news media; consequently, homosexuals have their clubs, organizations, and even churches. Homosexual practice has invaded institutions such as our armed forces and even some Christian denominations, and this invasion continues to increase daily. It is clear that the Old and New Testaments, canon law and Holy Tradition all condemn homosexual practice as being abnormal and inconsistent with both God's law and natural law. However, several Christian denominations, some traditionally prestigious among them, have distorted the message of these sources and cause an ever-increasing amount of consternation among the faithful.

As I have said in another presentation, there is a new theological trend which is sweeping the Christian world today called the theology of liberation. We Orthodox have been asked to define our position vis-à-vis this theology. Can the Church remain passive and silent in a world of hunger, racism, totalitarianism, economic exploitation and social injustice? And if not, can the Church advocate armed resistance and encourage social revolutions as ways and means to liberate oppressed nations? We need, the world needs, answers to this and to other new iconoclasms. We cannot merely refer our people to theological libraries to find the answers in the Fathers of the Church. The Church of the twentieth century must speak out against those who would destroy man, just as the Ecumenical Church of the eighth century spoke out against the heretical iconoclasts.

The Church in Diaspora

One of the topics on the agenda of the Great Council which does concern and interest the Orthodox in this hemisphere is the situation of the faithful in diaspora. I wonder, however, how much the venerable hierarchs of the Church in the Old World really know about our Orthodox situation in America. Who will speak for the American Church? I feel that it is imperative to provide our Orthodox brethren from across the ocean with a true and clear picture about our successes and failures, especially during the current century. Our brethren in the Old World must see that Orthodoxy on this continent is no longer a child.

Nearly two centuries ago our forefathers, driven by the horrors of tyranny, social injustice and despair, heard the Voice which Abraham heard: "Get thee out of thy country and from thy father's house unto a land that I will show thee." Thus, from the Middle East, the Balkans, Russia and Eastern Europe our fathers came and blessed these shores by planting the seeds of the glorious Orthodox Faith, the Faith of the Apostles, the Faith of the saints and martyrs. Faced with seemingly insurmountable obstacles, struggling for their daily bread, these pioneers had the courage and determination to establish in this land religious communities to perpetuate Orthodoxy.

Because of their various national backgrounds and strong ethnic ties which connected them with their mother churches, our people found themselves separated from each other and living under a multiplicity of administrative jurisdictions—a situation unparalleled in the history of the Church. If the first and second generation of Orthodox have tolerated this confusing situation, I assure you that the third and fourth generations will neither understand it nor accept it. The youth, perhaps more than any other age group, know full well the blessings to be derived from a united Church, and constantly reiterate their pleas for action in this direction.

On the occasion of the bicentennial of the American independence, celebrated in 1976, the first pan-Orthodox encyclical was released to the media. It stated, in part, that "The Divine Liturgy was first sung on this continent three decades before the American Revolution by Orthodox pioneers who were swiftly followed by Russian missionaries bringing the Faith of Jerusalem, Antioch and Byzantium to the Native Americans who still cherish it." There can be no doubt that Orthodoxy is deeply rooted in the American soil.

We will be forever indebted to our forefathers who planted and nurtured the Church in America, but our mother churches must realize once and for all that we are no longer a Church of immigrants. Our Orthodox children have died on the battlefields of many wars defending American principles and ideals. Our people have generously contributed to American life in business, education, the arts, science and medicine, law and government. Through them Orthodoxy has found a permanent home in the New World. This fact cannot continue to be ignored. If the mother churches are not aware of the special characteristics which distinguish the life of the Church in this hemisphere, we say to them, "Come and see." It was in this spirit that I invited His Beatitude Elias IV, Patriarch of Antioch and All the East, to visit the North American Archdiocese. After spending three months in 1977 traveling throughout the United States and Canada, meeting our people and experiencing firsthand the Church in the New World, he stated:

> In preparation for the upcoming Great Council, the Antiochian Holy Synod has studied in depth the situation of Orthodoxy in the Diaspora. Our position is clear. There must be established independent Churches in Western Europe, in North America, etc. The possibility for such an autocephalous Church is greatest in North America. The Antiochian See is ready to do her part to rectify the unfortunate situation of Orthodoxy in North America. We affirm that in North America there should be an autocephalous Church with its own Patriarch and Holy Synod.

To our other brothers in the Old World we issue the same invitation, "Come and see." Yes, come and see our churches and institutions, our liturgical and theological publications, our theological schools. But even more importantly, come and see our dedicated and faithful clergy, our devoted laity, and our dynamic youth movements.

My brothers and sisters in Christ, I am not suggesting that all is well with Orthodoxy in this hemisphere. We too have our problems. But the most cancerous is the administrative disunity which allows us to continue to live in our artificially constructed ghettos. Individually our various jurisdictions have done much. But collectively we have not yet even begun to explore our tremendous potentialities as one administratively united body.

We Orthodox are fortunate that we represent two thousand years of theology and spirituality. But where is our spiritual impact on the life of America? Who is articulating our Orthodox theology for the benefit of our American brethren who have been victimized and confused by all kinds of theological innovations? Where is our presence in the media? Where is our moral influence on our national and international politics? Orthodoxy, despite her past glories, remains the best-kept secret in this land because of our failure to speak with one united voice. America does not understand us because we are still speaking to her in a multitude of languages which she does not understand.

The problem of the diaspora, that tremendous exodus of millions of Orthodox Christians from their "Old Countries," constitutes a major and unprecedented experience in the history of the Church. The multiplicity of jurisdictions in one given territory contradicts the fundamental understanding and teaching of ecclesiology. No one can deny that we are dealing with a very serious and highly complex problem. But it is a problem which must be faced. Nine years ago His Eminence Archbishop Iakovos stated in response to a question about Orthodox unity in America: "The problem is not simple. But the simple thing is this, that we are not going back. We are going forward. Our relations with the mother churches will be severed unless the mother churches realize the American reality." It is the earnest prayer of six million Orthodox Christians throughout this land that this realization will be accomplished as a result of the forthcoming Great Council.

An American Synod

My own suggestion as a first step in the achievement of administrative unity in America would be for the mother churches to elevate the Standing Conference—which has already served its purpose—to the dignity of a Synod. Such a Synod will be able to speak to America and to the world with one voice and one accord. This Synod, which will truly represent six million free Orthodox Christian believers, will be able to respond effectively to the moral and social challenges of our time. Why should we, for example, issue ten Orthodox statements vis-à-vis abortion?

The most important task for this Synod, however, will be

the preparation for the establishment of an Orthodox Patriarchate in America, which will reflect both our organic unity and the richness and diversity of our ethnic cultures. I want to make it clear here, that this patriarchate can only be established by a common decision of all Orthodox Churches.

Finally, if this proposal is not Orthodox, I do not know what is. Orthodoxy in America must not be permitted to be victimized by historical feuding and comfortable inaction. The mission of the Church is to recreate life and constantly to transform history. How long can our mother churches continue to ignore the destiny and fulfillment of millions of Orthodox Christians in North America? How long?

In Memoriam: Patriarch Elias IV
1979

My Captain does not answer, his lips are pale and still,
My father does not feel my arm, he has no pulse nor will.
The ship is anchor'd safe and sound, its voyage closed and
  done,
From fearful trip the victor ship comes in with object won:
Exult O shores, and ring O bells!
But I with mournful tread,
Walk the deck my Captain lies,
Fallen cold and dead.
  —Walt Whitman

The day Elias IV died was one of the saddest days of my life. On June 21, early in the morning, I went to the dining room to eat breakfast. The deacon was waiting for me sorrowful and with much anguish. I told him that I spent a very restless night and I even heard the phone ring around four o'clock in the morning. The deacon looked at me with tearful eyes and did not utter a word. When I finished breakfast, the deacon, with a shaky voice, said: "The phone which you heard this morning was from Damascus. The patriarch is dead." We looked at each other and with much grief burst into tears.

It was impossible for me to believe that Elias IV was dead. I immediately placed a call to Damascus and the news of his death was confirmed. Anyone who knew Elias IV in his vitality, dynamism, mental and physical strength, would find it difficult to believe that this man of distinguished character is no longer with us.

Elias IV was born in the heights of the Lebanese mountains, and although he left the village very young, the village never left him. His spontaneity and simplicity reflected this reality. He combined in his personality the gentleness of a soft midnight summer breeze and the explosiveness of a man who was impatient with everything. He was in this world but not of it. He was born poor, lived like a hermit and died like a meteor. His childhood impressions from the village never left him, hence his individualism, impatience with bureaucracies and all kinds of organizational structures. Elias IV was a sensitive and intense poet; such sensitivity and intensity were always demonstrated in his prophetic words, penetrating eyes and constant hand gestures.

His love for the Fathers of the Church influenced all his theological thinking, and his rootedness in his people's soil made him live all the agony, misery and restlessness of the Middle East. In 1974, he became the first Christian leader ever to address a Pan-Islamic Conference in Lahor, Pakistan. His passionate plea on behalf of Jerusalem earned him the title of "Patriarch of the Arabs." In 1975, he became the first Christian leader to visit Saudi Arabia and to tell King Khaled, "We Orthodox Christians are more rooted in this land than you."

His devotion to theological education brought him to North America in 1977 and subsequently took him to South America in 1978. How fortunate we are that we had the opportunity to kiss his hand, look at his bright face and receive his apostolic blessing. One day in 1977, after we returned from a regional SOYO Conference, he was so elated that he said to me, "Now, I truly feel that I am the Patriarch of Antioch. This archdiocese is the 'new' Antioch."

Three days after the patriarch died, a little boy called me at the archdiocese and said, "Is it true that the holy man died?" I said, "Yes, he did." The boy paused for a while and then said, "Good-bye," and that was the end of our conversation.

It is difficult to believe that Elias IV is gone; however, it is not hard to believe that he died of a heart attack. The agony of Antioch, the suffering of his people and the heavy burdens of his office shattered the last vein in his heart. Elias IV now belongs to history. He will always live in the conscience of the Church. His penetrating eyes are closed. His bright face is dust.

His ever-moving hands are still and his restless heart is finally at rest. Elias IV is no more, but our consolation lies in the fact that he was born on the peak, he lived on the peak and like an eagle, he died on the peak.

May his memory be eternal!

Be Doers of the Word and Care for the Children
Florida, 1979

Once again our archdiocese convenes to examine the harvest of the past year. St. James the Apostle wrote:

> Be doers of the Word and not hearers only, deceiving yourselves. For if anyone is a hearer of the Word and not a doer, he is like a man who observes his natural face in a mirror; for he observes himself and goes away and at once forgets what he was like. But he who looks into the perfect law of liberty, and perseveres, being no hearer that forgets but a doer that acts, he shall be blessed for his doing (James 1:22–25).

The Word Which Bears Fruit
During the past year I have traveled extensively throughout the archdiocese. And I am happy to inform you that the state of the archdiocese is good despite our imperfection. All archdiocesan departments and organizations are doing their best to serve the eternal goals and ideals of our Church. We have intensified our efforts in the field of theological education and I am happy to report to you that we now have eighteen seminarians studying at St. Vladimir's Seminary in New York and Holy Cross Seminary in Brookline, Massachusetts.

Most of our missions are doing very well. They continue to receive financial assistance from our missionary fund and all their Christian education and sacred music materials as well as their liturgical books from the archdiocese, free of charge. I would like to remind you that the missionary zeal which you have demonstrated last year did not end with 1978. Such missionary efforts must continue if we want to remain faithful to our Lord's commission "to go and make disciples of all nations" (Matthew

28:19). The revitalization of our youth department which was effected in 1970 is bearing very good fruit. It is indeed a pleasure to see these young people at work, conducting meetings, attending religious services, receiving the sacraments, raising funds for hungry people, helping missions, delivering orations, participating in catechism bowls and committing themselves to the lofty ideals of our Church. Being with them always reminds me of this poem by Walt Whitman.

> I have perceived that to be with those I like is enough,
> To stop in company with the rest at evening is enough,
> To be surrounded by beautiful, curious, breathing, laughing
>   flesh is enough,
> To pass among them or touch any one, or rest my arm ever
>   so lightly
> Round his or her neck for a moment, what is this then?
> I do not ask any more delight, I swim in it as in a sea.

For the past nine years we have been trying to make the old SOYO Conventions into new Parish Life Conferences. The conferences which I have attended this year proved beyond doubt that this dream has been realized. We have finally succeeded in bringing to the conferences not only the youth but the entire family and archdiocesan organizations; mainly, teens, the parish councils, the Antiochian Women and the Order of St. Ignatius of Antioch.

Important Changes
This is the last annual Archdiocesan Convention. Our next Archdiocesan Convention will be held in 1981. There is no doubt whatsoever that our annual conventions have served a tremendous purpose during the past thirty-four years; they have kept our family together and they have cemented many beautiful relationships. For many practical reasons we can no longer hold these annual conventions. Now our task is to preserve and develop our archdiocesan programs through the regional

conferences. It is imperative, therefore, that we reach every Antiochian family within the region through direct mailings not only to the church office, but to each family.

Moreover, in order to strengthen the relations between our parishes and the archdiocese, I am going to create advisory regional councils for the metropolitan composed of the pastor, chairman and vice-chairman of every parish council within the region. The purpose of this advisory council will be to bring to the attention of the bishop the needs of the parishes on the local level. At the same time, the bishop will have the opportunity to dialogue with these individuals and bring to their attention the importance of the archdiocesan activities and programs on both the local and national levels. The meetings of such advisory councils will consist of two sessions: the first will be strictly with the bishop, and the second will be a workshop on stewardship which will deal with the spiritual and financial conditions of our parishes. We must realize once and for all that the archdiocese cannot be stronger than the parish. If you are weak, we are weak, but if you are strong, we are strong also. If our archdiocesan programs are not well implemented on the local level, then all our activities on the national level are to no avail.

The Antiochian Women continue to work diligently, striving ever forward. If you do not have a chapter in your parish, establish one. This organization is doing very good work in this archdiocese for the glory of God. The two television spots which the Antiochian Women sponsored are the beginning of greater things to come. I would like to take this opportunity to thank their spiritual advisors, the North American Board and all regional officers for a job very well done.

The Order of St. Ignatius of Antioch is indeed a miracle in the life of this archdiocese. I have never witnessed an organization grow so fast and accomplish so much so soon like the Order of St. Ignatius of Antioch. Undoubtedly, this progress is due to the dynamic leadership of the Order on both the national and local levels. Our Lord said: "Ye shall know them from their fruit." Let the warped-minded people who question the validity of the Order come and see what the Order is doing for our clergy and this archdiocese. The Order is still in its formative years and we will make some mistakes, but such mistakes will be corrected in a spirit of objectivity and love. The past year was a very fruitful year for the Order. I pray that during the coming year more men and women will join this tremendous spiritual venture for the glory of God.

A Glorious Dedication and Vision for the Future
Last year, as you well remember, we purchased the Antiochian Village for $350,000 from our archdiocesan funds. We did not raise this money from you because we wanted this Village to be a gift from the archdiocese to you and your children.

The Antiochian Village, my friends, is a manifestation of a new spiritual dimension in the life of the Church in this hemisphere. If we reflect carefully on the history of our people in North America, we may distinguish three main eras in the life of our archdiocese:

1. The "era of immigration," perhaps the most difficult one, which extended from the turn of the century to the end of the thirties.
2. The "era of organization," which extended from the early forties to the end of the sixties.
3. The "era of spiritual maturation" (I hope) which began in 1970 with the revitalization of our Youth Department and subsequently the creation of the Antiochian Women, the creation of the Order of St. Ignatius of Antioch, the visit of His Beatitude of thrice-blessed memory, Patriarch Elias IV in 1977, our missionary thrust, our many retreats and spiritual encounters, and last but not least, the acquisition of the Antiochian Village.

Last October, on the eve of the dedication of the Village, we celebrated an open-air Vespers service on that beautiful mountain. While the choir was chanting "O Gladsome Light," the bright sun was slowly sinking beyond the horizon, half covered by the yellow leaves of the Pennsylvania trees. I felt like bending down and kissing the ground because the place was holy. I saw God face to face in His eternal glory. I saw Him in every individual who prayed with me on the mountain.

We have spent enough time, energy and money chasing planes from one hotel to another and we have spent more than enough time talking and hearing about God. I am tired of that. My young people, I am sure, are also tired of hearing about God. I believe that the world is also tired of hearing about God. There is a deafening noise in the media about God, yet nobody sees Him. We no longer want to hear about Jesus of Nazareth. We want to meet Him face to face and talk to Him.

We Orthodox represent two thousand years of history. History can be a blessing if we penetrate its depths, or it can be a curse if we permit ourselves to be crushed by its weight. Modern Orthodox history leaves much to be desired. We have been chewing the past, imitating and reiterating. We are so afraid of writing a new song, seeing a new vision and creating a new day. We have imprisoned Christ in our icons, in our temples, in our libraries and in our rituals. Paul Evdokimov, writing about modern Orthodox spirituality, said:

> Its dynamism has taken refuge in national and juridical provincialism, the aestheticism of the elite, and the folk superstition of the masses. As soon as Orthodoxy hinders the forward movement of tradition, it degenerates into an immobile traditionalism and betrays its vocation.

The biggest disappointment during the thirteen years of my episcopate has been the lack of sincerity and genuine interest in inter-Orthodox relations.

Some of you might ask: What is the relation between these thoughts and the Antiochian Village? The answer is: We must develop a *philosophy* for the Village. We have acquired this Village to breathe new, spiritual, fresh air, to encounter Christ in His beauty and to ask Him questions just like the Samaritan woman did at the well of Jacob. I want this Village to serve everyone in the Orthodox Church, young and old. Presently, our facilities at the Village are excellent for children, teens and young singles. However, since the Orthodox Church and our archdiocese, in particular, is family-oriented, it is of the utmost importance to provide facilities for total family involvement in the programs offered at the Village.

To adequately meet this urgent need, a comfortable family conference and retreat center is indispensable. This center will provide the following facilities: (a) one hundred motel-type sleeping rooms (mixed doubles and singles) with private baths; (b) a dining room/assembly hall which will accommodate three hundred diners and approximately five hundred, theater style; (c) a fully equipped kitchen to service the dining room; (d) five meeting rooms; (3) a 15,000-volume research library. These facilities will help us to implement the philosophy which we will continue to develop for the future of our Church in this land.

The Year of the Child

What a beautiful coincidence that while we are talking about the Antiochian Village and the future of our children, we are at the same time celebrating the International Year of the Child. Writing about the Year of the Child, poet Paul Garrida said:

> 1979 is a gift,
> to give a chance,
> to let a child sing,
> to let him spread his wings,
> with your help the clouds will await him
> like open doors, to the blue sky above,
> the flight will last forever.

Little children are little poets. They are full of wonder and amazement. I wish we could see the world the way children see it and celebrate life the way children celebrate it. The most sincere love is the love of children and the most genuine innocence is the innocence of children. Our Lord said: "Except ye be converted, and become as little children, ye shall not enter the kingdom of heaven" (Matthew 18:2-4). Only if you are childlike, may you enter the kingdom of heaven. I think that God's kingdom will have more children than bishops, priests, philosophers, politicians or so-called leaders of this world.

I shall not bore you with figures and statistics about the plight of millions of children in this country and all over the world. You may read about that in many books and magazines. Since the dawning of the age of modern psychology and psychoanalysis, there has been a tremendous debate on how to raise children. High schools and universities are even offering courses in "parenting." I wonder how many of your parents and grandparents took such courses. I know my parents did not. Despite the fact that I left home when I was young, I still remember my childhood very vividly. My parents did not have much material wealth but they had much love. The few things which we had, we shared and that was the secret of our happiness. The report of the Carnegie Council on children states: "Where poverty is shared, in the security of a stable family and a functioning cultural environment, a child would not suffer."

In order for children to grow up well adjusted to life, they need more than money, bread and meat; they need love. There was a time when we did not have much money, much bread and much meat, and yet we were happy. Today, we have all these things, and yet we are unhappy. When Christ said: "Man shall not live by bread alone," He expressed the eternal truth. It is indeed unfortunate that millions of children are being raised by day-care centers in this country and by the state in communist countries. How can a child experience his parents' love if he is raised by faceless people? Mueller Fahrenhold said: "What a child has learned, no one can take away again and this applies to suffering as well as to happiness."

Traveling in this archdiocese during the past thirteen years, I have had the most wonderful encounters with our little children. They call me all kinds of names—for example, my niece calls me "Mee Moo," some call me "Your Innocence," some "Your M & M," some "St. Edna," and some believe that I am the "Imperial Margarine King." Children are the most precious gifts which we receive from God. I have a special file in my office which contains the most beautiful letters from children.

During this International Year of the Child, I would like to conclude with this verse by the Chilean poet, Gabriela Mistral:

> Many things can wait.
> The child cannot.
> Right now his hip bones are being formed,
> His blood is being developed.
> To him we cannot say "tomorrow"
> His name is "Today."

Editor's Endnotes:

1. In his 1979 address to the Archdiocesan Convention in Florida, Metropolitan Philip also reviews his visits to parishes and youth conferences; addresses the financial information relative to the Antiochian Village; reflects on his own childhood in Lebanon; and summarizes the impact of Patriarch Elias IV, who had recently fallen asleep in the Lord.

2. 1979 would be the last year of the **annual** Archdiocesan Convention. This gathering of all parishes and organizations in the archdiocese would begin meeting biennially. On even-numbered years there would be gathered a biennial **Clergy Symposium,** a new conclave created by Philip for purposes of continuing theological and pastoral education for his clergy. The first Clergy Symposium was being planned for 1980 in Chicago, logistically the central gathering point in the archdiocese.

Part II

The Second Decade
The 1980s

Chapter 10

BEHOLD THE NEW HAS COME:
New Challenges for the 1980s

> *St. Paul said, "If anyone is in Christ, he is a new creature, the old has passed away; behold the new has come" (2 Corinthians 5:17). Only God's love which we experience in Christ can transform our inner being and create new hearts in us ... make new minds, renew our families, transfigure our parishes, and ultimately transform the entire world. But all these things can happen only "if we do not accept the grace of God in vain."*
>
> Metropolitan Philip

- *Show Love and Do Good: The Paternal Bishop and the Clergy, 1980*
- *Now Is the Acceptable Time: Weaving a New Cloth, 1981*

Newness is the gift that Christ always offers in any age: "Behold I make all things new!" *(Revelation 21:5). The 1980s begin with this dominant theme. The two addresses in this chapter are both related to newness. The first address concerns a new phenomenon in the Church, the Clergy Symposium. In the second, Metropolitan Philip celebrates his fifteenth year in the episcopacy, and the theme of his address is precisely newness.*

In truth, it is most appropriate to begin this part on the 1980s with the first Biennial Clergy Symposium at which Philip addresses his priests gathered in Chicago. This can be said because throughout this decade, there are a multitude of occasions on which the clergy benefit from Philip's strong focus on their life and circumstances, both spiritually and temporally. Of course, the richness of the eighties cannot be limited to the clergy. It extends also into the establishment of programs and institutions which were set on course in the seventies, e.g.: two phases of the Heritage and Learning Center at the Antiochian Village will be completed in the eighties; a second patriarchal visit will occur, this time by Ignatius IV; the need becomes obvious and is satisfied for an auxiliary bishop, as Father Antoun Khouri is elevated to the episcopacy, etc. The reader will see these events, and many more, unfolding during the years captured in Part Two of our text.

What is different—and wonderful—about Philip's first talk at the Clergy Symposium is that, having reached a point of maturation through experience and physical suffering, he speaks out of that reservoir to his clergy. And, therefore, as he addresses the issues of worship, preaching and service, it is with a certain personal feel: "We cannot fool the people . . . do not be conceited . . . we do not preach ourselves . . . you are a servant, not a dictator . . . rule with love." *These are words spoken by the more paternal bishop of the eighties to those he appoints to* **"show love and do good."**

Our second piece included in this chapter is Philip's fifteenth anniversary address in Los Angeles, 1981. It is the first of the Biennial Conventions and, as noted earlier, its theme is "Behold I Make All Things New." *Here Philip* "weaves" *together a beautiful* "cloth" *by relating the newness prescribed in the Scripture with a call in the eighties to enact that newness within the structure of the Church and archdiocese. As the administrator that he has become by now, he reminds the people what has been accomplished in those fifteen years. But as had also become typical of his approach—restlessness, reaching, inspiring—he challenges them with this very theme: newness. He especially completes this weave as he elaborates upon the theology of ordination, rooted in the New Testament, which must now be applied to the need for another bishop in the archdiocese. As he develops this teaching, he reminds the Convention that they, as laity, have a critical part to play in the nomination process. They are the people of God, and now must fulfill that responsibility.*

In general, this feeling is clearly conveyed in these addresses: time is calling, needs are increasing, and the God who makes things new is presenting us with a challenge not to delay in our response: **Now is the acceptable time!**

J. J. A.

Show Love and Do Good
The First Clergy Symposium, 1980

With this Divine Liturgy, we conclude five days of beautiful fellowship for which we have longed for many years. When we made the decision in Houston to change to biennial Archdiocesan Conventions, I promised you biennial Clergy Symposia. I hope that this holy gathering has enriched your minds and hearts with meaningful spiritual encounters. You can make such gatherings even more rewarding if you tell us where we succeed and where we fail. Therefore, the feedback which we get from you is of utmost importance.

The purpose of this symposium was set forth a long time ago by the writer of the Epistle to the Hebrews: "Let us be concerned for one another, to help one another, to *show love and to do good.* Let us not give up the habit of meeting together as some are doing" (Hebrews 10:24, 25). The Book of Acts tells us that the early Christians came together for three main reasons: (1) to worship the Triune God and celebrate the Eucharist; (2) to preach the Good News and experience a genuine Christian *koinonia;* and (3) to glorify Jesus Christ through a life of witness and service. I believe that these principles were true yesterday, are true today and will always be true until the end of history.

I would like to comment briefly on each of these points. The Church started as a worshipping community. Even during the era of persecution, the Church never failed to come together for worship and the celebration of the Eucharist. Notice that I did not use the term "to perform the Divine Liturgy" because the early Christians did not "act" the Liturgy; they celebrated it. To celebrate an event is to observe it in a very special way. The priests and the congregation are the celebrators, while Christ is the celebrity *par excellence.* To celebrate the Eucharist is to encounter Christ in His manger, in His public ministry, in His suffering, death and Resurrection from the dead. No other Christian denominations celebrate these special and unique events in human history the way the Orthodox Church does.

Have you noticed that I do not prefer to hold church banquets after the Divine Liturgy? The reason is that after I celebrate the Eucharist, I feel physically and emotionally exhausted. I put into this celebration everything I have, my whole being, and unless we priests go through a spiritual experience during this celebration, neither we nor our congregations will encounter God. In that case, Christ, the sacraments, the Eucharist, the Church become empty acts; just things.

Preaching the Good News

St. Paul said: "Woe unto me if I do not preach the gospel" (1 Corinthians 9:16). Those who are not familiar with the Orthodox Church think that we are just a ceremonial church. This is very far from the truth. Preaching has always been an essential part of the eucharistic celebration. Otherwise, why the Liturgy of the Word? I believe that during the eucharistic celebration, two kinds of communion take place: communion with the Word and communion with the Body and Blood of Christ. I would dare say that communion with the Word is one of the sacraments. I have said this to impress on you the importance of preaching, the importance of the *kerygma*. But to nourish your children on Sunday with the Word, you must properly prepare your sermons. It is true that the Holy Spirit speaks through us. However, we must not be arrogant: we must cooperate with the Spirit through our struggle and prayer life, as we prepare to become an instrument of transmitting the Word.

I would, therefore, start preparing my sermon on Monday. If you do not like to write it and read it, at least make a written or mental outline of it. Remember that you are a healer; therefore, you must give your children the medicine which they need. Do not bore them with abstract theology which is not related to concrete problems. Any theology which does not touch man in his hope and despair, in his victory and defeat, in his faith and doubt, in his sickness and health, and in his life and death, is a meaningless theology.

Always be prepared and ready to preach regardless of the size of your congregation. St. John Chrysostom said:

> We, to whom the service of the Word is entrusted, have received from our dear God the command never to abandon our duty and never to be silent, whether anyone listens to us or not. There are those priests who make fun of us and say, stop the good advice, scrap the admonitions, they will not listen to you, let them go. What are you saying? Have you promised to convert all men in one day? If only ten, or only five, or indeed only one repents, is that not consolation enough?

Finally, a word of caution here concerning credibility and conceit. There must not be a credibility gap between what we say and who we are. We cannot fool the people. By the same token, if you are a good preacher, do not be conceited. Preach to glorify God and not yourself. People come to church to worship God and not the priest. St. Paul said: "For what we preach is not ourselves, but Jesus Christ as Lord with ourselves as your servants" (2 Corinthians 4:5).

Witness and Service

The last point that I would like to touch upon is the priest as witness and servant.

To glorify Jesus Christ through a life of witness and service is to love people, and to experience within your congregation a genuine Christian *koinonia* (communion). If you are not capable of loving, forget this life of service; go and do something else with your life. Before our Lord commissioned Peter to feed His sheep, He asked him thrice: "Do you love me?" You serve your people best when you love them and develop a spiritual sensitivity to each and everyone of them. Church historians tell us that Chrysostom's congregation numbered about one hundred thousand souls, yet he knew them, ministered to all of them and was always moved by a deep compassion for them. You are a father and a servant in the Church, not a dictator. If you have to rule sometimes, rule with love; otherwise, the Satan of authority will enter your heart and destroy all your mission.

The vocation to which you have been called is most challenging, but only if you take it seriously. You cannot face the challenge of your calling if you do not continue to grow spiritually. St. John Chrysostom likened life to a battle. Listen to him speak:

> You stand always in the front rank of battle, and are always receiving new wounds... now your wife irritates you, then your son worries you, an enemy sets his snare for you, a friend speaks badly of you, a neighbor abuses you, a colleague deceives you, poverty oppresses you, the loss of those related to you afflicts you, fortune makes you arrogant, and misfortune makes you downcast. All around us are numerous opportunities for inducing in us anger, worry, discouragement, affliction, vanity and despair. Therefore, we need the divine medicine by which we may heal the wounds we have received.

What an eloquent description of the human condition. This is pastoral theology. I have known you for many years. Many of you have received the grace of priesthood through the laying on of my unworthy hands. Throughout the years many of you, thank God, continue to grow in Christ and increase in wisdom; some of you have remained spiritually stagnant, and still a few have become cynical.

Stagnation and cynicism are the result of spiritual and intellectual slothfulness. Do you know that some of us do not read a book after leaving the seminary, let alone the Scriptures and the Fathers? How can we fight the good fight if we are empty from within? A contemporary theologian said, "Exterior pressures win their easiest victories over an interior emptiness."

Beloved coworkers in Christ, you are agents of change in your parishes. But we, ourselves, are not changed if we are not *renewed*, and if we are not inspired, how can we change, renew and inspire our flocks? I desperately need your help, especially with the youth and the elderly. I need your help to make our regional conferences true family gatherings. I need your help to build a conference, retreat and learning center at the Antiochian Village. Our people need a place where they can go and receive a glimpse of the divine.

Twenty years from now our Church will enter the twenty-first century. What our future Church will become depends on what we are today. I have tried to serve you to the best of my ability, and if I have stumbled along the way, it is because of human frailty. Do not forget, however, that I love you and care for each and everyone of you.

In conclusion, I would like to leave you with this prayer from one of the Western Fathers:

> Teach us, good Lord, to serve Thee as Thou deserve:
> To give and not to count the cost,
> To fight and not to heed the wounds,
> To toil and not to seek for rest,
> To labor and not to ask for any reward,
> Save that of knowing that we do Thy will.

Now Is the Acceptable Time
Los Angeles, 1981

"Even if the angels come and tell you 'division is good for you,' do not believe them."

The biblical text for my message to you this year is taken from Second Corinthians: "Working together with Him, we entreat you not to accept the grace of God in vain. For He says, 'At the acceptable time I have listened to you, and helped you on the day of salvation.' Behold, *now is the acceptable time;* behold, now is the day of salvation" (2 Corinthians 6:2).

As we gather at this convention to examine the harvest of the years, let us never forget for a moment that we are working together with God. Despite the evil days, despite the trials and tribulations of life, and despite the enemies which are on the attack from all sides, the Church will triumph because we are coworkers with Him who said: "I will build my church, and the gates of hell shall not prevail against her" (Matthew 16:18). Christ did not make just a visit to this earth to establish a Church and then leave it to the wolves, but as the Lord of history, He continues to work with us through His Holy Church, which is His extension in time and space. Did He not tell us, "I will be with you until the end of time" (Matthew 28:20)? In this biblical text, St. Paul admonishes us "not to accept the grace of God *in vain.*" How important it is to remember these words during this year of spiritual renewal.

The overall theme of our convention is: "Behold, I make all things new." Our study of history and the events which are shaping our world today prove beyond doubt that without Christ, this world will continue to be hopeless and aimless, and our lives will continue to be subject to decadence, corruption and death. St. Paul said: "If anyone is in Christ, he is a new creation, the old has passed away, *behold the new has come*"

(2 Corinthians 5:17). Only God's love, which we experience in Christ, can transform our inner being and create new hearts within us, new minds, renew our families, transfigure our parishes and ultimately transform the entire world. But all these things can happen only if we do not accept the grace of God in vain.

Fifteen Years of Service
Fifteen years have elapsed since my ordination to the episcopate to serve you. It is impossible to cover in this message all the important goals which you have achieved for the glory of God. I will, however, reflect with you on some of the issues which are of utmost importance to all of us.

Since my consecration as your bishop, the Mother Church has been at the top of the list of our priorities. Our clergy and our people in this archdiocese diverted a large sum of money from our treasury to build the Balamand Theological Academy, and when many projects were needed to strengthen the temporal and spiritual life of this archdiocese, we established a fund in the amount of $500,000 to help perpetuate theological education within the Mother Church. It is important to know, ladies and gentlemen, that this archdiocese is contributing more than half of the annual budget of the Balamand Academy, despite the fact that our archdiocese does not have one seminarian at the Balamand. In addition to that, every year we send between $10,000 and $15,000 as a gift to assist in the operating expenses of the patriarchate. We have never asked the Mother Church to do us any favors. After this convention, however, we are going to ask our Mother Church to elect for us one of the three individuals whom you will nominate to be an auxiliary bishop. Some might ask: Why do we need an auxiliary bishop?

You will find part of the answer to this question in the following statistics. In 1966, we had 78 parishes, 86 clergy and our budget was $77,000. Now, in 1981, we have 130 parishes, 200 clergy and our budget for the next fiscal year is $1,066,000. Such statistics prove beyond doubt that this archdiocese is very

Above: The young Metropolitan with students at the St. John of Damascus School of Theology (Balamand) immediately after his consecration in 1966.

Left: Metropolitan Philip delivering his State of the Archdiocese Address.

At the Liturgy: "Let us lift up our hearts!"

Metropolitan Philip receives his first Doctor of Divinity Degree from Metropolitan Theodosius, President of St. Vladimir's Seminary.

Metropolitan Philip preparing to consecrate a new church building.

His Eminence receives a warm kiss from a little girl at a Parish Life Conference.

Philip presents a gift to Father Alexander Schmemann for St. Vladimir's Seminary. Standing between them is Mansour Laham, long-time officer of the Archdiocese Board of Trustees.

A young child welcomes His Eminence with a flower during an archpastoral visit.

Above: His Eminence with Metropolitan Ilyas of Beirut and Bishop Antoun at the Archdiocese Headquarters.

Left: Metropolitan Philip with Father Joseph Allen, the editor of this book.

much alive and "working together with God" to fulfill His purpose in history.

During the past fifteen years, I have traveled hundreds of thousands of miles to serve you and, despite the tremendous help which I am receiving from my brother in Christ, Archbishop Michael, I feel that we need another bishop in the headquarters to help me in the daily administration of the archdiocese. Many times I feel very frustrated because I am not giving enough attention to our youth, the Order of St. Ignatius of Antioch, the Antiochian Women, the Antiochian Village and the rest of our departments and commissions.

We hope and pray that this bishop will be more than a ceremonial figure. We want him to be deeply involved in the total life of the archdiocese. I am sure that the election of another bishop is not a sign of death, but an expression of life and a renewed commitment to the eternal ideals and principles of our Holy Church. Let us hope and pray that the Holy Synod of Antioch will understand our situation and elect this bishop for us at the next session of the Synod, which will be held on August 17, 1981. *"Behold, now is the acceptable time."*

The Clergy

Our clergy are, indeed, the soul of this archdiocese and without them, we are dead. During the past fifteen years, we have done everything possible to improve the spiritual and temporal life of our priests. The new model constitution for parishes has restored the dignity of the priest; henceforth, our priests are no longer hired and fired. Priests are appointed and transferred by the bishop, with the advice of our parish councils.

We have continued to improve the educational and spiritual qualities of our clergy. Seven of them hold doctorate degrees in various fields of theology. Retreats and symposia have become a common practice for the clergy of our archdiocese. I am delighted to tell you that last year, we admitted twenty seminarians to study theology at Orthodox seminaries, and for the next academic year, we plan to admit no less than twenty seminarians. We have established the St. Stephen's Course of Theological Study for all those whose circumstances do not permit them to study at seminary. St. John Chrysostom said:

> The priestly office is indeed discharged on earth, but it ranks amongst heavenly ordinances; and very naturally so: for neither man, nor angel, nor archangel nor any other created power, but the Paraclete, the Holy Spirit Himself, instituted this vocation and persuaded men to represent the ministry of angels.

Retreat and Learning Center

Once again, I would like to remind you of St. Paul's admonition, "Now is the acceptable time." Let us not procrastinate and say, "Tomorrow we will do it, or next year, or next century." *"Now is the day of salvation."* What we do now, today, will determine what kind of archdiocese we will be tomorrow and next year. Whether you realize it or not, we are already on the threshold of the twenty-first century. Thus, the future of our archdiocese is not twenty-five or fifty years from now; the future of this archdiocese is now! Are we spiritually prepared to enter the twenty-first century? This is a challenging question which requires a courageous response.

Part of our response to this question is the proposed Heritage and Learning Center, which is indeed a challenging project. Can we do it? Yes, we can! I have been traveling in this archdiocese for the past fifteen years, and have experienced firsthand the faith, courage and determination of our people. I have dedicated many new churches and cultural centers which were built by twenty or thirty families. Moreover, what you have done for this archdiocese during the past fifteen years proves that nothing is impossible.

We urgently need this spiritual home, not only for the edification of our own people, but also to help our Orthodox brethren in Central and South America, in Western Europe, in Australia and New Zealand and, perhaps, in the Middle East.

Yes, we can do it because there is a new spirit, a new dedication and a new commitment in this archdiocese. I thank God that at long last we have learned the art of giving. I am proud to report to you that some of our people have already pledged very generously to this center. If we all do our share, we will build that spiritual home on the mountain and it will be a beacon of light. "A city set on a hill cannot be hid . . . let your light so shine before men, that they may see your good works and glorify your Father who is in heaven" (Matthew 5:14–16).

Orthodox Unity in America
The original purpose of SCOBA was to bring unity to our Orthodox people in this hemisphere. I am sad to report to you that SCOBA has failed utterly in this respect. This is not the time, however, to discuss the reasons behind this failure.

Since I came to this country twenty-five years ago, our annual conventions have been adopting resolutions in favor of Orthodox unity in America. Early this year, and in response to your mandate of past years, Metropolitan Theodosius, Primate of the Orthodox Church in America, and I appointed a bilateral commission to discuss ways and means of increased cooperation and eventual unity between our two jurisdictions, which share similar visions for the future. I made it clear to the Orthodox Church in America that this archdiocese will not take a major step in this direction without full consultation with the Holy Synod of Antioch. This commission has already met twice and many important issues are being discussed. Orthodox unity in America, however, cannot be achieved in one day; therefore, we ask you to be patient with us and pray that *"all may be one."*

I am sorry to report to you that some Orthodox hierarchs in this country and abroad are displeased with this commission, and their displeasure was officially conveyed to the Patriarchate of Antioch. I do not understand the reason behind their displeasure. If they can dialogue with the Jews about Christian-Jewish unity, and if they can dialogue with the Roman Catholic Church and all kinds of Christian sects all over the world, is it that sinful for us to dialogue with our Orthodox brothers and sisters in this country? The people of this archdiocese are not slaves to anyone. Thus, we shall continue the work of this commission until our shameful division is overcome and Orthodox unity is realized. For a long time the Orthodox Church has been victimized by an outdated and irrelevant feud between Moscow and Constantinople which is still suffering from the complex of a second and a third Rome that no longer exists. Unfortunately, nothing is happening in world Orthodoxy because of this continuing squabble. There is an Arabic proverb which says: "While the ship is sinking, the crew is busy painting the chimney."

We are tired of division. We want Orthodoxy to unite and face the challenges of our time, not only in North America, but all over the world. We of the Antiochian Archdiocese know well the agony of division. We have suffered this agony for sixty years; then in a bright moment of our history, our people were reunited in the strongest archdiocese in the Patriarchate of Antioch and, perhaps, in the entire Orthodox world. I want you to be vigilant, watchful, strong, and guard this unity with your mighty arms. The other day, I heard a rumor to this effect: *that after the death of Metropolitan Philip, this archdiocese will be divided.* Do you want history to repeat itself? Do you want brothers to fight brothers, cousins to fight cousins and neighbors to fight neighbors? We have already gone through our long, dark night. Do you want to be divided again? Even if the angels come and tell you, "Division is good for you," do not believe them!

Nomination of Auxiliary Bishop

During this convention, our clergy and laity, exercising their sacred right and duty, will nominate a bishop to join us in this fellowship of service. Due to the important significance of this event, I would like to devote this portion of my message to the meaning of this nomination. The office of bishop is deeply rooted in the New Testament teaching and in the apostolic and post-apostolic eras; thus, it is not an innovation in the life of the

Church. From the very beginning, deacons, priests and bishops have exercised a special ministry. They were members of a fellowship, who in addition to their membership in the Body of Christ have received the gift, the *charism* and the authority to preach the Word of God, to baptize the people, and to offer the sacrifices of the Holy Eucharist.

The apostles were the first bishops of the Church. We consider St. Peter to be the first bishop of the Patriarchate of Antioch. It is evident from the New Testament that the Apostles were elected, instructed and commissioned by Christ. After Christ's Ascension, the Apostles filled the vacancy created by the fall of Judas in the following manner. After much thought and prayer, Matthias was then elected "and numbered with the apostles." St. Paul begins his Epistle to the Philippians with these words: "Paul and Timothy, servants of Christ Jesus. To all the saints in Christ Jesus who are at Philippi with the bishops and deacons: Grace to you and peace from God, our Father and the Lord Jesus Christ" (Philippians 1:2).

The Book of Acts states: "Take heed to yourselves and to all the flock in which the Holy Spirit has made you guardians (*episcopoi*) to feed the church of the Lord which He obtained with His own blood" (Acts 20:28).

During their life, the Apostles kept the name "Apostle." Those, however, whom they ordained and appointed to take charge and to replace them in certain localities like Philippi, Ephesus, Crete and Corinth were called *episcopoi* or bishops. During the last decade of the first Christian century, St. Clement of Rome dealt clearly with this subject. He reminded the Corinthians that their leaders are *episcopoi* (bishops) who have succeeded the Apostles. The same concept is evident in the writings of St. Irenaeus, and St. Hippolytus, Bishop of Rome, and the testimony of St. Ignatius, Bishop of Antioch, who considers the Christian priesthood as the highest good illustrated to man. In his epistle to the people of Smyrna, he describes the threefold ministry of the priesthood in a way that leaves no doubt regarding the validity and historicity of the offices of bishop, priest and deacon. Since we have established the divine institution and the historicity of the *episcopoi*, the question now is: Did the clergy and laity play any role in the election of the bishops? The answer to this question is, yes, they definitely did. I would like to refer you to two incidents recorded in the Book of Acts.

In those days Peter stood up among the brethren (the company of persons was in all about a hundred and twenty), and said, "Brethren, the scripture had to be fulfilled, which the Holy Spirit spoke beforehand by the mouth of David, concerning Judas who was guide to those who arrested Jesus. For he was numbered among us, and was allotted his share in this ministry. . . . 'His office let another take.' So, of the men who have accompanied us during all the time that the Lord Jesus went in and out among us, beginning from the baptism of John until the day when He was taken up from us, one of these men must become with us a witness to His resurrection." And they put forth two, Joseph called Barsabbas, and Matthias, and they prayed and said, "Lord who knowest the hearts of all men, show which one of these two Thou hast chosen to take the place in this ministry and apostleship, from which Judas turned aside to go to his own place." And they cast lots for them, and the lot fell on Matthias; and he was enrolled with the eleven Apostles (Acts 1:15–17, 20–26).

Another incident is recorded in the same Book of Acts, Chapter 6:

Now in these days, when the disciples were increasing in number, the Hellenists murmured against the Hebrews because their widows were neglected in the daily distribution, and the Twelve summoned the body of disciples and said: "It is not right that we should give up preaching the Word of God to serve tables. Therefore, brethren, pick out from among you seven men of good repute, full of the Spirit and of wisdom, whom we may appoint to this duty. But we will devote ourselves to prayer and to the ministry of the Word." And what they said pleased the whole multitude and they chose Stephen, a man full of faith and of the Holy Spirit, and Philip . . . These they set before the Apostles and they prayed and laid their hands upon them (Acts 6:1–6).

There is no doubt, then, that the New Testament and Holy Tradition give testimony to the fact that since the inception of the Church, the people have had the right to participate in the election of their bishops. We know from the history of the Church that some laymen have even participated in ecumenical and local councils and have helped formulate Christian dogmas and doctrines. From the Orthodox viewpoint, the sacrament of priesthood encompasses all the faithful, clergy and laity alike. All the members of the Body of Christ constitute "a holy nation, a chosen people and a royal priesthood" (1 Peter 2:9). All of them constitute that sacred fellowship (*koinonia ayion*). Within this all-inclusive fellowship, there is a fellowship of charismatics, a fellowship of service (*koinonia diakonias*) composed of deacons, priests and bishops. All those, however, who were baptized in Christ have put on Christ and were called to perform a special ministry in the life of the Church.

The hierarchical principle in our Church is sometimes overemphasized to the extent that the fellowship of service becomes obscured. Christ did not enter history, was crucified and resurrected from the dead, for the hierarchy alone, but for all the people of God (*laos tou Theou*) which constitute the totality (the *pleroma*) of the Body of Christ. St. Paul describes the Church as the Body of Christ, and in this body there are many members, and each member has a specific function to perform. All members of this body are equal in the eyes of God, despite their different functions. St. Paul says:

There are varieties of gifts but the same spirit: and there are varieties of service, but the same Lord; and there are varieties of working but it is the same God who inspires them all in every one. To each is given the manifestation of the Spirit for the common good" (1 Corinthians 12:4–7).

Based on this, we may rightly say that there is a difference of purpose and of service, not of nature and substance, between the priesthood of the laity and the priesthood of the clergy.

Our Sacred Right to Nominate
I am saying all this to point out to you that the right which you are exercising at this convention, in nominating an auxiliary bishop for your own archdiocese, is deeply rooted in the Scripture and the Holy Tradition of the Church; thus, no one has the authority to deny you this sacred right. It is most unfortunate that in some Orthodox patriarchates, the clergy and laity have nothing whatsoever to say in the nomination of their bishops, let alone the administration of their Church. This is a flagrant violation of the understanding of the nature of the Church at a time when even the Roman Catholic Church, which is known for its extreme clericalism, is attempting to return to our ancient Orthodox practice. In January, 1968, 563 priests in the Roman Catholic Diocese of New York asked to be able to choose Cardinal Spellman's successor on a broad basis of participation. In February, 1968, *Le Monde* in Paris reported that a group of Roman Catholic priests and laity directed a letter to Pope Paul VI and to the Parisian Vicar General, asking for a preliminary consultation on the naming of their future archbishop.

Our historical findings, therefore, reveal a theological understanding in which the appointment of the bishops lies within the responsibility of the priests and congregations. It is amazing that this principle was followed in the early Church and in a milieu in which democracy, as we know it today, was foreign.

Yet, the young Church practiced completely democratic procedures which were compatible with the principle of hierarchy. The people in our Church have always been the defenders of Orthodoxy. Bishops, therefore, are not infallible, nor are they absolute rulers who must be obeyed blindly. *The Didache*, one of the most ancient Christian documents, states:

> Everyone who comes in the name of the Lord should be accepted; but then you must test him and thus get to know him; for you should apply your understanding to distinguish right from left.

Aside from the participation of the laity in the nomination of their bishops and the administration of their local parish and archdiocese, there is that most important lay participation in the worship of the Church. It is in this participation that one may easily comprehend the meaning of the priestly dignity of the layman, and his royal priesthood as a member of the Body of Christ. It is important to know that without the presence, the prayers, and the confessions of the faithful, our worship is impossible. No sacrament is validly offered in the Orthodox Church unless the faithful attend and join their prayers with those of the celebrant priest: "Thine own, of Thine own, *we* offer unto Thee," not "*I* offer unto Thee."

It is evident, therefore, that all of us clergy and laity share in the priestly, prophetic and royal office of Christ. And despite our diversity of service, all of us bear witness to the unity of the Body of Christ. The laity are not just guests in the Church; they are full citizens of the kingdom and full citizens of the Church. The two-class theory in the Church (hierarchy and people) emerged only after the Constantinian era. The laity are not to be ignored in the total life of the Church. Can you imagine where our archdiocese would be without the participation of the laity on both the parish and archdiocesan levels? I thank God daily for the faith, commitment and dedication of our laity.

Finally, fifteen years ago, on the top of a Lebanese mountain which overlooks the deep valley where I was born, I made this vow which I would like to renew today before God and this beloved flock: "I promise to visit and watch over the flock now entrusted to me, after the manner of the Apostles, whether they remain true to the faith, and in the exercise of good works, more especially the priests; and to inspect with diligence, that there may be no schisms, superstitions and impious veneration, and that no customs contrary to Christian piety may injure Christian conduct. And may God, who sees the heart, be the witness of my vow. And may our Savior Himself be my helper, in my sincere zealous government and performance thereof; and unto Him, together with the Father and the Holy Spirit, be glory, dominion, honor and worship, now and ever and unto all ages."

Editor's Endnotes:

1. With the first Clergy Symposium, Metropolitan Philip sets a precedent of the bishop celebrating the final Liturgy as a priest, rather than in a hierarchical Liturgy. This decision set future symposia in a brotherly and more informal setting in which discussion, sharing, workshops, etc., would prevail.

2. In 1980, the metropolitan establishes the St. Stephen's Course in Orthodox Theology, a directed reading course for those who are unable to attend seminary. St. Stephen's Studies, as it later becomes known, grows rapidly, includes students from all jurisdictions and from abroad; later includes a residency program, and includes ministerial projects in local parishes; eventually it is placed under the Antiochian House of Studies as the Diploma Program, along with an accredited Masters and accredited Doctoral program. However, the reader should know that Philip's vision for this oldest form of theological education, that is, with use of an Elder and with personal study and research, begins with St. Stephen's Studies.

Chapter 11

INCARNATING THEOLOGY:
The Roots of Pastoral Ministry

The priest is called upon to be a man of prayer, and at the same time a man of action, one who does not lose his soul: "For what shall it profit a man if he gains the whole world and loses his own soul?" (Mark 8:36). There is no doubt that being a priest calls for careful preparation, not only in terms of the knowledge and understanding of Scripture and the sacramental life, but also in terms of the various means through which the divine grace and God's Word come to man. Such means are found in preaching, organizing and caring.

        Metropolitan Philip

- *Commencement Address: On Receiving His First Doctoral Degree, 1981*

AND HE LEADS THEM

In 1981 Philip is granted his first Doctor of Divinity degree, **honoris causa** *("for the sake of honor"), at St. Vladimir's Orthodox Seminary in Crestwood, New York. The occasion is the annual commencement of the 1981 graduating class, and on this, his fifteenth anniversary, Philip delivers the commencement address. It is a talk rooted in that to which he often refers as "incarnational theology." To this he remains faithful throughout the following years; this, he says, is what any future servant of the Church must hear: "Any theology which does not touch man in his joy and sorrow, his hope and despair, his faith and doubt, his sickness and health, his poverty and wealth, and his life and death, is abstract and meaningless theology!" It is from this base that Philip delivers one of the finest talks in the area of pastoral theology, one which holds three* **foci:** *preaching, organizing and caring. Every Orthodox priest must certainly respond to this talk, but also, every Orthodox layperson will pray that his or her pastor will minister according to the message of this talk.*

This address, which we present **in toto,** *stands by itself as an independent chapter.*

J. J. A.

Commencement Address: On Receiving His First Doctorate Degree
1981

It is indeed a great honor to be asked to deliver this commencement address. Every time I return to this holy hill, I find myself immersed in delightful memories. In 1964, I took a year's leave of absence from parish life in order to continue my theological study in this fine institution. I will not be exaggerating if I tell you, that was the best year of my life. It is difficult to appreciate this kind of feeling until you leave this spiritual shelter and become totally involved, as ministers of the Word, in the complexities and problems of this world.

Some of you will be leaving soon, and some will follow in the years to come; thus, my remarks are directed to all. I want to warn you, however, not to expect a theological treatise from me because I am certain that, during the years which you have spent here, you have heard some of the best lectures on all matters pertaining to theology. Moreover, although I am aware of the theology of the Church, I do not consider myself a professional theologian. First and foremost, I am a pastor; this is how I lived as a priest and continue to live as a shepherd of my flock. My main concern for the past twenty-five years has been to find meaning in people, not in words, concepts or abstract theological speculation.

If we can define theology as the study of God and His relation to the world; if we can say, "The Word became flesh" (John 1:14); if we can say, "For God so loved the world" (John 3:16); if we can say that God became man in order to make us "partakers of the divine nature" (2 Peter 1:4); and if we can say that the purpose of the Incarnation was to redeem man and the entire cosmos, we can rightly say that any theology which does not touch man in his joy and sorrow, his hope and despair, his faith and doubt, his sickness and health, his poverty and wealth, and his life and death, is abstract and meaningless theology.

Sooner or later, you will leave this spiritual oasis for the wilderness of this world. In what kind of world will you be living? In the *oikoumene* of the Byzantine Empire, there was a definite Christian view of man, the world and history. Today, under the influence of technology, the Church is confronted with a secular and materialistic view of the world, which fundamentally contradicts all Christian principles and ideals.

Our modern culture is clearly marked by violence, brokenness, dislocation and rootlessness. Our crime and divorce rates have never been higher. According to statistics, five hundred thousand teenagers in America commit suicide every year. They feel estranged, rootless and abandoned. Sociologists say that three main factors have contributed to this phenomenon: (1) our violent culture; (2) human alienation and depression; and (3) the dissolution of the family.

When you start your mission to the world, you will discover that the dignity of man is threatened and that human relationships are strained by competition and suspicion. Such a world situation cries out for a Church, priests and church people that reach out with all their energy, through policies, priorities and programs into the troubled heart of the world. Yes, such a world situation demands from us a theology of reconciliation, healing and hope.

Confronted with this reality, there are those who suggest that we withdraw and pray for the Second Advent, for we can have little direct impact on these issues. It is a worldly enterprise; therefore, to demonstrate our commitment to Christ, we must be detached, withdrawn and isolated. And there are those who are tempted to reduce the gospel of Jesus Christ into nothing but social activism. Consequently prayer, self-renewal, sacraments, contemplation and spirituality are not to be taken seriously. In my humble opinion, both attitudes contradict the Gospel and the experience of the Church throughout history.

The great task of the priest is to live and help live in this tension between both attitudes, and to search for a synthesis. The priest is called upon to be a man of prayer and a social reformer who does not lose his soul, "for what shall it profit a man if he shall gain the whole world and lose his own soul?" (Mark 8:36). The priest is called upon to be a *man of action* and a *man of prayer* at the same time.

There is hardly a doubt that being a priest calls for careful preparation, not only in terms of the knowledge and understanding of the Scripture and the sacramental life of the Church, but also in terms of the various means through which divine grace and God's Word come to man. Such means are: celebrating, preaching, teaching, caring and organizing. Due to the limited scope of this address, I will restrict myself to three of the aforementioned aspects: namely, preaching, organizing and caring.

Preaching

The proclamation of the Gospel is the heart of the Liturgy of the Word. In his Second Epistle to Timothy, St. Paul said, "I charge you in the presence of God and of Christ Jesus who is to judge the living and the dead, and by His appearing, and His kingdom: preach the word, be urgent in season and out of season. Convince, rebuke and exhort, be unfailing in patience and in teaching" (2 Timothy 4:1–3). Again in 1 Corinthians, St. Paul said, "Woe unto me if I do not preach the gospel" (1 Corinthians 9:16). In Matthew, our Lord admonishes us to "go and make disciples of all nations" (Matthew 28:19).

How can we make disciples of all nations, if we do not preach the Good News? And to preach the Good News, you must study and be prepared. Make sure that your sermon is rooted in the Scripture, and related to concrete human conditions in your congregation and society. If you preach to your people from an ivory tower, you will completely miss the point. If you do not like to read your sermon, the least you can do is to make a written or a mental outline of it.

Furthermore, you must learn how to communicate with people. If you do not know how to help your people and heal them with the theology which you have learned in this school, the years which you have spent here are for naught.

I have never known a priest to fail because he did not know theology, but I have known several priests who failed because they could not communicate with people. If you know everything about horses and do not know how to ride a horse, what is the use of your knowledge? By the same token, if you know everything about God, but fail to make Him alive in the hearts of your people, what is the use of your theology? Some one recently said, "When God, Church, Sacraments and Liturgy become things, forget God; He is not there. But when God becomes a person who loves us and asks for a like response because He loves us, then the Church is real."

Put flesh on your words; people are tired of dry bones. If you are empty from within, your words will certainly reflect that emptiness. People are not interested in theories; therefore, your sermon must be the result of personal experience. If you do not experience love and compassion in a personal way, do not preach about love; you cannot fool the people. We are more transparent than we think. Do you remember the old saying, "What you are cries so loudly, I cannot hear what you say?" In his book, *Scenes of Clerical Life,* George Elliot wrote:

> Ideas are often poor ghosts . . . but sometimes they are made flesh; they breathe upon us with warm breaths; they touch us with soft responsive hands . . . and speak to us in appealing tones; they are clothed in a living, human soul, with all its conflicts, its faith and its love. Then their presence is a power, then they shake us like a passion.

You must be always prepared to preach regardless of the size of your congregation. St. John Chrysostom said,

> We, to whom the service of the Word is entrusted, have received from the dear God the command, never to abandon our duty and never to be silent, whether anyone listens to us or not. There are those priests who make fun of us and say, 'stop the good advice, stop the admonition, they will not listen to you, let them go.' What are you saying? Have you promised to convert all men in one day? If only ten, or only five, or indeed, one repents, is not that consolation enough?

To be a good preacher, you must observe three basic facts: when, where and to whom; time, place and people. You are neither in Byzantium nor in Imperial Russia. You are in the United States of America and on the threshold of a new century.

After my ordination to the priesthood in the early sixties, my bishop assigned me to a parish in the Midwest. I was hardly aware of the spiritual needs of my people. Thus, after I delivered a series of sermons on Christ and Wealth, some of my parishioners said, "This new priest is a Communist, let's get rid of him." It took me a while to find out that I was talking to the wrong people. During the Renaissance period, people used to gather in salons to read poetry and discuss various intellectual and artistic trends. Today, the average American comes home from work exhausted, depressed and in no mood to read volumes. He acquires his knowledge from watching the evening news, reading *Time* magazine and the headlines in some newspaper. His only indication of reality is the economic forecast. Despite such human conditions, priests must proclaim the Good News. But if the priest has no news to proclaim, then certainly he will add to his people's despair.

Last, but not least, if you are a gifted preacher, do not be conceited. Preach to glorify God and not yourself. People come to church to worship God, not the priest. St. Paul said, "For what we preach is not ourselves, but Jesus Christ as Lord with ourselves as your servants" (1 Corinthians 4:5).

Organizing

There is no doubt that we are living in the age of organization. Someone stopped at my office the other day, looked around and said, "You are behind the times; you have not yet computerized your system." Maybe he was right. We are living in an ever-changing society; thus, if we do not organize and reorganize and adapt to new conditions, we will indeed find ourselves behind time. We must be careful, however, not to become obsessed by the idea of organization, lest we organize for organization's sake. Organizing is not an end in itself; it is a means to an end. The ultimate goal of the priest remains the salvation of souls.

Some of our parishes are ultra-organized. As a matter of fact, one of my parishes has more organizations than people. No one can argue that the priest is the agent of change in the parish. However, changing structures and systems, changing the external, does not necessarily inaugurate the Kingdom of God on earth. What must be changed first is your inner being. St. Seraphim of Sarov said, "Save yourself and thousands around you will be saved." Therefore, it is impossible to separate between organizing and spirituality.

In organizing your future parish, I would like to caution you of three main dangers:

Concretism. Some of our priests go to a parish expecting to make it a song of praise to the Almighty God in one month or in one year. Thus, if their efforts do not bring forth concrete and immediate results, they become disappointed, bitter, angry or indifferent. We often forget that God does not make things happen according to our calendar. He makes things happen in His own way and in His own time. After all, He did not call you to succeed in restructuring the whole world, but to structure your priorities and remain faithful to His Word.

Power. People who organize are in constant danger of creating small kingdoms for themselves. It is extremely difficult to take initiatives and develop new plans without claiming them as something that is yours. How often do we hear priests saying, "I built this church and that hall; I established this mission and that parish; I...I...I..." as if God has nothing to do with our activities and daily lives. Our Lord said, "When you have done all that is commanded, you say we are unworthy servants; we have only done what was our duty" (Luke 17:10). Therefore, my humble advice to you is to concentrate on building God's kingdom, not yours. Our Lord was tempted once to change the stones into bread and to take the power and glory of all the kingdoms of all the world, but He overcame the temptation.

Pride. Finally, there is the great temptation of pride. Some of those who want to change society are in danger of putting themselves over it and being more conscious of the weaknesses of others than of the weakness of their own soul. Very often we get very busy going from meeting to meeting and from function to function. We want to be everywhere, and yet we are afraid to enter the sanctuary of our soul, to be alone and face the fact that we are in just as much need of change as the congregation we are trying to convert.

Remember, you are not in the parish to dominate, but to serve, to discover and cultivate talent. If the priest really wants to be an agent of spiritual change, the first thing he has to learn is how to share leadership. It is amazing to find that most priests are still working very much on their own and have not yet found the creative ways to mobilize the potential leadership in their parishes and share their responsibilities with others. Congregations can be transformed only when priests and laymen come together in a spirit of charity and humility.

Caring

The third aspect of your ministry which I would like to emphasize is pastoral care. Speaking about preaching and organizing, I stressed the fact that if you are not spiritually motivated, you can neither preach nor organize. By the same token, if you do not identify with Christ in His sensitivity and love for people, your pastoral efforts will be in vain. Christ cared for people in their most individual needs. He cared for the widow who lost her only son. He cared for the man who was paralyzed for thirty-eight years. He cared for the blind, the woman at the well, the sick and the sinner. Our Lord said, "If any man would come after Me, let him take up his cross and follow Me" (Mark 8:34). Again He said, "Greater love has no man than this, that a man lay down his life for his friends" (John 15:13).

You cannot give yourself in love and you cannot empty yourself unless you find that self, through meditation and prayer. Only after self-affirmation can self-emptying take place. It is unfortunate that modern psychology speaks much about self-affirmation and says hardly anything about self-denial and self-sacrifice. Why does a man lay down his life for his friends? There is only one answer to that question: to give new life.

All functions of the priesthood are life-giving. Whether a priest teaches, preaches, counsels, organizes or celebrates, his aim is to open new perspectives, to offer new insights, to give new strength and to create new life. To care for people is to share their joy and sorrow, their hope and despair, their triumph and defeat. Priesthood is not a job; it is a *vocation*. Priesthood is not a profession; it is a covenant between the priest and his parish.

One of my priests said to me once, "I will not serve that congregation unless I sign a contract with them." That immediately raised a very important question in my mind: Is God's relationship with us based on a contract or a covenant? A contract terminates when one of the parties does not adhere to his promise. We read in the Psalms, "If my father and mother desert me, God will care for me still" (Psalm 27:10). Thus, it is not the professional contract but the divine covenant which is the basis of a pastoral relationship. The covenant is unconditional; it is based on faithfulness, compassion and love.

In the final analysis, pastoral care must be rooted in that divine love which transcends everything. This love does not encompass only man but the entire cosmos. Listen to St. Isaac the Syrian speak:

What is a loving heart? It is a heart burning with love for the whole of creation, for men, for the birds, for the beasts, for the demons and all creatures. He who has such a heart cannot see or call to mind a creature without his eyes becoming filled with tears by reason of the immense compassion which seizes his heart; a heart which is softened and can no longer bear to see or learn from others of any suffering, even the smallest pain being inflicted upon a creature. This is why such a man never ceases to pray also for animals, for the enemies of truth and for those who do him evil, that they may be preserved and purified. He will pray even for the reptiles, moved by the infinite pity which reigns in the hearts of those who are becoming united to God.

In conclusion, my friends, I would like to leave you with these words from the First Epistle of St. Paul to the Thessalonians:

> We exhort you, brethren, admonish the idle, encourage the fainthearted, help the weak, be patient with them all. See that none of you repays evil for evil, but always seek to do good to one another and to all. Rejoice always, pray constantly, give thanks in all circumstances; for this is the will of God in Christ Jesus for you. Do not quench the Spirit, do not despise prophesying but test everything, hold fast to what is good, abstain from every form of evil. May the God of peace Himself sanctify you wholly; and may your spirit and soul and body be kept sound and blameless at the coming of our Lord Jesus Christ (1 Thessalonians 5:14–23).

Editor's Endnotes:

1. *During this same year, 1981, the book* **Orthodox Synthesis: The Unity of Theological Thought** *is published by St. Vladimir's Seminary Press in honor of Philip's fifteenth anniversary. It is an anthology of articles written by various Orthodox theologians in North America, and has been republished many times since that year.*

2. *The reader should know that "incarnational theology," as Philip would label it, eventually becomes one of the titles by which he names his approach to implementing the gospel in our human life. Although later he will use other words like applied theology, praxis in theology, practical theology, etc., they are all rooted in the appellation, "incarnational."*

Chapter 12

THE WHOLE PEOPLE OF GOD

> *On many occasions in the past I have told you that the Church is not the bishop alone, or the priest alone, or the deacon alone or the laity alone. The Church is the bishop, priest, deacon and laity ministering together like a symphony for the edification of the whole Body of Christ. Despite the existence of the ordained ministry which is deeply rooted in the New Testament, there is a ministry of all believers by virtue of their baptism: "For as many of you as were baptized into Christ have put on Christ" (Galatians 3:27).*
>
> Metropolitan Philip

- *Sharing Christ's Priesthood: Laity and Clergy in Symphony, 1983*
- *Funeral Oration for Alexander Schmemann, 1983*
- *Orthodoxy in America: Success and Failure, 1984*
- *Searching for a Spiritual Renaissance: The Second Holy Year, 1985*

The four addresses included in this chapter are best titled "The Whole People of God" because, in each of them, Philip addresses issues that require the laity, the **laos tou Theou** *(people of God), to work in symphony with the clergy. Furthermore, they are to do so cheerfully, "for God loves a cheerful giver," as Philip will emphasize in the last of these addresses given in Boston, 1985.*

But in truth, he already begins this call to the laity in 1983 in Toronto, where he chooses as his theme **First Peter** *to emphasize that they, as the "chosen race and holy nation," are to share in Christ's royal priesthood. Reminding them, indeed, that the Body of Christ is a symphony, that the Church cannot depend on the clergy alone, i.e., that there are not two theologies, he reviews their part in the election of a new bishop, now in their midst as Bishop Antoun. In that same talk, Philip announces that, during his visit to the Middle East, he invited Patriarch Ignatius IV to visit the archdiocese in 1985. The patriarch accepted that invitation, and the archdiocese begins preparation for the second Antiochian Holy Year.*

The second address in this chapter is the metropolitan's touching homily in 1983 at the funeral of Father Alexander Schmemann, longtime dean and professor at St. Vladimir's Seminary. Not since Philip preached at the death of Patriarch Elias IV did the sound of his voice ring with such truth and sorrow.

The third address is Philip's challenging sermon given at Worcester, Massachusetts, in 1984. It was delivered on the Sunday of Orthodoxy. However, this is a very different sermon from those which were delivered in the 1970s. Again, in reference to the "whole people of God," he asks, "Is there not a place where we can dream of a better Orthodox future? I believe that there is a place, and this place is the North American continent. . . . We have a tremendous opportunity . . . but we must put our house in order. . . . We are no longer a Church of immigrants," etc. Philip ends this sermon with a rousing call to the laity to rise up, "as the conscience of the Church and the defenders of the faith," and to demand Orthodox unity on the basis of his "three visions" for the future of the Church. It will not be the last time, as the reader will discover, that Philip will raise these "three visions."

The fourth and final address in this chapter is delivered during the visit of Patriarch Ignatius IV. It is now the second Antiochian Holy Year, and the talk, delivered in Boston in 1985, is often directed to the patriarch himself. In this address, Philip not only speaks of the critical role of Antioch in the Christian world, but he also uses the completion of phase I of the Heritage and Learning Center at the Antiochian Village to call for a "real spiritual renaissance." The "whole people of God," he says, should realize that this center is the "beginning of greater confidence in ourselves and in the future." Why? Because we can "do all things through Christ who strengthens us" (Philippians 4:13). As history shows, Philip's confidence in the people to respond to God's call is not misplaced.

J. J. A.

Sharing Christ's Priesthood: Laity and Clergy in Symphony
Toronto, 1983

Our theme is taken from First Peter, chapter two, verse nine: "You are a chosen race, a royal priesthood, a holy nation, God's own people, that you may declare the wonderful deeds of Him who called you out of darkness into His marvelous light." I have chosen this theme in order to reemphasize our true identity as it was revealed to us by St. Peter. We are a chosen race because God has chosen us before the foundation of the world. We are a royal priesthood because Christ is the High Priest and all of us share in His priesthood. We are a holy nation, God's own people, because we were "bought with a price" (1 Corinthians 7:23), and the price was the blood of the Lamb. Therefore, we must declare the wonderful deeds of Him who called us out of darkness into His marvelous light.

The Gentiles walked in utter darkness, and in less measure the Jews, but we, as Christians, have been called out of all races and all lands, in order to be God's own people. What a privilege! And yet, what a responsibility! God took the initiative by choosing us and by allowing us to share in His priesthood. What, then, should our response be to Him? And how can we declare His wonderful deeds?

The Symphony of Believers

We all know that Christ is the perfect priest and the suffering servant, and since we are His own people, we are called to be the extension of His priesthood and His ministry in time and space, and whether we are clergy or laity. Hence the whole Body of the Church is priestly, and the whole Church is the *laos*, the people of God. On many occasions in the past I have told you that the Church is not the bishop alone, or the priest alone, or the deacon alone, or the laity alone. The Church is the bishop, the priest, the deacon, and the laity ministering together like a symphony for the edification of the whole Body of Christ. Despite the existence of the ordained ministry which is deeply rooted in the New Testament, there is the ministry of all the believers by virtue of their baptism. "For as many of you as were baptized into Christ have put on Christ" (Galatians 3:27).

For centuries, the priestly nature of all the believers has been neglected and misunderstood in our Church. No wonder, then, that many of our laity still exist on the margin of the Church as spectators, without any significant involvement in the liturgy, discipline and ministry of the Church. Could it be that we, the clergy, have stifled the spirit of the laity and neglected their many gifts? Could it be that the hierarchy of the Church has overemphasized the hierarchical principle at the expense of the lay ministry? In his Epistle to the Romans, St. Paul said, "Having gifts that differ according to the grace given to us, let us use them: if prophecy, in proportion to our faith; if service, in our serving; he who teaches, in his teaching; he who exhorts, in his exhortation; he who contributes, in liberality; he who gives aid, with zeal; he who does acts of mercy, with cheerfulness" (Romans 12:6–8).

Not the Clergy Alone

Surely, St. Paul did not direct these words to the clergy alone, but to the entire people of God, clergy and laity alike. There was a time in the history of our archdiocese when we experienced a terrible dichotomy of two classes opposing each other—the clergy on one side and the laity on the other. The priest preached the sermon upstairs and the parish council counted the money downstairs. Perhaps there were historical reasons for this dichotomy which no longer exist; consequently, in my message to the 1968 Convention, we put an end to this upstairs–downstairs theology once and for all. The laity, as the royal priesthood, must be concerned with all the needs of the Church, and the ordained clergy must also be concerned with all the needs of the Church. "To each is given the manifestation of the Spirit for the common good" (1 Corinthians 12:7). "As each has received a gift, employ it for one another, as good stewards of God's varied grace" (1 Peter 4:10).

The clergy have the responsibility of assembling and building up the Body of Christ. They preside over the eucharistic gatherings, perform the sacraments and proclaim the Word. They exercise this authority, however, in the name of Christ. Thus, their authority is not and must not be of domination and despotism. It is an authority based on love and service (*diakonia*). Otherwise, it will be void of any Christian significance. In the Gospel of St. Mark, our Lord said, "You know that those who are supposed to rule over the Gentiles lord it over them and their great men exercise authority over them. But it shall not be so among you; but whoever would be great among you must be your servant, and whoever would be first among you must be slave of all" (Mark 10:42–44).

Not Two Theologies

The Church does not have one theology for the clergy and another for the laity. Christ cannot be divided. After we are resurrected from the baptismal font, we receive the sacrament of chrismation through the priest, who says, "The seal of the gift of the Holy Spirit." All gifts, therefore, "are inspired by one and the same Spirit, who apportions to each one individually as He wills" (1 Corinthians 12:11). We have the same Spirit but different gifts, and rightly so. The members of the body are equally important; however, they perform different functions.

The apologist Justin Martyr restated the principle of the priesthood of all believers when he wrote, "Being inflamed by the word of Christ's calling, we are the true higher priestly race of God." St. Clement of Rome specified what he meant by the lay ordination when he wrote, "Let each of us brethren in his own order make Eucharist to God, keeping a good conscience and not transgressing the appointed rule of his liturgy." In the second Christian century, St. Irenaeus said, "All who are justified through Christ have the sacred order."

Based on the witness of the Scripture and the Fathers, the laity therefore have a definite ministry to perform in the life of the Church. As a matter of fact, in today's secular and pluralistic world, the ministry of the layman or laywoman has a wider scope and a bigger dimension than the ministry of the ordained clergy. I would like to qualify my statement: The priest's activities, for example, are, in most instances, confined to the boundary of his parish. His many parochial duties in this age of organization do not leave him enough time to transcend the boundaries of his parish and reach out to the world at large.

Some theologians might say, "But the world is evil, filthy and corrupt; thus, let us flee from the world and let the world go to hell." This world-denying attitude, my friends, is not Christian at all. In the Gospel of St. John we read, "For God so loved the world that He gave His only Son, that whoever believes in Him should not perish but have eternal life" (John 3:16). If this were not so, what then was the purpose of the Incarnation?

The layman, whether he is a farmer, a truck driver, a teacher, a businessman, a doctor, a lawyer, an engineer, a physicist or a scientist, is much more involved in the affairs of this world than any priest. The priest's parish is limited, but the layman's parish is the whole world. It is mainly through its laity that the Church enters into contact with the world. It is at this meeting point of the Christian and non-Christian, the sacred and the profane, the religious and the secular, that the layman stands, and there that he encounters the problems.

The Ministry of the Laity

The laity, however, cannot fulfill their ministry to the Church and the world if they are not regular members of the worshipping community. We need Christ-bearing laity, conscious of their royal priestly responsibilities, to which they were called by baptismal ordination. Although we do not expect all our laity to be expert theologians, we do expect them to be theologically illiterate. It is the sacred duty of our priests to encourage the ministry of the laity in their communities and cultivate their talents.

When we speak about the ministry of the laymen in the Church, we do not exclude the ministry of the laywomen. Women have been ministering to the Church since the inception of the early Christian community. Both the Scripture and the apostolic teachings testify to this fact. Women were the first to announce the most joyful news of the glorious Resurrection, and their icons adorn our iconostasis and walls of our churches. In his Epistle to the Philippians, St. Paul wrote, "And I ask you also, true yokefellow, help these women, for they have labored side by side with me in the gospel together with Clement and the rest of my fellow workers, whose names are in the book of life" (Philippians 4:3). And in his Epistle to the Romans, St. Paul wrote, "Greet Prisca and Aquila, my fellow coworkers in Christ Jesus, who risked their necks for my life, to whom not only I, but all the churches of the Gentiles, give thanks" (Romans 16:3, 4).

The Consecration of a Bishop

On August 1, 1981, you nominated three of our beloved clergy for the office of auxiliary bishop for our archdiocese. This nomination was made according to the tradition of the Church, our constitution and the tradition of the Patriarchate of Antioch. It took the Synod of Antioch fourteen months to meet and elect one of your nominees. During that time, we experienced a great measure of anxiety and frustration. The main issue was: Do the clergy and laity have the right to nominate their bishops? I believe that this question was answered when the Synod met on November 4, 1982, and elected one of your nominees, Archimandrite Antoun Khouri, to be my coworker in this fellowship of service. Your perseverance and adherence to the Holy Tradition of our Church made the Synod reflect more deeply on the true ministry of the laity in the Church. Consequently, in December 1982 our Father in Christ, Patriarch Ignatius IV, issued the following statement to the press:

We felt that circumstances at one time or another have dictated to us that our people no longer participate with us, the clergy, in finding the effective, reasonable, spiritual leadership; namely, the nomination and election of bishops. We have decided henceforth that the spiritual leadership in the Patriarchate of Antioch will be a leadership chosen by and acceptable to the people. . . . Our theological point of view is: The Church is all of its people and not merely one group alone.

The statement of His Beatitude and the decision of the Synod last November constitute a victory for the true teachings of our Holy Orthodox Church.

On January 9, 1983, Archimandrite Antoun Khouri was elevated to the rank of the Holy Episcopate. His elevation was a moment of transfiguration for the entire archdiocese. More than fifteen hundred people filled St. Nicholas Cathedral of Brooklyn and its hall. All our national organizations were very well represented. Many of our clergy traveled from near and far to participate in this historic event. All of us who were there felt a tremendous outpouring of the Holy Spirit. Our hearts and minds were captured by a sense of the supernatural. Once again, Bishop Antoun, we say to you from the depth of our hearts—AXIOS! AXIOS! AXIOS!

Our Trip to the Middle East

I thank the Almighty God for your faith and concern with the needs of the oppressed and the poor. You have seen in the faces of the poor, the face of Christ Himself. "For as you did it to one of the least of these My brethren, you did it to Me" (Matthew 25:40). The poor of the world, whether they are in Latin America, Africa, the Middle East or Southeast Asia, are our unfortunate brothers and sisters. There is nothing more important in our Christian concerns than binding a wound or wiping a tear.

After the June War of 1967, we raised money to help the

needy Palestinians; and after the October War of 1973, we raised money to help the Syrians. Last year, after the Israeli invasion of Lebanon, we raised money to help alleviate some of the suffering of the Lebanese people. In every instance, I took the money personally to the Middle East to avoid administrative costs and to make sure that the money was distributed according to your wishes.

Last April, before I left for the Middle East, I had a very friendly and pleasant meeting with President Reagan. The president was very hospitable and kind. I brought to his attention two major issues: (1) the withdrawal of the Israeli troops from Lebanon, and (2) the future of the West Bank and Gaza. In the first issue, the president was very clear and emphatic. "We are committed to the withdrawal of all foreign troops from Lebanon," he said. In regard to the West Bank and Gaza and the future of the Palestinian people, the president said, "King Hussein and Mr. Arafat are meeting now, and the result of their meeting will affect the future of the Palestinians." I left the White House with the impression that, if the president would be reelected for a second term, he would try very hard to solve the Middle East problem in its entirety.

On April 8, I left for the Middle East on Alia Airlines. We reached Amman, Jordan, Saturday evening. Sunday, we were informed by the Jordanian Ministry of Information that the talks between King Hussein and Mr. Arafat had broken down. This was a setback to President Reagan's initiative of September 1, 1982. Monday morning, we flew to Damascus, Syria, and went straight to our patriarchate to receive the blessings of our Father in Christ, Patriarch Ignatius IV. His Beatitude was most kind, hospitable and friendly. I spent the whole day and evening with him discussing church problems, especially in the Middle East. Then on your behalf, I extended to him a tentative invitation to visit our archdiocese in 1985.

My invitation to His Beatitude was unanimously confirmed by our Board of Trustees Friday, June 3, in Charleston, West Virginia. His Beatitude has accepted our invitation; thus, 1985 will be proclaimed another Antiochian Holy Year in our archdiocese.

Tuesday, on very short notice, I met with President Hafez Assad for two hours. We discussed many issues related to Lebanon and the Middle East situation. President Assad unequivocally stated that, if and when the Israelis withdrew from Lebanon, without infringing on Lebanese sovereignty, he would immediately withdraw all his army from Lebanon. I was very much impressed by his sincerity and friendliness.

Wednesday, we flew to Lebanon and were received by our beloved brother in Christ, Metropolitan Elias (Audi) of Beirut, the Metropolitans of Lebanon and many government officials. The news media covered our movements in Lebanon on a daily basis. On Friday, April 15, we met with the President of Lebanon, Amin Gemayel. Friday afternoon, we met with all the Orthodox archbishops of Lebanon and their lay representatives at the Archbishopric of Beirut, and equally distributed the funds which you have raised among them.

I left Lebanon with these impressions: The psychological and sectarian wounds are very deep and they need a long time to heal. Almost all Lebanese villages, let alone the cities, have been affected by the war. Lebanon will need billions of dollars for reconstruction. The devastation which we saw reminds us of Stalingrad and Berlin at the end of the Second World War. The majority of the Lebanese people, however, still want a free and a united Lebanon. In the final analysis, the future of Lebanon depends on the outcome of the regional struggle between Israel and the Arab countries, and the international struggle between the Soviet Union and the free world.

The Heritage and Learning Center
In 1978, we were very fortunate to purchase the Antiochian Village in Western Pennsylvania, which consists of 280 acres of land, for $350,000. We did not ask you to raise a cent for this land; we paid for it from archdiocesan funds. Subsequently, we renovated our camping facilities, which cost the archdiocese

hundreds of thousands of dollars, and again, we did not ask you to contribute a cent for this renovation. All of you know the wonderful time your children are having at the Village. Two years ago, we presented to you a comprehensive plan for the Heritage and Learning Center and launched a campaign to raise the necessary funds to build this center. Some individuals responded generously to our appeal, some responded moderately, and others responded rather poorly.

Some of the defeatists among us still ask, "Why do we need the center?" "It is too far from us." "It is too elaborate." "It is too expensive," etc. To these people, I say, "Why do we need camping facilities? Why do we need christian education? Why do we need insurance and retirement for our clergy? Why do we need priests? Why do we need bishops? Why do we need seminaries and churches? And why do we need anything? Why do we not just wallow in our apathy and do nothing?" Are these the kind of questions which your fathers and grandfathers asked when they came to North America and established parishes for you? Certainly not!

We need this center in order to focus on our Antiochian and Orthodox spirituality. We need it for clergy symposia. We need it for workshops for our parish councils, church school teachers and choirs. We need it in order to perpetuate a unique spiritual and cultural heritage. Those who do not know us think that the best we can offer to North America is Arabic food and belly dancing. Is this the kind of legacy we want to leave for our posterity? We represent six thousand years of cultural and spiritual values. The preservation of such values transcends the boundaries of ethnicism and chauvinism. Every nationality has made its contribution to our North American culture. What about us? If you remove *The Prophet* of Gibran from our bookstores, we will have nothing left. Hence, the importance of this retreat and learning center is apparent.

Besides the many facilities which this center will contain, its two most important focal points will be the Heritage Library and the Heritage Museum. In addition to the religious and cultural books which we will have, and in addition to our past which will be preserved and displayed in the Heritage Museum, we are going to ask every family in our archdiocese, whether from Middle Eastern descent, Russian, Greek, Eastern European, etc., to write its own history, which will be put on microfilm and treasured in the Heritage Library. Unfortunately, many of the early immigrants are no longer with us, but fortunately, many of the first generation are still with us and do remember where their parents and grandparents came from. If we neglect this task, our children's children and our future generations will know absolutely nothing about us. Consequently, we will be nobody, from noplace, going nowhere.

Finally, in his first Epistle to the Corinthians, St. Paul said, "Therefore, my beloved children, be steadfast, always abounding in the work of the Lord, knowing that in the Lord, your labor is not in vain" (1 Corinthians 15:58).

Brothers and sisters, let not our labor be in vain!

The Burial of Rt. Rev. Alexander Schmemann
December, 1983

In the Name of the Father and Son and Holy Spirit, Amen.

Beloved in Christ Jesus:
We are gathered here this evening in this chapel and on this holy hill to pray for the repose of the soul of our departed friend, Father Alexander Schmemann. Death in human experience has never been easy, whether it comes in youth or in old age; whether it strikes suddenly or after a long illness, it always leaves in its wake loneliness, tears and longing. Let us pray that our merciful Lord will give Matushka Schmemann and her family divine comfort and consolation.

We are not here to mourn like those who have no hope. We are here to contemplate and to celebrate the life of Father Alexander Schmemann, a great theologian, a distinguished professor and articulate lecturer, a renowned author, an organizer and a builder. The sixty-two years which Father Schmemann lived on this earth have been a pilgrimage and a journey which started in Estonia, went through France and ended here at this seminary, which consumed his life and to which he gave every ounce of his energy.

I honestly do not know of any contemporary Orthodox theologian who has left more impact on our theology, spiritual lives and thoughts than the Right Reverend Alexander Schmemann. "Whosoever shall do and teach, the same shall be called great in the kingdom of heaven" (Matthew 5:19). Certainly his untimely departure shocked all of us, but in the final analysis, it is not how long we live; it is rather how deeply we live, how many candles we light and how many chapters we write in the Book of Life.

I am sure that all of you are aware of the many books Father

Schmemann authored during his life. I would like to mention, however, only one of them, *For the Life of the World.* This excellent work has been translated into eight languages, and as *The New York Times* stated yesterday, "This book remains one of the most widely read books on Orthodox Christianity written for the general public." Father Schmemann has popularized Orthodox theology and brought it down from its ivory tower to the people's level. He lectured to academicians as well as to the smallest congregations in North America. Father Schmemann was a pioneer in the field of liturgical theology, and I would dare say he is the father of liturgical theology in the Orthodox Church. His relentless emphasis on the eucharistic experience as a journey to the Kingdom created a spiritual renaissance in thousands of parishes throughout the Orthodox world.

I was fortunate to have been one of his students. He touched my life as well as many lives in this country and abroad. As professor of liturgical theology, his lectures were never dull. No matter how serious the subject was, Father Schmemann would always inject his wit and humor and make it most interesting. We looked forward to his lectures with much longing because he made God, the Church, the sacraments, the liturgy and even Byzantine history very much alive in our minds.

Both in France and in the United States, he has educated patriarchs, scores of bishops and hundreds of pastors. As Dean of St. Vladimir's Seminary he worked tirelessly to bring the seminary from its humble beginning to the fine institution it has become today. Since the beginning of my episcopate, Father Schmemann and I developed a very deep friendship and shared many, many intimate thoughts about the seminary and the future of Orthodoxy in this hemisphere. Oh, how hard he worked and preached about Orthodoxy in this land. His burning desire was to see Orthodoxy organically united in North America. Unfortunately, he died before the realization of his dream. We shall continue to struggle for this unity and we shall dedicate our efforts in this regard through the Bilateral Commission to the blessed memory of Father Alexander Schmemann.

Despite his tragic illness, he continued to travel and speak on behalf of the seminary and Orthodox unity in this hemisphere. Last July, he honored the Antiochian Archdiocese with his presence at the convention banquet. At the conclusion of his speech, in which he reflected on the conditions of Orthodoxy in America, he said, "It may have been very useful, very necessary to discuss in detail various ecclesiastical problems, but when Christ touches us with the light and the joy of our ascension with Him to the Kingdom of God and the Table of the Lord, then we understand the real scope of American Orthodoxy. Defeat transformed into victory; death destroyed by death; darkness absorbed by light; suffering made into a way to Christ. Such, for us, is the meaning of the Church, and one cannot escape it."

Nothing worthwhile in this life can be achieved without struggle, and suffering will always lead to Christ if it is understood in the light of the Cross. This was the firm conviction of Father Alexander Schmemann. The German poet, Goethe, once said, "He who does not eat his bread with tears, and he who does not spend the midnight hours weeping and waiting for the dawn, does not know you, ye heavenly powers."

On December 1, at the end of the dinner with the Board of Trustees of St. Vladimir's Seminary, knowing perhaps that his days on this earth were numbered, Father Schmemann spoke to us in simple and direct words which I am sure penetrated every heart. His words were reminiscent of St. Paul's words recorded in 2 Timothy 4:6–8, "I am already on the point of being sacrificed; the time of my departure has come. I have fought the good fight, I have finished the race, I have kept the faith." Father Schmemann's words to the Board of Trustees were his will and testament. "I am sorry," he said, "that I cannot meet with you tonight because I have just had a chemotherapy treatment. Please take good care of the seminary. Remember our humble beginning and how hard we fought to be where we are today." Father Schmemann uttered these words, then excused himself and vanished into the darkness of the night. There were misty eyes in the room and a strong, silent determination that the seminary will live and that the torch which Father Schmemann has lighted on this holy hill will never be extinguished.

On behalf of the Antiochian Orthodox Christian Archdiocese of North America, I would like to convey my sincerest condolences to Matushka Schmemann and her family, to Andre Schmemann, to Metropolitan Theodosius and the members of the Holy Synod, to the clergy and laity of the Orthodox Church in America, to the Board of Trustees, the faculty, the student body and the staff of St. Vladimir's Seminary.

Farewell, my dear friend. I am sure you have already heard these divine words. "Well done, thou good and faithful servant; you have been faithful over a little. I will set you over much; enter into the joy of your Master" (Matthew 25:21).

Orthodoxy in America: Success and Failure
Worcester, March, 1984

Once every year, on the Sunday of Orthodoxy, the Orthodox people in America emerge from their ethnic islands to celebrate the triumph of the Orthodox Faith over the iconoclastic heresy. This victory happened in A.D. 787—1,197 years ago. The icons were restored to the Church after much suffering, much bloodshed and much sacrifice. We are indeed grateful to the Church of the eighth century, for her courage to stand against emperors and governments in order to defend the faith, "which once and for all was delivered to the saints" (Jude 3). Heroes such as John of Damascus, Theodore the Studite, Patriarch Germanos and Patriarch Nicephorus will live in the memory of the Church forever.

It is not my intention, today, to elaborate on the historical circumstances which led to the iconoclastic controversy, nor will I attempt to present a new theology in defense of the holy icons. I doubt if anyone can add much to the brilliant thoughts of St. John of Damascus on this subject. I am not trying, by any means, to minimize the historical events which led to this Orthodox victory in A.D. 787. I am proud of our history; for those who have no past, and have no present, there will be no future. There is a difference, however, between *contemplating* history and *worshipping* history.

During the first one thousand years of her existence, the Church was courageous enough to respond to the challenges of her time. Many local councils were called and seven Ecumenical Councils were convened to deal with important issues which the Church had to face. The question now is: What happened to that dynamism which characterized the life of the Church between Pentecost and the tenth century? Did God stop speaking to the Church? Did the action of the Holy Spirit in the

Church cease after the tenth century? Why are we always celebrating the remote past? Have we been lost in our long, long history? I wish we could gather to celebrate an event which happened five hundred years ago, or two hundred years ago, or even perhaps something which happened last year.

In the Gospel of St. John, our Lord said, "My Father is working still, and I am working" (John 5:17). Thus, we cannot blame God for our inaction. History, from a Christian perspective, is a dynamic process because it is the arena of God's action in the past as well as in the present. But if we do not fully, creatively and faithfully respond to the divine challenge, no change can be effected in our Church, our values and the human situation. Our forefathers, motivated by the power of the Holy Spirit, have fought valiantly and triumphantly against iconoclasm and all kinds of heresies; but the triumphalism of the past will not save us from the sterility of the present and the uncertainty of the future!

Frozen History

It is indeed astonishing that we have not had an Ecumenical Council since 787 despite the many changes which the Church has encountered during the past 1,197 years. I shall mention but a few of these global events which affected the life of the Church directly or indirectly since the last Ecumenical Council:

1. the 1054 schism between East and West;
2. the fall of Constantinople;
3. the European Renaissance with all its implications;
4. the Protestant Reformation;
5. the discovery of the New World;
6. the French Revolution;
7. the Communist Revolution and its impact on the Orthodox Church;
8. the First and Second World Wars;
9. the dawning of the nuclear age;
10. the exploration of space and all the scientific and technological discoveries which baffle the mind.

Despite all these significant events which have already touched our lives, we Orthodox are still debating whether or not we should convene the Eighth Ecumenical Council!

A few days ago, I was glancing through the 1932 Arabic issue of the *WORD Magazine* and came across the following news item entitled: "Pan-Orthodox Consultations for an Ecumenical Council Were Postponed." The news item continues:

> The Orthodox world was expecting that the representatives of the Orthodox Churches would meet on Mount Athos during the Pentecost Season in June of this year for serious preparation for the Great Ecumenical Council. There was great concern as to what the pan-Orthodox consultations would decide regarding important and urgent issues facing the Church. What a disappointment to have learned that the meeting was postponed to the forthcoming year.

That meeting never took place, and I doubt if an Ecumenical Council will be convened in the foreseeable future.

You may ask, what is the reason behind this Orthodox stagnation? Did our history freeze after A.D. 787? There is no doubt that the rise of Islam, the collapse of the Byzantine Empire, and the fall of Tsarist Russia have contributed much to our past and present stagnation. The sad condition of our mother churches across the ocean is indicative of this reality. The Patriarchate of Jerusalem is living under the heel of a Zionist state. The Coptic Orthodox Patriarch of Egypt is still living under house arrest. And what can I say about Antioch? If I may apply biblical words for my purposes, I would say the following: "A voice was heard in Lebanon, wailing and lamentation—Antioch weeping for her children; she refused to be consoled because they were no more" (Matthew 2:18).

The Church of Cyprus is suffering the consequences of a badly and sadly divided island. The Ecumenical Patriarchate is slowly, but surely, dying from Turkish oppression. Furthermore, the Patriarchate of Moscow and those of Eastern Europe continue to suffer under the yoke of communism.

Have we then lost all hope for an Orthodox Renaissance? Is there not a place on this planet where we can dream of a better Orthodox future? I believe that there is a place, and this place is the North American continent. We have a tremendous opportunity in this land to dream dreams and to see visions—only if we can put our house in order. Where in the whole world today can one find seven million free Orthodox except in North America?

We are no longer a Church of immigrants; the first Orthodox liturgy was celebrated in this country before the American Revolution. Many of our Orthodox young people have died on the battlefields of various wars, defending American ideals and principles. We have contributed much to the success of this country in the fields of medicine, science, technology, government, education, art, entertainment and business. We consider ourselves Americans and we are proud of it—except when we go to church, we suddenly become Greeks, Russians, Arabs, Albanians and so forth. Despite our rootedness in the American soil, our Church in America is still divided into more than fourteen jurisdictions, contrary to our Orthodox ecclesiology and canon law, which forbid the multiplicity of jurisdictions in the same territory.

Rising above Ethnicism
Individually, Orthodox jurisdictions have done much for themselves. We have some of the finest theological institutions in the world. We have excellent religious publications. Many volumes have been written in English on Orthodox theology. We have some of the best Christian education programs. Our clergy are highly educated and deeply committed to the Orthodox faith. We have built multimillion dollar churches and cathedrals, and our laity are well organized and have contributed generously to the financial and spiritual well-being of our parishes. Collectively, however, we have not been able to rise above our ethnicity

and to work together with one mind and one accord for the glory of Orthodoxy. Our efforts continue to be scattered in different directions. Why should we have fifteen departments for Christian education, media relations, sacred music, youth ministry, clergy pensions and so forth?

Where is our spiritual and moral impact on the life of this nation? Where is our voice in the media? Why is it that every time there is a moral issue to be discussed, a Protestant, a Roman Catholic and a Jew are invited for such discussions? How can we explain our Orthodox absence, despite the authenticity of our theology and moral teachings?

The answer to these disturbing questions is simple: it is ethnicism. Unfortunately, we have permitted ourselves to become victims of our ethnic mentalities. We cannot be agents of change in full obedience to the truth unless we transcend ethnicism and establish a new Orthodox reality in North America. I am not asking you to deny your own history and your own culture. What I am asking is to blend your old and new cultures into some kind of an integrated reality. I am not against ethnicism, if ethnicism means a return to the spirit of the Desert Fathers, the Syrian Fathers, the Greek Fathers and the Slavic Fathers. But if ethnicism means a narrow, fanatic, ghetto mentality which separates us from each other, then I am definitely against such ethnicism.

The mission of the Church is not to be subservient to any kind of nationalism. The mission of the Church is the salvation of souls—all souls. In his Epistle to the Galatians, St. Paul said, "There is neither Jew nor Greek, there is neither slave nor free, there is neither male nor female; for all are one in Christ Jesus" (Galatians 3:28).

Brothers and sisters in Orthodoxy, I have shared with you today some of my reflections on our past and present, on our success and failure. I would like to share with you, now, some daring visions about the future. My first vision concerns the role of our Orthodox laity in this relentless quest for Orthodox unity. After eighteen years in the episcopate, I have become convinced that Orthodox unity in America must begin on the grassroots level. You, the laity, are the conscience of the Church and the defenders of the faith. Consequently, I would like to see a strong pan-Orthodox lay movement, totally dedicated to the cause of Orthodox unity. Without the laity, our churches would be empty and our liturgical and sacramental services would be in vain. The clergy and laity, working together, are the *laos tou theou* ("the people of God"), and they constitute the Orthodox Church.

My second vision concerns the Standing Conference of Orthodox Bishops in America (SCOBA). Since the purpose of SCOBA is to bring organic unity to our churches in America, I believe that SCOBA should be elevated to the rank of an Orthodox Synod which will have the power to deal effectively and decisively with our Orthodox problems in this country.

My third vision, ladies and gentlemen, concerns the Ecumenical Patriarchate. There is no doubt that we need a catalyst to lead us from the wilderness of division to the promised land of unity and fulfillment. I do not know of a better catalyst than the Ecumenical Patriarch, himself, who continues to live like a prisoner in Istanbul. Let us prevail on him to leave Turkey, come to America and unite our various jurisdictions under his wings. The Greek remnant in Istanbul can be shepherded by an exarch who would represent the ecumenical throne. The Ecumenical Patriarch will preserve his traditional role in the world regardless of where he resides. We have unlimited opportunities in this free land, but if we do not move forward with faith and courage, our Church on this continent will remain an insignificant dot on the margin of history.

Finally, I would like to conclude this sermon with the words of the late Alexander Schmemann:

> One can almost visualize the glorious and blessed day when forty Orthodox bishops of America will open their First Synod in New York or Chicago or Pittsburgh with the hymn, 'Today the grace of the Holy Spirit assembled

us together,' and will appear to us not as representatives of Greek, Russian or any other jurisdictions and interests, but as the very icon, the very Epiphany, of our unity within the Body of Christ; when each of them and all together will think and deliberate only in terms of the whole, putting aside all particular and national problems, real and important as they may be. On that day, we shall taste and see the oneness of the Orthodox Church in America.

Searching for a Spiritual Renaissance: The Second Holy Year
Boston, 1985

The biblical text of my message to you this year is taken from the Second Epistle of St. Paul to the Corinthians:

> He who sows sparingly will also reap sparingly, and he who sows bountifully will also reap bountifully. Each must do as he has made up his mind, not reluctantly or under compulsion, for God loves a cheerful giver. And God is able to provide you with every blessing in abundance so that you may always have enough of everything and may provide in abundance for every good work (2 Corinthians 9:6–8).

Two years ago, when I addressed you in Toronto, some of the points which I emphasized were: the role of the laity in the Church, and the need for a Heritage and Learning Center to help us preserve our precious spiritual and cultural heritage. Last year, on July 15, and in the presence of more than one thousand faithful, we broke ground for this edifice and implored the Perfect Builder, our Lord and Savior, Jesus Christ, to build with us for the glory of His Church. On July 14, exactly one year after the ground-breaking, our Father in Christ, Patriarch Ignatius dedicated this magnificent center which stands on the mountain as a monument to your courage, perseverance and faith in the future of Orthodoxy in this great land.

July 14 was an historic day in the life of this archdiocese. It was reflective of the day which the Lord has made. July 14 was the fulfillment of a dream, which for a while, seemed impossible. But, what is "impossible to man is possible to God" (Matthew 19:26). July 14 was a day of victory of faith over doubt, a victory of determination over procrastination and stagnation.

July 14 marked the end of our small dreams and the beginning of greater confidence in ourselves and in the future. By building this center, we proved that we can dream big dreams, climb high mountains and achieve greater things. We proved to ourselves and everyone else that if the sons and daughters of Antioch can build such a Heritage and Learning Center, then the sons and daughters of Orthodoxy in this land, if united in one mind and one heart, can build hospitals, universities, colleges and many other institutions in this country and abroad. Yes, we proved beyond that "we can do all things through Christ who strengthens us" (Philippians 4:13).

The Heritage and Learning Center is a living memorial to your parents and grandparents who planted the seeds of Orthodoxy in this North American soil and fought valiantly to preserve our eternal ideals and principles. And if some of you still ask, "Why the center?" the answer is this: We must realize once and for all that we are on the threshold of the twenty-first century. The third millennium will be upon us more swiftly than the twinkling of an eye. The question therefore is: Are we prepared to face the challenges of the next century? In my humble opinion, the center is an important step in our preparation to face the future. We hope that this center will inaugurate a *real spiritual renaissance* in the life of our archdiocese in particular, and in the life of Orthodoxy in general. We did not spend all that money just to have a white elephant on the mountain. On the contrary, we spent our money to witness to the truth and the faith which "once and for all was delivered to the saints" (Jude 3). We expect you, therefore, to spend weeks and months learning, praying and planning so that you may breathe life into the dry bones and put flesh and blood on the great spirituality which you represent.

We expect our youth, the Antiochian Women, the Order of St. Ignatius of Antioch, our clergy, our parish councils, our Archdiocese Board of Trustees, our choirs, our church school teachers, our altar servers, and all the faithful to hold retreats, seminars, workshops, marriage encounters and symposia in this center. We also invite our Orthodox brothers and sisters from various Orthodox jurisdictions to use this center for the edification of their faithful.

The Place of Antioch in History

On Thursday, May 16, this North American continent was blessed by the arrival of our Father in Christ, His Beatitude, Patriarch Ignatius IV and his entourage. When we welcomed His Beatitude at Kennedy Airport, we said from the depths of our hearts, "Blessed is he that cometh in the name of the Lord." Just think how fortunate we are, during this Antiochian Holy Year, to behold the head of our Patriarchate, embrace him, listen to him, kiss his hand and receive his apostolic blessing. His Beatitude is the 165th successor of St. Peter, the first Bishop of the Holy See of Antioch.

The Patriarchate of Antioch was established before the Patriarchates of Jerusalem, Alexandria, Constantinople and Rome. It is the most ancient patriarchate in the Christian world. During the apostolic era, Antioch was the main center of missionary activities. There was a time when the See of Antioch encompassed the whole East. Antioch was glorified by the martyrdom of its third bishop, St. Ignatius of Antioch, by the melodies of St. Romanos of Homs, by the poetry of St. Ephraim the Syrian, by the eloquence of St. John Chrysostom and by the genius of St. John of Damascus. This is to mention but a few of the great Antiochian saints.

I am not trying to be parochial by stating these facts. I do not know of anyone who has focused on the catholicity of the Church more than the Antiochian Fathers. In a lecture which His Beatitude, Patriarch Ignatius, delivered two years ago at the Sorbonne University in Paris, he said, "The Christianity of the Church of Antioch, just as Christ Himself, belongs neither to the East nor to the West." During the early Christian period, Antioch developed its own school of architecture, monasticism and theology. What we call today the incarnational school of theology is deeply rooted in the Antiochian Fathers.

Patriarch Ignatius IV represents much glory and yet much suffering. As a matter of fact, the land of Antioch is still drenched by the blood of confessors and martyrs. I shall briefly mention some of the calamities which Antioch suffered throughout history. From Calvary to the Edict of Milan, Antioch has suffered the most barbarous and longest holocaust under the pagan Roman Empire. This was followed by the Persian invasion and the internal heresies which have torn Antioch asunder, the Muslim conquest of the Near East, the Crusades, the Ottoman Turks, the Western missionaries, the Melkite schism and last, but not least, international Zionism. It is a miracle, indeed, that Antioch is still alive. Perhaps it is the destiny of Antioch to wash away the sins of the world with her tears and blood.

From Antioch to America
Your Beatitude, around the end of the last century, thousands of Antiochian faithful were forced to leave their motherland, seeking freedom and social justice in the New World. Unfortunately, some of them died in North Africa and Europe and never made it here. Fortunately, however, many of them did reach Ellis Island in the New York Harbor. They had no money, no skills and did not speak the language. The blessed ones had an address of a friend somewhere in this land. Many of them had to sleep in the streets before they found a humble shelter. They purchased some light merchandise and peddled it from city to city, town to town and state to state. While walking in this vast land, some died from heat and exhaustion, and some froze to death.

When they reached a city and could no longer walk, they would settle there, perhaps for the rest of their lives. The first thing they did was to establish a church in some house, in order to preserve their spiritual heritage. It is important to note here that many of our parishes were established by lay people before our bishops and priests arrived on this continent. Hence, the strong lay orientation of our Church in North America. Our people were blessed if a priest visited them once a year to marry them, baptize their children and pray for their dead.

These simple, early pioneers were the true heroes of Orthodoxy in this New World. Besides their stubborn clinging to the Holy Orthodox Faith, they proved to be good citizens of their new, adopted country. They were determined to educate their children and instill in them their traditions and values, such as hard work, honesty and decency. Their children and grandchildren have excelled in every walk of life, namely, business, science, medicine, law, education, government and entertainment.

Antioch in America Today
Your Beatitude, the early immigrants have laid the foundation of this archdiocese. Today, almost one hundred years later, if we reflect on the history of our archdiocese, we may distinguish three main eras: the era of immigration, which was the most difficult, the era of organization and the era of spiritual maturation. The third era began with the rejuvenation of our youth movement, the founding of the Antiochian Women, the Order of St. Ignatius of Antioch, the acquisition of the Antiochian Village, the erection of the Heritage and Learning Center and the establishment of about sixty new parishes.

Your Beatitude, these humble achievements and many others [that] were realized, especially during the past nineteen years, are not the fruit of my efforts alone. They are the result of perfect cooperation between the bishop, the clergy and the laity. We in this archdiocese cherish this sound Orthodox principle, and whenever this principle is violated, the whole life of the Church is violated.

Your Beatitude, this archdiocese is blessed with faithful, active and productive organizations. The Board of Trustees was organized in the late forties and has served this archdiocese without interruption. It consists of men and women who are totally dedicated to the eternal ideals and principles of our Church. Our youth movement, which began in the thirties, has combined Eastern spirituality with Western practicality. These young people pray and work, and have given us some of our very dedicated clergy. One of their most important projects is Food for Hungry People. Through this project, they have raised hundreds of thousands of dollars to feed the hungry in North, Central and South America, in Africa, in the Far East and certainly in the Middle East. Every year our Teen SOYO sponsors the Special Olympics at the Antiochian Village to help handicapped children from the Commonwealth of Pennsylvania.

The Antiochian Women have emulated the ointment-bearing women in faith and good deeds. Besides their retreats and study of the Bible, they have also raised hundreds of thousands of dollars to help the projects of this archdiocese and the needy everywhere. It is important to note that last year, more than fifteen percent of the archdiocesan budget was spent on charity. And speaking about our organizations, I cannot say enough about the Order of St. Ignatius of Antioch. Words are inadequate to describe the impact this Order has left on the life of our archdiocese.

On the local level, our parish councils continue to be responsive to the needs of our archdiocese; most of the time, cheerfully, and sometimes, reluctantly. Our clergy are the heartbeat of this archdiocese. They continue to preach the Word, "in season and out of season." Without them, our spiritual and humanitarian goals cannot be realized.

Last, but not least, Your Beatitude, I want to say a few words about our little children. The children of our archdiocese are the real source of my inspiration. They never cease to amaze me with their curiosity, humor, innocence and genuine love. After the June War of 1967, I was raising funds for the Palestinian refugees in Allentown, Pennsylvania. When I finished my sermon on the plight of the refugees, an eight-year-old altar boy reached into his pocket and handed me a quarter. I am sure that quarter was all that he had. Five years ago, during the dark days of the Lebanese War, after preaching about the agony of the Lebanese children, a little girl in Boston took off her ring and gave it to me saying, "This is for the Lebanese children."

Your Beatitude, your memorable visit to us coincides with the tenth anniversary of the reunification of our Antiochian people in North America. Our people on this continent were sadly divided by internal and external forces—first, between Russi and Antaki, and second, between Toledo and New York. Ten years ago, Archbishop Michael and I met in Pittsburgh, Pennsylvania, and signed the Reunification Agreement which was subsequently blessed by the Holy Synod of Antioch. After that long, dark night of shameful division, our people in North America have resolved, by the grace of God, that henceforth no power on earth will be able to divide them again. Despite the vastness of this archdiocese, we live like a big, happy family. Someone sneezes in Boston and he is instantly heard in Los Angeles.

Orthodox Unity Is Lacking

Your Beatitude, what I have already said indicates that all is well with Antioch in North America. All is also well with the Greek Archdiocese of North and South America. All is well with the Orthodox Church in America and the other Orthodox jurisdictions. Collectively, however, we have not achieved significant goals because of our ethnic ghetto mentality which characterizes the life of the Church in this hemisphere. It is incredible, indeed, that eight million Orthodox have not made any lasting spiritual or moral impact on the life of this nation, despite the sound and authentic theology which we represent. Thus, the most pressing issue which Orthodoxy is facing in North America, Your Beatitude, is the question of Orthodox unity. Some Orthodox sources say that the problem of the Orthodox diaspora can only be discussed in the context of a pan-Orthodox council. But how soon will this pan-Orthodox council convene?

Modern history moves extremely fast. We cannot, therefore, afford the luxury of inaction. The past is glorious indeed, but how long can we sleep on the glory of the past? It is time that we wake up. Despite the progress which Orthodoxy has made on this continent, we seem to have reached a dead end because of the unprecedented canonical chaos which is plaguing the life of the Church in this hemisphere. We are in the process of developing our own schools of architecture, iconography, hymnology and theology. But where do we go from here? It is true, Your Beatitude, that the roots are in Antioch, Jerusalem, Constantinople, Greece, Eastern Europe and Russia; but the branches are here, and these branches are very deeply rooted in this fertile and beautiful North American soil. We will never forget our roots; what we are seeking is unity with diversity.

Your Beatitude, all the Orthodox in North America, regardless of national background, look up to you for guidance and leadership. They have been very encouraged by the positive statements you have made vis-à-vis Orthodox unity on this continent. With all my respect for all Orthodox Patriarchs, you are the only patriarch in the world today who has enough freedom and courage to dialogue sincerely and effectively with both the Greeks and Slavs. Antioch, as you well stated, does not have the "illusions of the first, second or third Rome." Being fully cognizant of this reality, please permit me to borrow an expression from the president of our country and ask you, "If not you, who? And if not now, when?"

Finally, Your Beatitude, your visit to this archdiocese has been an explosion of love. During the past two and a half months, you have traveled to every region of this archdiocese and touched every heart. You have seen us in our strength and in our weakness. Rest assured, Your Beatitude, that the beautiful memories of your visit will linger in our minds for many, many years to come and wherever you go, you will always be surrounded by our love and prayers.

Our fervent supplication shall always be: "Among the first be mindful, O Lord, of our Father, Patriarch Ignatius, whom do Thou grant unto Thy Holy Church in peace, safety, honor, health and length of days and faithfully proclaiming the Word of Thy truth."

Editor's Endnotes:

1. In the 1983 address to the Toronto Convention, Metropolitan Philip also announces that, now that Bishop Antoun is serving the archdiocese, the three hierarchs, Philip, Michael and Antoun, will share in overseeing the various departments; he lists the responsibilities of each hierarch; speaks of the poor response of some of the parishes to raise the necessary funds for the development of the Heritage and Learning Center, and that, therefore, a three-year assessment will have to be implemented in each parish.

2. In 1983, Philip meets with President Ronald Reagan at the White House to discuss International Relations and the Middle East.

3. In 1985, while Patriarch Ignatius IV is visiting the archdiocese, Philip arranges a meeting with him on behalf of the group known as the Evangelical Orthodox Church (EOC). This begins the process of accepting thousands of Christians into the canonical Orthodox Church which will be realized two years later in 1987.

4. In 1986, Philip receives his second honorary Doctorate Degree from Wayne State University in Detroit, Michigan. He graduated from the University in 1958 when he arrived in the United States. The degree he now receives is Doctor of Humane Letters, given for his humanitarian work throughout the world.

5. On July 1, 1986, Philip receives the cherished Liberty Award given by Mayor Ed Koch on behalf of the City of New York.

Chapter 13

TENDERNESS AND JOY:
Speaking from the Heart

> *Twenty-one years ago the Almighty God entrusted me with this vineyard to serve, to nourish and to protect. Needless to say, the first five years of my episcopate were the most difficult years of my life. I will never forget my response as I entered the old archdiocese headquarters in Brooklyn after my consecration. There I was, the Archbishop of New York and All North America, working alone without a deacon, a priest, a secretary or even a cook. My experience in administrating an archdiocese of such vastness was simply inadequate. But "what is impossible to man is possible to God."*
>
> Metropolitan Philip

- *Funeral Oration for Ellis Khoury, 1987*
- *A Man Obsessed by the Word: The Twenty-fifth Anniversary of John Estephan, 1987*
- *Two Joys: The Evangelical Orthodox and The West Coast Chancery, 1987*
- *Struggling Against New Iconoclasms, 1987*

AND HE LEADS THEM

In 1987, Philip delivers three talks unlike any others he has hitherto presented. They are invested with his personal emotion, his fondest hope, his untiring quest. He speaks from the heart in each one.

The first is the funeral oration which he delivers at the departure from this world of the beloved Ellis Khouri, the venerable Archimandrite and Protosyngelos of the archdiocese. Father Ellis, he says, is a "living icon" that will "live in the consciousness of the archdiocese forever." The reader cannot but be impressed with the tenderness of heart, the flood of compassion, and the pathos of love which is exhibited by Philip; God Himself is present in these words.

The second unique address is delivered in that same year at the twenty-fifth anniversary of Father John Estephan. While it is just as sincere as the first address in this chapter, the pace and feel of this talk is altogether different. Strong and generous of spirit, Philip speaks of his admiration for this priest and his power of the Word. And because of that power, we leave the Arabic in place since the ambience cannot truly be captured in translation. Nevertheless, those who do not read the Arabic language will miss nothing of the unique power transmitted in Philip's talk.

The third address is delivered at the historic acceptance that year of the group known then as the Evangelical Orthodox, a mass acceptance reflecting nothing less than the baptism of Rus one thousand years earlier. This was to be the welcoming home of those who longed for, and energetically sought, the ancient apostolic faith; they discovered it in Orthodoxy. And now Philip will begin sealing that faith on February 8, 1987, in Van Nuys, California. The address is given the night before, February 7, at the West Coast Chancery in Los Angeles; it is a landmark occurrence in the history of Orthodox Christianity. Philip never regrets his acceptance and openness in response to their longing.

But there is another historic landmark which brings a unique touch: this is also the opening (not the dedication) of the West Coast Chancery, which begins the process of preparing it for the hierarchy. Taken together, these two events offer the reader a glimpse at the sincere joy which emanates from Philip's words.

Finally, we include an address on the occasion of the twelve hundredth anniversary of the restoration of iconography. He delivers this talk in Dearborn, Michigan, in 1987, and demonstrates the impact of iconography relative to the teaching and doctrine of the Holy Orthodox Faith. Mentioning the triumph of the Church over the iconoclasts (icon-breakers), he points to the multitude of contemporary iconoclasms against which the Church must continue to struggle. This address, delivered to the Archdiocesan Convention, also finds Philip explaining those historical events and procedures by which the Evangelical Orthodox were entered into canonical Orthodoxy. This final address, in a sense, completes that joy which Philip expresses in the former talk earlier that year in California.

Thus, in the last address of the year, Philip points to three events: the restoration of iconography, the acceptance of the Evangelical Orthodox and the establishment entitled the Benefactors of St. George Orthodox Hospital in Beirut. The latter is a response to the war that is then raging in Lebanon.

J. J. A.

Funeral Oration for Ellis Khouri
1987

"Who shall ascend the mountain of the Lord? And who shall stand in His holy place? He who has clean hands and a pure heart, who does not lift up his soul to what is false, and does not swear deceitfully" (Psalm 24:3, 4).

These beautiful words from the prophet and poet, David, illustrate perfectly the distinguished personality of the most beloved priest of our archdiocese, Protosyngelos Ellis Khouri. Father Ellis was born around the turn of this century in Khiam, South Lebanon, a land which was blessed by the footsteps of Jesus of Nazareth and was stained by the blood of saints and martyrs. From time immemorial, Khiam has been embraced by Haramon [Hermon], the Holy Mountain, always basking in its eternal beauty. From the snow of Mount Haramon, Father Ellis acquired the purity of his heart and the beauty of his soul. "Blessed are the pure in heart for they shall see God" (Matthew 5:8).

God endowed Father Ellis with a sensitive spirit; thus his words always reflected both the freshness of a Lebanese summer dawn and the sadness of the last ray of a sunset on Mount Haramon. David the poet asks: "Who shall ascend the mountain of the Lord?" Surely, Father Ellis has ascended this mountain because, from his youth, he was destined to live on the peaks. For only when you reach the peak, you may experience the depth of the valley. Sensitive and restless souls despise flatness, and it is the nature of eagles to shun the swamps and aim for the summit.

Sometimes in the presence of Father Ellis you felt the serenity of a man who had transcended the boundaries of this world. And many times you felt that he was embracing you in your joy and sorrow, in your hope and despair, in your faith and doubt, and in your triumph and defeat. Many times the thorns of my crown have pierced my flesh and the weight of my cross has crushed my shoulders, but Father Ellis, the man, the companion, the friend and the brother, was always there to wipe a tear, a drop of blood and to help carry a piece of that heavy cross.

Ellis Khouri, the priest, the man and the poet, could not live in this world without sharing its agony and restlessness. One might ask: Was it not this restlessness which brought him to our shores? Was it not this restlessness which drew him to his contemporaries: Khalil Gibran, Amin Al-Rayhani, Mikhail Naimy, Elia Abou-Mady, and was it not this restlessness which ultimately threw him in the bosom of God?

From the peak of the mountain, Father Ellis looked across the ocean and saw in his dreams a vast land equal to the vastness of his soul. Thus he joined the procession of heroes in an eternal march to conquer the unknown. Despite the distance which separated him from Khiam, Lebanon, he could never forget his roots, his people and his beautiful heritage. In his conversations and writings, he would paraphrase the poet Neruda by saying:

I am here watching, listening with half of my soul in Lebanon and half of my soul in America. And with both halves of my soul, I watch the world.

What I have said about Father Ellis, I have already said before, namely this past June as he celebrated his fortieth anniversary as advisor to SOYO. Last month when he got sick I visited him twice, once in the hospital and once at his home. It was not difficult to notice that he was melting away like a candle; and despite the fact that cancer was eating his frail bones, Father Ellis was concerned with the affairs of the archdiocese and he expressed his tremendous enthusiasm about the reception of the Evangelical Orthodox into canonical Orthodoxy.

In the Gospel of Saint John we read, "He who believes in Me, even though he dies, yet shall he live. And whoever believes in Me shall never die" (John 11:25, 26). Every time Father Ellis celebrated the Eucharist, he died with the Lord and was resurrected with Him. Three weeks ago, when I said goodbye to him for the last time, he was prepared to die, in order never to die. Saturday morning, his light having faded, he cried, "It is finished!" and he gave up his spirit.

In 1966, when we lost Metropolitan Antony, a group of us young clergy begged Father Ellis to accept the nomination to the office of metropolitan. Father Ellis firmly but humbly declined, and said, "This archdiocese needs a younger man to carry the heavy burdens." After the Archdiocese Nominating Convention, there was some hesitation on the part of the Synod of Antioch to proceed with the election of a metropolitan for our widowed archdiocese. It was then that Father Ellis led a delegation of faithful clergy to the Middle East to fight for the unity and integrity of this archdiocese, and in the face of the storm, Father Ellis stood firm like a rock and used his strength and eloquence in order to convince the Holy Synod of Antioch to respect the will of God and the wishes of our people.

During the past twenty-one years of my episcopate, he was my companion in many trips throughout this country and to the Middle East. I can honestly say that I do not know of any clergyman or layman who is more revered, more loved and more respected than Father Ellis Khouri. I do not know of any priest who was more loyal to his archdiocese and his metropolitan than Father Ellis Khouri. I do not know of any priest who loved and cared for his brother priests more than Father Ellis Khouri. I do not know of any individual who was more committed to the Board of Trustees, SOYO, the Order of St. Ignatius of Antioch, and the Antiochian Women than Father Ellis Khouri.

We very often referred to Father Ellis as the "living icon," and rightly so. Icons which are made of wood, color, silver and even gold sooner or later get old, tarnish and decay. But Father Ellis, the living icon, will never get old, will never tarnish and will never decay. He will always be our window to heaven. He will live in the consciousness of this archdiocese forever.

Farewell my dearest friend, you have lived with dignity and died with dignity. You have indeed "fought the good fight"; enter into the joy of your Lord.

A Man Obsessed by the Word: The Twenty-fifth Anniversary of John Estephan
1987

We are gathered here this evening to express our deep gratitude to Father John and Khouriya Souaad for twenty-five years of fruitful ministry. I am sure that all of you have known Father John, the priest, and loved him. I wonder, however, how many of you have known Father John, the writer and the poet. Please permit me to reveal to you the other dimension of Father John's personality as much as I can.

When you read Father John Estephan, you feel as if his body cannot contain his soul. You read Father Estephan and you discover in him the vastness of the spirit, after he discovered in himself that boundless man. The uniqueness of Father John lies in the fact that he never strived after empty fame, nor did he like artificial lights. God has given him much, and when you receive from God, you live satisfied with God's gifts.

I do not know of any writer who has tamed the Arabic language more than Father John Estephan. When you read him, you feel that he is completely obsessed by the word. He does not write poetry; he bleeds poetry. Father John loves his people and the land which he "never left" to the point of drunkenness. When he writes about the tragedies of his people, he dips his pen in their tears, and when he writes about their past victories, his words dance with joy to the point of ecstasy.

One of the things which I treasure most is a personal collection of precious letters which I have received from Father John on various occasions. The best tribute I can pay him on his twenty-fifth anniversary in the priesthood is to share with you excerpts from some of his letters.

In November, 1975, he wrote to me on the occasion of the

Feast of St. Philip, the Apostle, my patron saint. Speaking about the Church, Father John said:

> لم تدعوا خطها العمودي المفضي إلى الملكوت ينسيكم خطها الأفقي الممتد في إتجاه الأرض. عموديا حرصتم على قدسية الكنيسة وعصمة تعاليمها ورهبة أسرارها وجمالات طقوسها، وأفقيا نافحتم عن القيم الإنسانية في دعوتكم إلى العدالة والسيادة والإخاء والحريات، كل الحريات........

You did not let her vertical line which leads to the kingdom, make you forget her horizontal line which leads to the earth. Vertically, you have preserved the sanctity of the Church, the infallibility of her teachings, the awesomeness of her mysteries, and the beauty of her rituals. And horizontally, you have fought for human values in your emphasis on justice, sovereignty, brotherhood, freedom and all freedoms.

In July of 1980, after the unfortunate loss of his eye, he wrote to me the following:

> أحببتك بعيني الإثنتين، وأحبك الآن بعيني الواحدة التي بقيت لي. فضياع البصر في عين لا يعني ضياع البصيرة". . . ثم يمضي ليقول:
> "إنها معاناة من نكب ببصره، وهو دون بصر نعش يمشي، وصندوقة فارغة تركل بالأقدام. إنظروا إلى الزنابق .... الحق أقول لكم ان سليمان في كل مجده لم يلبس كواحدة منها ... قلت في نفسي والآية ترن في مسمعي رنين بلور يتكسر على رخامة: كيف يريدني مبدع الجمال ان انظر إلى الزنابق وقد اختُطِفْ مني البصر ؟؟ وانى لي ان اميز البهاء عن القبح وقد ساوت الظلمة بينهما في ناظري........"

I loved you with my two eyes, and now I love you with the one eye which is left to me. The loss of sight does not mean the loss of comprehension. . . . My tragedy is the tragedy of one who loses his sight. A man without sight is like a walking casket or an empty box trodden by feet. Behold the lilies of the field ... Verily, I say unto you, even Solomon in all his glory was not arrayed like one of these (Matthew 6:28). I said to myself while these words were ringing in my ears like the ringing of broken crystal on a sheet of marble. How does the Creator of beauty want me to behold the lilies after my sight was snatched away from me? And how can I distinguish between beauty and ugliness after darkness has made them equal?

In 1983, after my trip to the Old Country, Father John wrote to me the following:

"قرأت مانقلته عنك النهار والسفير. تقديم نفسك للقـراء "ابـن فلا ح" رائع. ابن الفلا ح يستشعر ماتستشـعره يا ابـن الفلا ح. عندما يطأ العدو أرضه، انما صدره يطأ. وعندما يقتلع شجرة من شجرات بلا ده، انما شريان من شرايين قلبه يقتلع..."

I have read what you have said to the Lebanese press. Telling the readers that you are the son of a peasant is marvelous. The son of a peasant feels exactly what you feel, O son of peasant. When the enemy steps over his land, he steps over his chest and when he uproots one tree from the trees of his country, he uproots a vein from the veins of his heart.

St. Augustine once said: "I am what I am, O Lord, because you have given me such a good mother." Father John's mother was one of those good mothers. Her thoughts have influenced his thinking and were the basis of his intellectual and spiritual formation. Unfortunately, this good mother passed on to life eternal in 1985. In May of that year, Fr. John wrote to me the following:

Tenderness and Joy

"وكانت امي تخص المعمدان بالتكريم فتحرق البخور امام ايقونته وتغطيها بالورد والرياحين. قلت لها مرة: المعمدان يا امي "كان طويل اللسان. كان لا يرهب ولا يخاف. كان اذا عاث ملك في الارض فســـادا او خان الامانات، يجلده بكلمات من نار. تألقت اسارير امي وقالت: لذا سميتك حنا......"

My mother always favored John the Baptist. Thus she burned incense before his icon and covered it with roses and flowers. I said to her once, Mother, John the Baptist had a big mouth. He did not fear anyone. Even if a king betrayed his trust, the Baptist would lash him with fiery words. The Baptist had a big mouth. My mother smiled and said, that is why I named you John.

In July, 1985, my father passed away in Lebanon. Father John sent me a most moving letter in which he said:

"تلفن لي منذ ساعة تقريباً الارشمندريت الياس الخوري ينعى الي ابا فيليب. لقد تطيبت الارض بجثمانه بعد ان طوع الارض وطبعها بجثمانه. ارضنا في منظوري تضاهي الملكوت قداســة وبــهاء اذ انها تغتذي بأجســاد آبــائنا وامهاتنا، وتتشرب دماء شهدائنا وابطالنا وتستضيف في حناياها الراحلين من احبابنا والغالين علينا.
لا اعرف ابا فيليب ياسيدي. اذكر انك قلت لي في حفلة الذكرى العاشرة لتتويجك انه فلا ح. فلا ح يعني الروح الذي يتجســد من كل ما تطلع الارض من خيرات. فلا ح يعني اليدين اللتين تنســجان من الازاهير ملاءة للحــواكير وتزينانها بافانين الالوان وتضمخانها بافخر الاطياب......"

About an hour ago, Archimandrite Ellis Khouri phoned me and told me that your father passed away. His remains have filled the earth with fragrance after he tamed the earth and left his imprint on it.

In my opinion, our land is equal to the heavenly kingdom in brightness and sanctity. It feeds on the remains of our fathers and mothers and drinks the blood of our martyrs and heroes, and hosts our precious loved ones.

I did not know your father. But I remember your telling me during the celebration of your tenth anniversary in the episcopate that he was a peasant. Peasant means the spirit which incarnates all the gifts of the earth. Peasant means the hands which weave from the flowers a garment for the gardens and decorate it with all kinds of color and bathe it with the most precious fragrance.

Father John is deeply rooted, spiritually and intellectually, in the soil of Lebanon. In one of his letters, he said, "I am away from Lebanon, but I never left it." Perhaps the most tragic event in Father John's life is that cruel, meaningless and uncivil war which is still raging in that country. In a letter to one of his very dear friends in Lebanon, Father John wrote:

"كم مسيحياً في اعتقادك درس القرآن دراسة علمية ايجابية اكاديمية ليدرك كنهه؟؟ والمحمدي هل طالع عظة الجبل ليسوع؟ هل تصفح الانجيل؟ هل ألم بتعاليم من قال فيه القرآن "سلام عليه يوم ولد ويوم مات ويوم يبعث حيا" لا لا فالمسيحي اللبناني والمحمدي اللبناني كلاهما عدو للعقل. العلة ليست في اديانا، العلة هي في ان ابناء هذا الدين يجهل جهلا مطبقا ما يؤمن به ابناء ذاك الدين. فهم لو وعوا "الكتب" لاهتدوا الى ان ما فيها يجمع لا يفرق ويرتق لا يفتق.

هل قرأ المسيحي قول القرآن "يا ايها الذين آمنوا انا خلقناكم من ذكر وانثى وجعلناكم شعوبا وقبائل لتعارفوا ان اكرمكم عند الله اتقاكم"

وهل قرأ المحمدي قول الانجيل "من سألك فاعطه، ومن اراد ان يقترض منك فلا تمنعه. صالح أخاك قبل ان تقدم قربانك الى المذبح. أحسن الى من يبغضك ......

ولم القراءة ... أيسر على عدو العقل أن يقتل وينسف الجسور من أن يقرأ ويعي ..."

How many Christians, in your opinion, have studied the Quran in a scientific positive and academic way in order to understand its essence? And what about the Mohammedan! Did he read Christ's Sermon on the Mount? Did he read the Gospel? Did he understand the teaching of whom the Quran said, Peace be unto him the day he was born, the day he died and the day he will be resurrected? The Lebanese Christian and the Lebanese Mohammedan both are the enemy of reason. The problem is not in our religions. The problem lies in the fact that the followers of this religion are completely ignorant of what the followers of the other religion believe in. Had they studied the books they would understand that religion does not divide, but unites. Did the Christian read what the Quran said? People, we have created you from male and female and made you nations and tribes to understand that the most righteous among you before God is the most pious. And did the Mohammedan read the saying of the Gospel? Ask and you shall receive. If anyone wants to borrow from you, do not turn him away. Make peace with your brother before you bring your bread to the altar. Love your enemy. But why read? It is easier for the enemy of reason to kill and dynamite bridges then to read and understand.

Ladies and gentlemen: These are but a few excerpts from Father John's letters which have nourished my soul. My tribute to him this evening is what he has generously given. "Thine own of Thine own, we offer unto Thee." Castles, palaces and skyscrapers some day will turn into ashes. Wealth, power, fame and glory sooner or later will fade away. In the final analysis, nothing remains except the living word and "in the beginning was the Word."

You have known Father John and Khouriya Souaad for the past twenty-five years and you have loved them. You have known

Father John as your priest, but I have known him as the priest, the writer and the poet. In my opinion, poets are the closest to God's heart because they are the true partakers of the divine nature. They see what we cannot see and they hear what we cannot hear. Their eyes are always focused on the horizon and their ears are always attentive to the silent music of the universe.

Father John, you have labored in His vineyard for twenty-five years. I am sure that the fruit of your labor will nourish your soul forever and ever.

"Well done, thou good and faithful servant."

Two Joys:
The Evangelical Orthodox and
The West Coast Chancery
1987

How significant it is, indeed, that we are gathered here on the eve of a most historic event in the life of Orthodox Christianity, not only in North America, but all over the world. Tomorrow morning, at St. Michael's Church, hundreds of Evangelical Orthodox will be received into canonical Orthodoxy. This mass conversion into Orthodoxy has not occurred since the conversion of the Slavic nations into Holy Orthodoxy almost one thousand years ago. I pray that Sunday, February 8, 1987, will be the dawn of a new era of Orthodox evangelization of this great nation.

We also gather this evening to officially open this West Coast Chancery. On these two occasions, unique in our history, I have been asked to reflect briefly on our early days in this country, thus leading us up to this present evening.

It is not my intention, however, in this brief message, to cover the entire history of our archdiocese. This would require more than a speech this evening. I will try, however, to point out where we were twenty-one years ago at the beginning of my episcopate, where we are now, and what our vision is for the future.

What I Found—and Did
Twenty-one years ago, the Almighty God entrusted me with this vineyard to serve, to nourish and to protect. Needless to say, these first five years of my episcopate were the most difficult years of my life. I will never forget my feelings as I entered the old archdiocese headquarters in Brooklyn, New York, after my consecration. There I was, the Archbishop of New York and all North America, working alone without a deacon, a priest, a

secretary, or even a cook. My experience in administering an archdiocese of such vastness was just inadequate. But "what is impossible to man is possible to God."

Despite his greatness, Metropolitan Antony, unfortunately, did not prepare anyone to succeed him in shepherding this beloved archdiocese. He was a one-man organization and it is amazing how much he accomplished by himself, alone. In 1966, the year he left this world, the budget of the entire archdiocese was $60,000. Our annual financial report consisted of one and a half loose sheets of paper. Half of our clergy were not prepared, either theologically or liturgically, to serve the archdiocese adequately.

There was no retirement plan to give our priests some financial security in the twilight years of their lives. Our theological education program was limited to three or four seminarians, and some of them did not even graduate, due to difficult circumstances. The New York–Toledo war was still raging, and in many communities there were hard feelings among relatives, among neighbors and even among priests.

We had only two departments in the archdiocese, namely the Department of Christian Education and the Department of Sacred Music, and the chairmen of these departments were serving without any financial compensation. Both the constitution of the archdiocese and that of the parishes were outdated and had to be rewritten in order to fit our needs. We had only seventy parishes and the Department of Missionary Activities did not exist.

The entire Western Region, in those days, consisted of four parishes, namely St. Nicholas of Los Angeles, St. Nicholas of San Francisco, St. George of Phoenix and St. George of Portland, Oregon. Our youth movement was getting stagnant, and there was much restlessness in the archdiocese due to the lack of a future vision. Ladies and gentlemen, without any further elaboration, that is where we were.

Faced with such monumental challenges, which caused me many sleepless nights, I was determined more than ever to face these problems head-on and not surrender to the luxury of inaction, heart attack and open-heart surgery notwithstanding. I remember one of our lay people, in the fall of 1966, telling me, "Your Eminence, you do not need a staff, you need a broom." I embarked on the reorganization of the archdiocese, deeply convinced that the challenges could not be met by the bishop alone, because the Church is not the bishop alone, but the totality of all the believers.

First and foremost on my mind was to know my flock. Thus, in one and a half years, I visited every parish within the archdiocese. A new financial system was initiated. More seminarians were sought to study theology and more than twenty departments were created. A staff was hired to assist in our work and a new archdiocese headquarters was acquired in Englewood, New Jersey. Our youth movement was rejuvenated and I am happy to inform you that the office of our youth director has already been transferred to the Chancery of the West Coast.

Our Spiritual Roots in Charity and Unity
The successive wars in the Middle East have caused much destruction and much pain in that area. We have sent millions of dollars to help alleviate the needs and some of the suffering of these unfortunate people in that region. I have met with almost every American President since Dwight D. Eisenhower on behalf of a just and lasting peace in the Middle East. The Middle East was not the only area of our human concern. Consequently, we have helped Mexico, Africa, Southeast Asia, let alone needy people here in our own country. We have been spending fifteen percent of our annual budget on charity; I believe that our people should be commended for that.

We have organized the Antiochian Women of North America. We have founded the great Order of St. Ignatius of Antioch. It is heartwarming, indeed, to note here that since its inception ten years ago, the Order has contributed more than $2,000,000 to various archdiocesan projects in this country and abroad.

We have hosted two patriarchs, thus giving our people the opportunity to rediscover their spiritual roots. We have purchased the Antiochian Village and initiated a very elaborate camping program for our young people. We have erected the Heritage and Learning Center to house our spiritual and cultural library and heritage museum. This center has already become the educational and spiritual home for our clergy and laity.

We have reunited our Antiochian people on this continent after sixty years of division between Russi and Antaki, and subsequently between New York and Toledo. The long dark night of division is over, I hope forever.

I have mentioned to you that in 1966, our annual budget was $60,000. Our budget for the current fiscal year is $1,356,300. I still feel that this budget is inadequate.

In 1966, we had seventy parishes. Today, we have 135 parishes, and with the reception of the Evangelical Orthodox into canonical Orthodoxy, the number of our parishes will increase to 150. Twenty-one years ago, we had seventy-five priests; today we have about two hundred priests and deacons and ninety-five percent are graduates of universities and seminaries. This tremendous progress which we have made is unprecedented in the modern history of the Orthodox Church.

Looking to the Future

We are where we are today because of your hard work and Christian commitment during the past twenty-one years. I believe that we have come a long, long way. Where do we go from here? What about the future? I have been preaching to you that spiritual progress has no limits; consequently, we cannot accept the status quo and surrender to stagnation. Our destiny is to continue the struggle until "we rest in Him," as St. Augustine put it. Thus, we still have many frontiers to explore, many horizons to discover, many stars to reach and many dreams to dream.

Ladies and gentlemen, as we anticipate with great joy the events which will take place tomorrow morning at St. Michael's Church in Van Nuys, and the events which will take place at St.

Nicholas Cathedral in Los Angeles the following Sunday, our immediate challenge is the chancery on the West Coast. Since my first archpastoral visit to California, twenty-one years ago, many of you have been stressing the need for a bishop on the West Coast. When we had only four parishes on the West Coast, I did not feel that the time was ripe for such a move, but now we have a different situation. With the help of God and you, the number of parishes in the Western Region has increased from four to twenty and our future possibilities are unlimited.

Based on these facts, last year, I appointed a committee of distinguished individuals to help me find a place to house this bishop. The committee worked hard, and thanks be to God, its efforts were crowned with success. Thus, the West Coast Chancery is no longer a dream; it is a reality.

Tonight, because of a financial deficit in preparing this chancery, we must raise the balance of this money which is required. I am appealing to your generosity to help us raise this needed sum of money. Our pledge system is based on a three-year period, and I look for your response. And please remember that "God loves a cheerful giver."

Finally, tomorrow morning we will witness the first Orthodox spiritual invasion of America. Let us pray that we may be worthy of this sacred moment. We do have a great future in California in particular, and in this country, in general. Thus, for the sake of Orthodoxy and our future generations, let us ask the Almighty God to accept the prayers of our sincerity, from this new West Coast Chancery, that He will continue to guide us in carrying the Gospel "to the ends of the earth" (Acts 1:8)!

Struggling Against the New Iconoclasm
Michigan, 1987

The text of my message to you this year is taken from the Epistle of St. Paul to the Ephesians: "For we do not wrestle against flesh and blood, but against principalities, against powers, against the rulers of the darkness of this age, against spiritual hosts of wickedness in the heavenly places" (Ephesians 6:12).

Two years have elapsed since we last met in Boston. Let us take a few minutes to reflect on some of the significant events which have taken place during the past two years. First and foremost, as you know, we are commemorating this year the twelve-hundredth anniversary of the triumph of the Church over the heresy of iconoclasm. The war against icons has led to a tremendous Christological controversy. The iconoclasts claimed that "the form of the servant assumed by Christ, was no longer in the realm of realities. It is important, therefore, that Christians, if they desire to anticipate the glory that is His, should contemplate God in the purity of their hearts, and not in artificial images of a historical past that is now over." Briefly, this was the argument of the iconoclasts.

Response to the Iconoclasts

The Church was fortunate, indeed, to have brilliant and articulate luminaries such as John of Damascus, Theodore the Studite, Patriarchs Germanos and Nicephoros, who valiantly and courageously defended her theology vis-à-vis iconoclasm. These theologians emphatically stated that it is indeed possible to make an image of Christ, because "the Word was made flesh and dwelt amongst us, and we beheld His glory, the glory of the only begotten of the Father, full of grace and truth" (John 1:14). Thus, since Christ became man and was seen, heard and touched by us, the Christian iconographer can represent his human character, because He became like one of us by assuming the totality of our human nature, except sin. The representation, however, of Christ's divine and incomprehensible essence is beyond the realm of iconography and art.

St. John of Damascus clearly stated this reality as follows:

> If we made an image of the invisible God we would certainly be in error, but we do nothing of the sort; for we are not in error if we make the image of the Incarnate God, who appeared on earth in the flesh, and who in His ineffable goodness lived with human beings and assumed the nature, the thickness, the shape and color of the flesh.

We are most grateful to the Church of the iconoclastic era for defending the Orthodox Faith, and thus preserving for us the beautiful icons which adorn our churches and instill in us a deep sense of the holy. Moreover, the icons in our churches remind us that the Church of the Old Testament, the Church of the New Testament and the Church throughout history is praying with us and interceding for our salvation. Briefly then, to deny the representation of the human nature of Christ is to deny the reality of the Incarnation. Such denial poses a tremendous Christological problem for the Church and destroys her foundation.

New Iconoclasms
Despite the victory which the Church scored against the iconoclastic heresy, iconoclasm continued to challenge the Church relentlessly through many philosophical, political and socioeconomic ideologies. Such ideological challenges are no longer aimed at church icons, but rather at man, the living icon of God. In the Book of Genesis, we read that God "created man in His own image, in the image of God created He him; male and female, created He them" (Genesis 1:27). The Bible reveals to us that man is God's most precious creation. He gave him "dominion over the fish of the sea, and the birds of the air, and over the cattle and over all the earth, and over every creeping thing

that creepeth upon the earth" (Genesis 1:26). Surely, the incarnation has a cosmic dimension; however, the primary purpose of God's marvelous intervention in human history was to embrace man and restore him to that divine sonship and, consequently, that divine image which was distorted by sin.

The so-called Age of Enlightenment in Europe inaugurated a new era of iconoclastic heresies such as godless humanism, godless secularism, and godless Marxism, just to mention a few. Man, in both capitalist and communist societies, is enslaved and reduced to a mere tool of production. In a speech delivered on the occasion of accepting the Templeton Award at Buckingham Palace in London, the famous Russian author, Alexander Solzhenitsyn, said:

> The failings of human consciousness, deprived of its divine dimension, have been a determining factor in all the major crimes of this century . . . the contemporary developed West demonstrates by its own example that human salvation can be found, neither in the possession of material goods, nor in merely making money. Our life consists not in the pursuit of material success, but in the quest of worthy spiritual growth. Our entire earthly existence is but a transitional stage in the movement toward something higher, and we must not stumble and fall, nor must we linger fruitlessly on one rung of the ladder.

On the global level, the Church today is beset by all kinds of iconoclasm, such as abortion, euthanasia, genetic engineering, test-tube babies, world hunger, totalitarianism, social injustice, and above all, the horrible threat of nuclear war which will destroy our entire civilization. But why should we be subjected to this kind of dehumanization? We read in the Psalms that God made man "a little lower than the angels and has crowned him with glory and honor" (Psalm 8:5). Where is that glory and where is that honor if we treat each other like mere objects?

On the national level, we are not faring any better. If the decade of the sixties was marked by some kind of romantic idealism and the reduction of the Gospel into social action, and if the decade of the seventies was marked by the theology of personal salvation as a reaction to the sixties, this decade is clearly marked by greed, selfishness, and moral relativism. It is the decade of "the end justifies the means."

In the May 25, 1987, issue of *Time* magazine, in an article entitled "Ethics," I read the following:

> Large sections of the nations' ethical roofing have been sagging badly, from the White House to churches, schools, industries, medical centers, law firms, and stock brokerages—pressing down on the institutions and enterprises that make up the body and blood of America.

Since the beginning of this decade, the symptoms of this moral decadence have manifested themselves in the insider trading scandal on Wall Street, the Iran Contra scandal which involved top leaders of this nation, the sports scandal at Southern Methodist University, the moral collapse of Christian fundamentalism, child abuse, teen suicide, drug addiction and the continuing disintegration of the American family. This is to mention but a few of the cancerous trends which are eating at the heart of this nation. The Woody Hays philosophy, which is winning at any price, is sweeping the whole country. What happened to St. Paul's admonition to Timothy "that an athlete is not crowned until he competes according to the rules" (2 Timothy 2:5)? And what would happen to our world if each one of us sets his or her own rules? Do you see such iconoclastic signs in America? May our merciful God grant us wisdom to discern between the Kingdom of God and the kingdoms of this fallen world.

The Second Event: Meeting the Evangelical Orthodox
The second event which we are celebrating this year did not happen in the remote past, but rather a few months ago. It is

indeed refreshing to celebrate the present once in a while, instead of always celebrating the past. I do not intend to elaborate on the history of the former Evangelical Orthodox Church, because that history was published both in *The WORD* and *AGAIN* magazines.

In June, 1985, while visiting our faithful on the West Coast, with our Father in Christ, Patriarch Ignatius IV, Bishops Peter Gillquist, Richard Ballew and Jon Braun asked for an appointment to see us. The appointment was granted immediately. The meeting between our visitors and us was very cordial, frank and friendly. I asked the bishops to send me whatever literature they had written on the Orthodox Faith. His Beatitude, Patriarch Ignatius, asked me to do everything possible to help the Evangelical Orthodox. A few weeks later, I received books, pamphlets, magazines and essays written by members of the Evangelical Orthodox Church. My aides and I spent days reading and examining the contents of this literature and found it very Orthodox, if not super-Orthodox.

In March, 1986, I received Bishop Peter Gillquist at the archdiocesan headquarters, and after a lengthy and fruitful discussion, I submitted to Bishop Peter a proposal and told him, "If your Synod accepts this proposal, soon you will be within canonical Orthodoxy." Bishop Peter asked if the entire Evangelical Synod, with some of their clergy and laity, could meet with me in September, 1986; his request was immediately granted.

On September 5, 1986, I was delighted to receive at the archdiocesan headquarters the members of the Evangelical Orthodox Synod, together with some of their clergy and laity. Needless to say, the meeting was marked by frankness, sincerity and openness. After four hours of intensive theological discussion, something happened which I will never forget. Bishop Gordon Walker of Tennessee broke down and with tears in his eyes, said to us, "Brothers, we have been knocking on Orthodox doors for ten years, but to no avail. Now, we have come to your doorsteps, seeking the Holy, Catholic and Apostolic Faith; if you do not accept us, where do we go from here?" I was deeply touched and moved by the sincerity of Bishop Walker and from that moment on, I had no doubt whatsoever that that dialogue, baptized with tears, will be crowned with heavenly joy.

On Saturday, September 6, we viewed a liturgy which was served by the Evangelical Orthodox at St. Anthony's Church in Bergenfield, New Jersey. The liturgical remarks which we made to them were welcomed and graciously accepted. On Monday, September 8, the members of the Evangelical Orthodox Synod and their clergy and laity met alone at St. Vladimir's Seminary to make their final decision.

That Monday afternoon, their presiding bishop, Peter Gillquist, called me and informed me that they would like to come and see me. They did and after we prayed, the first gentleman to ask for the floor was Peter Gillquist, who said, "Your Eminence, we have met and in one mind and one accord have decided to accept your proposal in its entirety; therefore, we humbly ask you to receive us into canonical Orthodoxy through the Antiochian Orthodox Christian Archdiocese of North America." At that historical moment, I felt that the Holy Spirit was indeed filling the room and with tearful eyes, I said, "Brothers, welcome home!"

Chrismation and Ordination
The next step in this process was to chrismate about two thousand people and ordain sixty-seven priests and eighty-four deacons. It was my intention to finish this task before Holy Pascha, 1987, in order to give the Evangelical Orthodox the joy of celebrating Easter within the bosom of the Holy Orthodox Church; hence my decision to begin the chrismations and ordinations on February 8, 1987. The question then was: How do I ordain sixty-seven priests and eighty-four deacons within two months? Thus, I began thinking about multiple ordinations. But is there anything wrong with multiple ordinations? Faced with this difficult question, I decided to examine three main sources: (a) the Scripture, (b) the Holy Canons of the Ecumenical

and local Councils, and (c) the patristic writings.

As a result of much research, I found that the Scripture supports my position vis-à-vis multiple ordinations. The Prophet Joel, foretelling the events of Pentecost, says: "And it shall come to pass afterward, that I will pour out My Spirit on all flesh; your sons and daughters shall prophesy, your old men shall dream dreams, and your young men shall see visions" (Joel 2:28). Notice here the words, "pour out My Spirit on all flesh." He did not say "pour out a little tiny bit of My Spirit on one head only," but rather, "pour out My Spirit on all flesh." Do we not, in reality, blaspheme against the Holy Spirit when we try to limit the limitless and bind the boundless? Cannot the Holy Spirit who descends on one deacon and one priest, during the same Liturgy, descend on two deacons and two priests, or ten deacons and ten priests, or even more, and do we not chrismate through the power of this same Holy Spirit, hundreds and thousands of people at the same service?

In the Gospel of John, chapter 20, verse 22, we read: "And when He had said this, he breathed on them, and said to them, receive the Holy Spirit." Notice here the words, "He breathed on *them* and said to *them*, receive the Holy Spirit." He did not breathe on one of them only, but on all of them.

Let us now examine the Book of Acts, which is one of the most authentic documents in the New Testament. Chapter 2 of Acts begins with these words:

When the day of Pentecost had come they were all together in one place. And suddenly a sound came from heaven like a rush of a mighty wind, and filled all the house where they were sitting. And there appeared to them tongues as of fire, distributed and resting on each one of them. And they were all filled with the Holy Spirit.

Let us look at chapter 6 of the same book, and examine the following text:

Now in these days, when the disciples were increasing in number, the Hellenists murmured against the Hebrews because their widows were neglected in the daily distribution. And the Twelve summoned the body of the disciples and said: It is not right that we should give up preaching the Word of God to serve tables. Therefore, brethren, pick out from among you, seven men of good repute, full of the Spirit and of wisdom, whom we may appoint to this duty. But we will devote ourselves to prayer and to the ministry of the Word. And what they said pleased the whole multitude, and they chose Stephen, a man full of faith and of the Holy Spirit, and Philip, and Prochorus, and Nicanor, and Timon and Parmenas and Nicolas, a proselyte of Antioch. These they set before the apostles, and they prayed and laid their hands upon them (Acts 6:1–6).

If this was not a multiple ordination, I do not know what it was.

Having examined the Scripture and finding nothing against multiple ordinations, I proceeded to examine the Holy Canons of both the Ecumenical and local Councils. I challenge anyone to produce one single canon against multiple ordinations. To solidify my position even further, I have examined certain patristic texts related to ordination and found nothing whatsoever against multiple ordinations. I do not think that the Fathers of the early Church, and especially the Fathers of the Ecumenical and local Councils, were stupid.

There is historical evidence that multiple ordinations were practiced both in the East and in the West. The Church of Constantinople stopped this practice after the twelfth century, while the practice continued in the Church of Alexandria until now, and in the Church of Russia until the sixteenth century. In his *Polemics Against the Latin West*, Patriarch Photios accused the Latin clergy of so many things such as, "shaving their chins, eating strangled meat, bathing with women, fasting on Saturdays during Lent, and eating cheese and dairy products during

Lent." He surely could have come up with a condemnation of the practice of multiple ordinations, if this practice was wrong.

Ladies and gentlemen, based on these facts, I traveled to California, Tennessee, Alaska and Seattle; and Bishop Antoun traveled to Mississippi, Indiana and Saskatoon, Canada, to accomplish this holy mission. I wish I could go beyond words to describe to you the joy which I experienced as I was chrismating these little children of the Evangelical Orthodox faithful. Every experience I had was like a chapter from the Book of Acts. I felt as if the Church was recapturing her apostolic spirit and rediscovering, once again, her missionary dimension.

Negative Reactions
Unfortunately, while we were immersed in this joy, some of our Orthodox brethren in this country were busy pointing fingers at me and accusing me of wrongdoing. We have challenged those brethren, more than once, to produce one theological, ecclesiological or canonical reason to justify their hostile attitude, but to no avail. Someone said to me, "You should know, these people are jealous of the Antiochian Archdiocese." But why should they be jealous? The Evangelical Orthodox visited them before they came to us. I asked one of our Evangelical Orthodox clergy, "You mean to tell me that you have been knocking on Orthodox doors for ten years and no one opened?" He said, "No, your Eminence, the doors were opened, but there was nobody in."

Instead of rejoicing with us, they were angry with us. Instead of sending us bouquets of roses, they were throwing stones at us. Instead of congratulating us, they were spreading all kinds of rumors and insinuations against us. Indecisive people never make history. History was made by visionary and courageous leaders who were not afraid to explore new frontiers and discover new horizons. I was not worried that the Evangelical Orthodox will pollute my *ethnos*. Christ did not die on the cross and was resurrected from the dead to save Arabs, Greeks and Slavs, only; for in Christ, "There is neither Jew nor Greek, there is neither slave nor free, there is neither male nor female, for you are all one in Christ Jesus" (Galatians 3:28).

Finally, for those who have ears to hear, I cannot but reiterate the words of our Lord in Matthew 23, verse 13: "Woe unto you scribes and Pharisees, hypocrites! Because you shut the kingdom of heaven against man; for you neither enter yourselves, nor allow those who would enter to go in." I am tired of empty and meaningless slogans. They talk about evangelization and do not evangelize. And when I received the Evangelical Orthodox, they criticized me. I want everyone to know that if I had to do it again, I would do it a million times. They talk about Orthodox unity and do not unite. They talk about brotherly love and close their churches in my face. I am not angry; I am hurt, but this will never deter me from pursuing my most cherished dream, which is Orthodox unity in America.

The Third Event: Beirut

Ladies and gentlemen, the third event which we are celebrating at this convention is the most welcome visit of a very beloved brother and a very dear friend, His Eminence, Elias Audi, Metropolitan of the Archdiocese of Beirut, Lebanon. Metropolitan Elias brings with him wounds and suffering of the Lebanese people, especially our Orthodox brothers and sisters who have suffered most in Lebanon and continue to suffer. I am sure that all of you have seen on your television screens the tragedy of Lebanon, and in particular, the tragedy of Beirut. The last time I saw that city was in 1983. I am not exaggerating if I tell you that the destruction of Berlin and Leningrad during World War II is nothing to compare with the devastation which befell the beautiful city of Beirut.

In order to give you a true picture about this cruel, uncivil and devastating war which has been raging in Lebanon for the past thirteen years, I would like to share with you the following statistics. Bearing in mind that the population of Lebanon does not exceed three million, you can see the extent of this tragedy.

600,000 people have been displaced and made refugees in their own country.
150,000 have been killed.
250,000 have been wounded.
70,000 have been disabled.
50,000 have been made orphans.
224 villages have been destroyed. Shreen, my home town, was one of them.
50 villages have been completely bulldozed.
400 churches, mosques and schools have been destroyed.
45 religious leaders have been murdered.

The Orthodox have suffered most because they do not have a militia. They have chosen to be victims, rather than butchers.

After the near-collapse of the American University Hospital in West Beirut, our St. George Orthodox Hospital in East Beirut has emerged as the primary hospital in the entire country of Lebanon. This hospital is under the direct supervision of Metropolitan Elias of Beirut. There was a time when the Archdiocese of Beirut, through its institutions and especially St. George Hospital, was helping the entire Patriarchate of Antioch. The thirteen years of war have left a tremendous financial strain on the hospital, and yet, St. George Hospital continues to minister to the poor and needy, free of charge, regardless of political and religious affiliation. St. George Hospital cannot continue this ministry indefinitely, and it will be a sad and shameful day when the poor will wither away and die at the gates of our hospital because of the lack of funds.

In his article entitled, "St. John Chrysostom, the Prophet of Charity," Father George Florovsky said:

> The Christians are called to renounce all possessions and to follow Christ in full confidence and trust. Possessions can be justified, only by their use; feed the hungry, help the poor, and give everything to the needy. Here is the main tension, and the main conflict between the

spirit of the church and the mood of the worldly society. The cruel injustice of actual life is the bleeding wound of society. Chrysostom goes so far as to denounce even the splendor of the temples. The Church, he says, is a triumphant company of angels and not a shop of silversmiths. The Church claims human souls, and only for the sake of the souls does God accept any other gifts. The cup which Christ offered to the disciples at the Last Supper was not made of gold. Yet, it was precious above all measure. If you want to honor Christ, do it when you see him naked, in the person of the poor. No use if you bring silk and precious metals to the temple, and leave Christ to suffer cold and nakedness in the outside. No use if the temple is full of golden vessels, but Christ himself is starving. You make golden chalices, but fail to offer cups of cold water to the needy. Christ, as a homeless stranger, is wandering around begging, and instead of receiving him, you make decorations."

This powerful statement by John Chrysostom made me tremble. I hope it does the same to you. It is, therefore, our Christian and moral responsibility to do our utmost to help the poor and the needy in Lebanon.

My fellow coworkers in Christ, today we are announcing the establishment of a new charitable organization called the Benefactors of St. George Orthodox Hospital in Beirut. This organization will encompass the whole archdiocese on the local, regional and North American levels. More details will be sent to you from our headquarters when we complete our organizational structure.

My dear friends, it is impossible for this message to cover all the events which have taken place in the life of this archdiocese during the past two years. We must, first and foremost, thank God, who is the source of "every good and perfect gift," for His sustenance and continued blessings.

Finally, I would like to leave you with these words from the second letter of St. Paul to the Corinthians:

> But we have this treasure in earthen vessels to show that the transcendent power belongs to God and not to us. We are afflicted in every way, but not crushed; perplexed, but not driven to despair; persecuted, but not forsaken, struck down, but not destroyed; always carrying in the body the death of Jesus, so that the life of Jesus may also be manifested in our bodies (2 Corinthians 4:7–10).

Editor's Endnotes:

1. *On February 8, 1987, Metropolitan Philip begins the chrismations and ordinations of the Evangelical Orthodox at St. Michael's Church in Van Nuys, California, followed by a similar celebration at St. Nicholas Cathedral in Los Angeles.*

2. *Also in the fall of 1987, Philip meets with Pope John Paul II in Columbia, South Carolina, and undertakes a fundraising campaign for St. George Orthodox Hospital in Beirut.*

3. *The dedication of the West Coast Chancery will not take place until 1990; the address here presented is the opening of the chancery, i.e., the beginning of preparation for the hierarchy.*

4. *Announcing the Benefactors of St. George Orthodox Hospital in Beirut, Philip presents the first archdiocesan portion of what eventually totals one million dollars for the suffering people of Lebanon.*

Chapter 14

LOOKING TO NEW HORIZONS

> *There is no doubt in my mind that we Orthodox have the richest spiritual heritage and the most glorious history. But for heaven's sake, let us not become prisoners of our history. Many times I feel that we Orthodox are crushed by the weight of our long history to the point that we cannot lift up our eyes to look at the horizon, and beyond the horizon.*
>
> Metropolitan Philip

- *Reflecting on the Past, Rejoicing in the Present, Focusing on the Future: The Fiftieth Anniversary of St. Vladimir's Seminary, 1988*
- *How Youth Can Affect Their Culture: The Pan-American Youth Conference, 1988*

In 1988, the Metropolitan is invited to speak at two occasions of importance: the fiftieth anniversary of St. Vladimir's Seminary, and the Pan-American Youth Conference. We have entitled this chapter **"Looking to New Horizons,"** *taken from his first talk, because in both addresses Philip is calling his listeners to look to the horizon of their future, and then to find the way to get there, according to the Christian vision.*

The first presentation is given before Metropolitan Theodosius of the Orthodox Church in America (OCA), many other hierarchs, the dean of the school, Father John Meyendorff, and a multitude of other clergy and distinguished laity. But this is not merely a congratulatory speech; it is a call to be "creative instead of frozen, dynamic instead of paralyzed," as he says. The reader will quickly discover in what sense Philip means these words; they are to look for a horizon which is truly relevant to the contemporary world.

The second address in this chapter shows that Philip truly understands the complexity of the youth as they must confront the society and culture in which they live. Clearly, His Eminence is informing the youth that it is the Church which presents them with the only horizon toward which they should aim; secularism and humanism are empty, and as he says, will leave them "divorced from God." This horizon of the Church is based on the truth that "they are created in the image and likeness of God ... that they are a little less than angels ... and that, therefore, they are somebody, from someplace, going somewhere!" Thus they are not to think so little of themselves that they will follow the herd. Finally, then, these young people are encouraged by Philip "not to be conformed to the world, but to be transformed by the renewal of the mind" (Romans 12:2).

J. J. A.

Reflecting the Past, Rejoicing in the Present, Focusing on the Future
The Fiftieth Anniversary of St. Vladimir's Seminary, 1988

I greet you this evening in the name of the Risen Lord. May the eternal light of the empty tomb always shine in your hearts. It is indeed an honor and a pleasure to celebrate with you the Golden Jubilee of St. Vladimir's Seminary. Since its inception, St. Vladimir's Seminary has been a spiritual oasis in a world thirsty for the living water and hungry for the heavenly bread. Undoubtedly, the establishment of this institution was one of the brightest moments in the history of Orthodoxy on this continent. Thus, to celebrate the fiftieth anniversary of the seminary is to *reflect on the past, rejoice in the present and focus on the future.*

The history of St. Vladimir's Seminary can be described as a journey which began in Russia and reached our blessed shores, via Europe. Surely, the courageous and dedicated founders of this school deserve our love, gratitude and admiration. Despite the difficulties and many obstacles which they faced, they were determined to persevere and succeed. From humble and inadequate headquarters on West 121st Street in New York City, under the brilliant and charismatic leadership of the former dean, the Very Reverend Alexander Schmemann, the seminary made a tremendous leap forward to its present location in Crestwood.

In the beginning, the seminary emphasized two important goals: first, to prepare priests and bishops to shepherd the flock, and second, to publish theological books for the edification of the Orthodox faithful and the enlightenment of those who seek Christ "in spirit and in truth." In both areas, the seminary has done a magnificent job. No wonder that after fifty years of struggle and hard work, we find hundreds of priests and many bishops shepherding our communities, which are spread across this continent from the shores of New Jersey to the shores of California and from Florida to Alaska.

Where Do We Go from Here?
I have stated before you this evening that the basic goals of the seminary, which were the publication of theological books and the education of priests to serve our ethnic communities, were very well realized. The question now is: "Where do we go from here?" Do we have a mission to America and are we prepared for this mission? Can Orthodoxy in America acquire an American expression to appeal to mainstream America? These are serious questions which challenge all of us, especially St. Vladimir's Seminary.

In 1985, writing about mission, the scholarly dean of the seminary, the Very Reverend John Meyendorff, said, "Is our liturgical life meaningful enough to be shared with newcomers? Or is it functionary only in terms of providing comfort and satisfaction to our present membership?" To whom does Father John refer when he speaks about "newcomers"? They are the millions of unchurched and churched Americans who are diligently searching for apostolicity, catholicity, holiness and meaning in religion. But can we impose on "newcomers" the cultural and religious expressions of the Middle East, Byzantium and Tsarist Russia? Is it not time that we seriously reexamine some of our liturgical and theological expressions in the light of our experience on this continent? I am not speaking here about changing the fundamentals of our faith, which "once for all was delivered to the saints." I am just referring to certain liturgical and cultural expressions which are foreign to the American mind.

Who on earth, except St. Vladimir's Seminary, can face this challenge and provide answers to these agonizing questions? And where on earth, except at St. Vladimir's Seminary, can scholarly research begin on the future of Orthodoxy in America? We cannot evangelize and "Orthodoxize," if you please, America without a clear vision of the future. I am a firm believer in the struggle of ideas, for in the final analysis, the best idea will be the winner. St. Vladimir's Seminary is the perfect arena for such spiritual and intellectual struggle, and not SCOBA. I want to confess to you this evening that the biggest disappointment of the twenty-two years of my episcopate has been SCOBA. Every time I return home from a SCOBA meeting, I feel as if I have been a false witness before the judgment seat of the Almighty God.

Let Us Not Become Prisoners

Beloved friends, there is no doubt in my mind that we Orthodox have the richest spiritual heritage and the most glorious history. But for heaven's sake, let us not become prisoners of our history. Many times, I feel that we Orthodox are crushed by the weight of our long history to the point that we cannot lift up our eyes to *look at the horizon* and beyond the horizon. When we lose the creative spirit to make history, we spend the rest of our lives reading history, and when the present becomes frozen and the future seems paralyzed, we tend to focus on the past.

As we celebrate the millennium of Orthodoxy in Russia and the Golden Jubilee of our seminary, let us bridge the distance between the past and the present. Let us beseech the Risen Lord to help us recapture the spirit of Ss. Peter and Paul, Ss. Cyril and Methodius, St. Nina and St. Herman of Alaska.

I always look back with nostalgia to the beautiful time which I spent at St. Vladimir's Seminary. From personal experience, God at the seminary is more than an object for abstract theological speculation. He is real and very much alive in the eucharistic and liturgical celebrations, the classrooms and even at the "breaking of the bread." And the students at the seminary are more than statistics and sociological concepts. They are icons of the living God, always surrounded with love and care in their joy and sorrow, in their success and failure, and in their hope and despair.

Congratulations, St. Vladimir's Seminary, on this most auspicious occasion. Our eternal gratitude goes to the Board of

Trustees, to our Dean, the Very Reverend John Meyendorff, the members of the faculty and all generous benefactors who continue to help us keep this torch burning. We have walked with God for fifty years. I pray that the Risen Christ will walk with us forever.

How Youth Can and Must Affect Their Culture
The Pan-American Youth Conference, 1988

At this glorious occasion I have been asked to discuss with you the following topic: "How Youth Can and Must Affect Their Culture." To begin my discussion of this very important topic this evening, I have chosen three quotations: two from First Corinthians, and the third is one of my own. Unfortunately, it reflects the thinking of so many people who have become slaves to our modern culture.

St. Paul said, "All things are lawful for me, but all things are not helpful. All things are lawful for me, but I will not be brought under the power of any" (1 Corinthians 6:12).

The second quotation is also from First Corinthians: "Do you not know that your body is the temple of the Holy Spirit which is in you, whom you have from God, and you are not your own?" (1 Corinthians 6:19).

The third quotation which reflects the sickness of this age reads as follows: "We are nobody, from noplace, going nowhere."

Let us now dwell, for a while, on the main topic of this discussion, "How Youth Can Affect Their Culture." Youth can either affect their culture or become slaves to it. As we go through life, from the cradle to the grave, we experience different stages of development. Perhaps the most important and most dynamic one is youth. Studying the life of young people, we cannot help but notice three main developments.

Biological Development
The first stage in youth development is a biological one. Young people usually experience radical biological changes. Arms and legs grow so fast, at times they are difficult to control. In addition to this, the reproductive organs develop, noses may grow and pimples may appear. For example, teens oftentimes feel

uncomfortable with their own bodies. Things are happening which they do not quite understand and they simply cannot control. The teenage years are the time when we must begin realizing our heterosexual identity. We begin to discover who we are as a male or a female. Our sexual identities are discovered as we relate to persons of the opposite sex. To protect yourself from the temptations of modern culture, it is best for you to be in the company of other teens in a sexually nonthreatening environment such as your youth group, where you are free to relate with persons of the opposite sex as persons, in a healthy and intimate atmosphere without overt sexual expression.

I understand that in our schools today, these biological developments are discussed. The Church and the family, however, must be prepared to discuss with young people the ethics of sex, church values and responsibilities. The morality of sex is left untouched by the schools. For example, while the possible methods of abortion may be discussed in school, the moral implications of abortion are left open-ended for each person to decide on his or her own. Where, then, are we going to find the criterion to make our decisions? Can we rely on the decisions of the Supreme Court of 1973 vis-à-vis abortion? Absolutely not. Here we find ourselves as Orthodox Christians in complete conflict with the state. What is legal is not necessarily moral. The standards of the Church are different from the standards of the state. Thus, we must rely here on what the Gospel of Jesus Christ, the Apostles, the saints and the canons of our Church state on this matter. The answer seems obvious. Abortion is murder. Issues such as premarital sex, abortion, homosexual practice and AIDS may be discussed in school. The Church, however, has the final answer because she is the eternal truth.

Emotional Development
The second stage in youth development is an emotional one. The adolescent can experience rapid emotional swings. Teens are often very moody. Within the course of a day, and some-

times within the course of a phone call, you may be experiencing huge mood swings, all the way from happiness to depression; hence the high percentage of teen suicide in our society. Young adults go through a type of mourning. Their childhood is gone and responsibility is fast approaching. Teens now see their parents in a different light and often say "no" to their values.

Youth is a time of restlessness, rebelliousness, questioning and doubt. I remember when I was a teenager, I used to see question marks stretched from earth to heaven. To illustrate this difficult stage, I would like to mention to you the biblical story of the Prodigal Son. Here is a young man who rebelled against his father and said to him, "Give me my share of your wealth." His father gave him what he asked. The Bible says that this young man took his money and went to a far-off city and wasted his money on his own pleasure. When he spent all he had and tasted the pain of starvation, he "came back to himself," and returned home to be received by his father with great joy. He repented; he turned around. St. Isaac the Syrian describes repentance as "the trembling of the soul at the gates of paradise." The good thing about this prodigal son is the fact that he "came back to himself." In other words, he repented. The trouble with many young people today lies in their lack of repentance, and thus, they end up committing suicide or become eternally lost.

To make things more difficult, our culture provides no absolutes. Everything is relative, they say. One of the major problems which young people are facing in this culture is the problem of relativism. What is relativism? Relativism teaches that knowledge of truth is relative and dependent upon time, place and individual experience. According to this philosophy, the Bible is no longer relevant because it was written almost two thousand years ago and there is no absolute truth.

This fundamentally contradicts what the Church always proclaimed: Jesus the Messiah is the Alpha and the Omega, and He is the eternal truth, yesterday, today and forever. "I am the way, the truth and the life," our Lord said. The eternal and absolute truth is not rooted in philosophy, psychology, or sociology. On the contrary, it is rooted in the biblical truth. There is a tremendous tension in this culture between the Kingdom of God and the kingdom of Caesar. If everything is relative, where then is our point of reference?

For example, I want you to consider this: A few years ago homosexual practice was considered to be deviant behavior. Now many people accept it as a new lifestyle and it is openly advocated in the media without reservation. But is homosexual practice an acceptable lifestyle? Let us turn to the Scripture, our point of reference, and find out what it says.

In his Epistle to the Romans, chapter 1, verse 22, St. Paul said:

Claiming to be wise, they became fools, and exchanged the glory of the immortal God for images resembling mortal man or birds or animals or reptiles. Therefore God gave them up in the lusts of their hearts to impurity, to the dishonoring of their bodies among themselves, because they exchanged the truth about God for a lie and worshipped and served the creature rather than the Creator, who is blessed forever! Amen.

For this reason God gave them up to dishonorable passions. Their women exchanged their natural relations for unnatural, and the men likewise gave up natural relations with women and were consumed with passion for one another, men committing shameless acts with men and receiving in their own persons the due penalty for their error.

And since they did not see fit to acknowledge God, God gave them up to a base mind and to improper conduct. They were filled with all manner of wickedness, evil, covetousness, malice. Full of envy, murder, strife, deceit, malignity, they were gossips, slanderers, haters of God, insolent, haughty, boastful, inventors of evil, disobedient to parents, foolish, faithless, heartless, ruthless. Though they know God's decree that those who do such things deserve to die, they not only do them but approve those who practice them (Romans 1:22–32).

What you have just heard from St. Paul is the divine truth and we must take it very seriously. A relativist will tell you, "What revealed truth? St. Paul is old fashioned and outdated. *I* decide what is moral and what is immoral." Again in Romans 6:23, St. Paul said, "For the wages of sin is death, but the gift of God is eternal life in Christ Jesus our Lord."

Intellectual Development
The third stage in youth development is an intellectual one. Throughout my adult life, every time I have an encounter with young people, especially high school and college students, I have always been challenged with so many questions, such as: the existence of God; the origin of the universe; the origin of life; evolution; genetic engineering. Where did we come from? Who are we? Where are we going? Is there life after death? Will history really end? Most of the time young people do not ask questions to learn, but to challenge, and to show that they also know something. In Arabic we say, "The most dangerous thing about knowledge is half-knowledge." The Church does have answers to all these questions. All we have to do is to pray and read. We must realize first and foremost that Christianity is not an intellectual adventure. Christ did not perform miracles once, "because of their disbelief."

Our modern culture seriously lacks a healthy and sound theological world-view. The European Renaissance and the so-called Age of Enlightenment have inaugurated two dangerous philosophies, namely secularism and humanism. What is secularism? Secularism is a system of beliefs which rejects all forms of religious faith and worship; the view that public education and other matters of civil policy should be conducted without the introduction of a religious element. And what is humanism? Humanism is a system or mode of thought or action in which human and secular interests predominate. You can see from these two definitions that the aim of both secularism and humanism is to divorce God from our world and culture. Unfortunately, many of our teachers today believe in such philosophy, and all our political and social actions reflect this decadence. Do we have to accept secularism and humanism? Is there not an alternative?

Yes, this alternative is the Orthodox view of God, man, history and nature. The Orthodox view states that we are somebody, from somewhere, going someplace. The Orthodox view states that we are created in the "image of God and His likeness" and that God made us "a little less than the angels," and that He "crowned us with glory and honor." The Orthodox view interprets history as creation, fall and redemption and that we are living now between the first and second coming of Christ. "And He shall come again with glory to judge the living and the dead."

The Body and the Soul; Images of Sexuality

The last thing I would like to discuss with you this evening is perhaps the most challenging question. How can Orthodox youth affect their culture? Orthodox youth have two choices: either accept relativism, secularism and humanism and thus become a part of this decadence; or reject the distorted values of this culture by adhering to a wholesome Orthodox view of God, man and history.

Almost everything in this culture leads to corruption. There is so much emphasis on the body at the expense of the soul. There is so much talk about physical fitness and very little about spiritual fitness. Most of our TV advertisements are geared toward the satisfaction of our primal instincts and are full of deceit. For example, buy this kind of perfume and the boys will fall all over you. Drive this kind of car and the girls will flock around you. Wear this or that kind of jeans and you will look as sexy as Brooke Shields. Buy this kind of deodorant and you will be very popular. Use this or that kind of hair spray and you will look beautiful. Use Ragu spaghetti sauce and you will eat a ton of spaghetti. Buy this or that bone for your dog and he will smell wonderful.

And what about the deafening, erotic music, such as, "I Want Your Sex," by George Michael; "Gonna Dress You Up in My Love," by Madonna; "We Will Make Heaven a Place on Earth," by Belinda Carlisle. She implies here that mere human love affairs can do this. And what about, "Boom, Boom, Boom, Let's Go Back to My Room," "Do You Want to Ride in My Mercedes, Boy?" and songs like, "Get out of My Dreams and into My Car," "Anything for You," "Girls, Girls, Girls," "Touch Me," and last but not least, by Tina Turner, "What's love got to do with it? What's love but a secondhand emotion?"

In addition to this, I feel that we are living in a disposable culture. We have disposable dishes, disposable glasses, disposable spoons, disposable forks and even disposable lovers. We treat each other like objects and not like God's icons. We even have disposable marriages. If you ever marry and your wife cannot have children, you may "rent a womb" and when the child is born, you take him or her from the natural mother. The Church teaches us that marriage must be holy and without blemish, and that what "God joined together, let no man put asunder."

The brokenness of the American family today screams at us. Just think of how many children are being raised by single parents. The Church teaches that marriage is a sacramental bond between two persons and not a social experience or a civil contract—if it succeeds, fine, and if not, there is always the civil court. We must understand that Christian marriage is theocentric and not egocentric. The late Father Alexander Schmemann said: "The problem with marriage today is the identification of marriage with happiness and the refusal to accept the cross in it."

The mission of Orthodox youth, then, is to transform this culture and this world and bring it back to God. We are God's stewards and everything we have belongs to Him.

The mission of Orthodox youth is to say "no" to homosexual practice, "no" to sex outside the community of marriage and "no" to divorce. Do not be afraid to be different. Do not become part of the herd. Cling to the sacred values which your Church represents. Walk in the light and you will never stumble. "All things are lawful for you, but all things are not helpful. All things are lawful for you, but you must not be brought under the power of any."

Finally, I say to you what St. Paul said to the Romans:

I appeal to you therefore, brethren, by the mercies of God, to present your bodies as a living sacrifice, holy and acceptable to God, which is your spiritual worship. Do not be conformed to this world, but be transformed by the renewal of your mind, that you may prove what is the will of God, what is good and acceptable and perfect (Romans 12:1, 2).

Chapter 15

BEARING WITNESS TO THE LIGHT

> *This "One Holy, Catholic and Apostolic Church" cannot be Eastern or Western, Northern or Southern, Greek or Russian, Japanese or American. This Church, which was established by Christ Himself through the power of the Holy Spirit, cannot be limited by geography or culture.... Unfortunately, some of us Orthodox have failed to differentiate between external cultural forms and fundamental spiritual expressions... between Holy Tradition and human tradition.... The question now is: Where do we go from here? Do we have a mission to America and are we prepared for this mission? Can Orthodoxy in America acquire an American expression to appeal to the mainstream America?*
>
> Metropolitan Philip

- *Even So I Send You: Bringing America to Orthodoxy, 1989*

AND HE LEADS THEM

Metropolitan Philip closes out the decade of the 1980s with one of the strongest presentations he has ever made. It is delivered in 1989 at Anaheim, California, where the archdiocese gathered for the biennial convention. If he began the 1980s speaking about newness, he ends the 1980s with the manifestation of the fruits of newness. The call to bring America to Orthodoxy requires that we bear witness to the light; that that light is offered in Orthodox Christianity; that we must sincerely distinguish between old forms and the true substance of the Faith, which is always new; that we observe the entry of the Evangelical Orthodox into canonical Orthodoxy as proof of bearing witness; that we need to be aware of both the potentials and dangers of the culture in which we bear witness; and finally, that the oldest form of giving, the tithe, must become the newest form of bearing witness.

The reader will note that Philip by this point is so committed to bringing America to Orthodoxy that he devotes little time, as was the case in the past, to the administrative and more perfunctory matters of the archdiocesan affairs. This issue is one from which he will not deviate; for him it is larger than life!

This address is presented in its entirety.

J.J.A.

Even So I Send You:
Bringing America to Orthodoxy
Anaheim, 1989

The theme of our convention this year is, "Bear Witness to the Light: Bringing America to Orthodoxy." In John 20:21, our Lord said, "As the Father has sent Me, even so I send you."

Last year, we celebrated the first millennium of the baptism of the Russian people. Five years from now, we will celebrate the bicentennial of Orthodoxy in North America. Eleven years from now, we will celebrate the second millennia of Christianity. When I welcomed the former Evangelical Orthodox Church into canonical Orthodoxy, I extended a genuine invitation to America to come home and embrace the New Testament Church, the Church which was born on Pentecost Day, the Church of Peter and Paul, the Church of Ignatius of Antioch, Athanasius of Alexandria, John Chrysostom, the Cappadocian Fathers, the Church which preserved the Faith and which was "once for all delivered to the saints."

Being Orthodox Christians
Some might ask, "Why has America not come home?" We have been on this continent for two hundred years. The answer is that while it is true that we have been on this continent for two hundred years, we have yet to introduce ourselves to America. We have done a good job building homes in America for Orthodox who have come from the Middle East, Greece, Russia and Eastern Europe; but unfortunately, we have failed to build an Orthodox home for America. Orthodoxy in North America continues to be identified with foreign cultural forms and liturgical expressions.

A few years ago, I was invited to a dinner party. Most of the invitees were not Orthodox. During the course of the evening, a gentleman, with much curiosity, asked me, "Bishop, are you Catholic?" I said, ""If you mean Roman Catholic, I am not." He asked, "Are you Episcopalian?" I said, "I am not." Then he asked, "Are you Greek Orthodox?" I said, "I am Orthodox, but not Greek." Then he asked, "Are you Russian Orthodox?" I said, "I am Orthodox, but not Russian." The poor man was utterly confused. He asked, "If you are not Roman Catholic, and if you are not Episcopalian, and if you are not Greek Orthodox, and if you are not Russian Orthodox, then what on earth are you?" I said to him, "I am a Christian Orthodox." I tried to explain to him our jurisdictional situation, but he remained more confused than ever.

Afterward, he told me about a visit that he made to an Orthodox Church on the Feast of Epiphany. Although he did not understand our iconography, which is quite different from the Renaissance art, he was overwhelmed by the mitred bishop, his long flowing beard and his glittering vestments. "The bishop," he said, "circled the baptismal font chanting in a foreign language. Then he dipped his hands into the water and sprinkled the people, and I saw the East." Most Americans think that the Orthodox Church is some exotic and mystical cult from the East.

In the May, 1989, issue of the *Atlantic Magazine*, there was an article entitled, "Eastern Orthodoxy." The author began his article with the following words:

> The celebration, last year, of one thousand years of Orthodox Christianity in Russia, offered us a number of televised reports, many showing bearded priests wearing tall, odd-looking hats, moving gravely through incense-filled rituals.

This is precisely how the West perceives the Orthodox Church.

Preaching Orthodoxy to America
When the American media refer to the main religions in this country, it always mentions Protestantism, Roman Catholicism

and Judaism. Can we blame America for its ignorance of Orthodoxy? I think not. It is we Orthodox who are to blame. In his Epistle to the Romans, St. Paul says: "How are men to call upon Him in whom they have not believed? And how are they to believe in Him of whom they have never heard? And how are they to hear without a preacher?" (Romans 10:14).

After two hundred years on this continent, we have yet to preach Orthodoxy to America. Instead, we have been busy being Eastern, Arabs, Greeks, Russians and everything else except Orthodox Christians. I am not anti–national cultures; as a matter of fact, I have urged you in the past to study all cultures, if you really want to be educated. We must differentiate, however, between cultures and ethnocentrism. Ethnocentrism or philetism was condemned as a heresy by the Synod of Constantinople in 1872. I consider ethnocentrism a form of racism, which is not compatible with the Christian message.

In his famous work, *The Mystical Theology of the Eastern Church*, Vladimir Lossky says:

> The Orthodox Church, though commonly referred to as Eastern, considers herself, nonetheless, the universal Church; and this is true in the sense that she is not limited by any particular type of culture, by the legacy of any one civilization (Hellenistic or otherwise) or by strictly Eastern cultural forms.

This One Holy Catholic and Apostolic Church cannot be Eastern or Western, Northern or Southern, Greek or Russian, Japanese or American. This Church, which was established by Christ Himself through the power of the Holy Spirit, cannot be limited by geography or culture. St. Paul put it this way: "There is neither Jew nor Greek, there is neither slave nor free, there is neither male nor female; for all are one in Christ Jesus. And if you are Christ's then you are Abraham's offspring, heirs according to the promise" (Galatians 3:28, 29).

Forms and Substance
Unfortunately, some of us Orthodox have failed to differentiate between external cultural forms and fundamental spiritual expressions, and conversely, between Holy Tradition and human traditions. A few months ago, on a cold, wintry morning, I was having coffee in my little dining room, when one of our priests arrived to do some work for us. I invited him to have coffee with me. He obliged. I said, "How is everything?"

He said, "Well, yesterday I was at the seminary working on my thesis, and decided to have lunch with the seminarians. While we were eating, one of the seminarians sitting across the table from me asked, 'Are you an Antiochian priest, Father?' I said, 'Yes.' 'Tell me, Father,' he said, 'how come your metropolitan does not have a beard? How come your metropolitan does not wear his jibbee (rasson) all the time? How come he does not wear the bishop's hat and veil?'" The priest told the seminarian, "Although I have a beard, which I am sure pleases you, my metropolitan feels—and he is right—that these things which you have mentioned are not necessary for life eternal."

In 1950, while in Damascus serving the Church as a deacon and secretary to the late Patriarch, Alexander III, I wrote an article in one of the leading Syrian newspapers about some external forms in the Church such as beards, cassocks, etc. The reaction of the ecclesiastical authorities to my article was one of the reasons which prompted me to leave the Middle East for the New World. I want you to know, however, that the seminarian at St. Vladimir's Seminary was not the only one who felt that way about me. After my consecration to the episcopate in 1966, every time I traveled to the Middle East on Church business, my own father would look at me, shake his head and ask, "Are you really a bishop? Where is your beard?"

Ladies and gentlemen, I am now fifty-eight years old and still do not know the significance of beards in the history of salvation.

Last year, on the of the fiftieth anniversary of St. Vladimir's

Seminary, I said the following which I would like to share with you:

> The basic goals of the seminary, which were the publication of theological books and the education of priests to serve our ethnic communities, have been well realized. The question now is, where do we go from here? Do we have a mission to America and are we prepared for this mission? Can Orthodoxy in America acquire an American expression to appeal to mainstream America? These are serious questions which challenge all of us.

In 1985, writing about mission, Father John Meyendorff said, "Is our liturgical life meaningful enough to be shared with newcomers? Or is it functionary only in terms of providing comfort and satisfaction to our present membership?" To whom does Father John refer when he speaks about newcomers? They are the millions of unchurched and churched Americans who are anxiously searching for oneness of faith, apostolicity, catholicity, holiness and meaning in religion. But, can we impose on newcomers the cultural and religious expressions of the Middle East, Byzantium and Tsarist Russia? Is it not time that we seriously reexamine some of our liturgical and theological expressions in the light of our experience on this continent? I am not speaking here about changing the fundamentals of our faith, which "once for all was delivered to the saints." I am just referring to certain liturgical and cultural expressions which are foreign to the American mind.

Despite the tremendous improvement in modern communication, we have not been able to create one global culture. Thus the Church must continue to missionize, evangelize, teach and serve in the context of many cultures. We all know that the Church which was born on Pentecost Day was deeply rooted in Jewish concepts and traditions, yet the early Christians struggled not to impose such Hebraic concepts and traditions on the newly baptized Christians. It is also true that the early Christian preachers preached Christ in the context of Jewish history,

Jewish culture and Jewish expectation, but they never confused the reality of the new covenant with the old one. "The shadow of the law has been annulled by the coming of grace." The Incarnation was the fulfillment of all Old Testament prophecies.

This is not to say that everything was harmonious among the early Christians who embraced the new religion. The Book of Acts and especially the writings of St. Paul prove otherwise. There was conflict between Paul and Peter about circumcision. Listen to the Book of Acts: "But some men came down from Judea and were teaching the brethren, unless you are circumcised according to the custom of Moses, you cannot be saved" (Acts 15:1). There was dissension among the brethren. Thus Paul and Barnabas and some others were appointed to go to Jerusalem to settle the matter.

As a result of this controversy, the first council in the history of the Church was convened in Jerusalem. James presided, and when the discussion was over, he made the following announcement: "Therefore, my judgment is that we should not trouble those of the Gentiles who turned to God. But we should write to them to abstain from the pollutions of idols and from unchastity and from what is strangled and from blood" (Acts 15:19, 20). And thus the practice of circumcision was dismissed as unnecessary.

Another example about the interaction between the new religion and the prevailing culture is the Christian transformation of the meaning of the word *logos*. The Greeks believed that all knowledge stems from the *logos*. St. John the Evangelist and Justin Martyr continued to use the term *logos*, but in a Christian context. Thus the Christian Logos is the Word, the Christ who became incarnate and died for the sins of the world. This is how the early Church succeeded in maintaining the content of Christian truth, but formulated it in such a way that it was understandable to the Hellenistic mind.

It is evident, therefore, that the Church must interact with culture without becoming enslaved by any culture. Consequently, the Church can use the good elements in every culture for divine purposes, and by the same token, oppose the demonic elements which can be found in every culture, in order to transform civilizations and bring the world back to God.

Bringing America to Orthodoxy
Some of you might ask, "What is the bishop talking about?" Well, I am talking about bringing America to Orthodoxy. The dilemma which we are facing is: To what kind of Orthodoxy do we want to bring America? Can we bring America to an Arabized, Hellenized or Russianized Orthodoxy? Is it possible that the life-giving Spirit which is always vivifying the Church made her freeze at one point in history? If you look at some Byzantine icons of the Pantocrator, you would think that Christ is a Byzantine emperor. Do we want to impose this culture on America? Moreover, can we impose our Byzantine and Slavonic melodies, which are the product of other cultures, on America? It is time to stop romanticizing the past and listen to "what the Spirit is saying to the Church."

Last year, I had the pleasure of meeting at the Heritage and Learning Center with the chairman of our Sacred Music Department and some good members of this department to discuss the state of our sacred music in this country. During our discussion, one of our outstanding choir directors asked me this question: "Which one is our music, the Byzantine or the Slavonic?" I said to her, "If you are asking this question as an American Orthodox, I would say neither one is your music." Both Byzantine and Slavonic music, despite their beauty, reflect cultures which are foreign to the American mind. This does not mean that we should take all that beautiful music and throw it in the fire. On the contrary, we should use it as our reference and our source of inspiration.

If we can say, "No man is an island," we can rightly say also, no culture is an island by itself. While preserving their authenticity, all cultures are influenced by other cultures. No one can create anything *ex nihilo* (out of nothing), except the Almighty God. I believe as we grow in this country and become more and more rooted in the North American soil, we will develop our own schools of iconography, hymnology and even theology.

Robert E. Webber in his book, *Common Roots*, says:

> We have argued that missions should be engaged in the translation of Christian principles from one culture to another, rather than the imposition of a western culturized Christianity upon a non-western culture. The Christian principle which stands behind this effort is that of the incarnation. As God in Christ entered into humanity and history and became one of us, so we are to enter into another culture and to participate in it fully in order to communicate the Gospel.

Four Critical Points

If we are serious about bringing America to Orthodoxy, and I know we are, then we have to have an agenda with the following items:

1. We Orthodox must realize once and for all that we are on this continent to stay, and that we should integrate our old cultures into the new cultural reality of this land. Moreover, we must not stifle the creative and artistic spirit of our young people, but rather encourage them to experiment in all matters related to the cultural expressions of Orthodoxy, strictly under the supervision of the Church.

2. It is very difficult to bring America to a divided Orthodoxy, and it is even more difficult for America to understand our jurisdictional problems. Therefore, in order to evangelize and missionize America, we Orthodox must first put our own house in order. In 1984, in Worcester, Massachusetts, I said the following:

> We cannot be agents of change in full obedience to the truth unless we transcend ethnocentrism and establish

a new Orthodox reality in North America. I am not against ethnicity, if ethnicity means a return to the spirituality of the desert fathers, Syrian fathers, Greek fathers and the Slavonic fathers. But if ethnicity means a narrow, fanatic, ghetto mentality, which separates us from each other, then I am definitely against such ethnicity.

3. As you well know, we have in this country an organization called The Standing Conference of Canonical Orthodox Bishops. The primary purpose of this Standing Conference, since its inception, was and still is to unite Orthodoxy in North America. Unfortunately, this conference has not been "standing" at all! Last February, Metropolitan Theodosius of the Orthodox Church in America and I called for the restructuring of SCOBA and the creation of a commission on Orthodox unity. I believe that SCOBA can serve a tremendous purpose in the life of the Church if we take it seriously and remain faithful to its original goal. But, if it continues to be peripheral, ineffective and absent from the American scene, then we have no choice except to pursue our goal without SCOBA. In the final analysis, the Church and those responsible for her life are under judgment if they do not make disciples, baptize, teach and faithfully proclaim the word of His truth. In his book, *Incarnate Love*, Vigen Guroian wrote:

> Orthodoxy in America is at a critical moment. Until now, the Orthodox churches have been immigrant churches retaining, in bold relief, the stamp of their national origin. The time has come, however, when to persist as such risks not only estranging vast numbers of American-born Orthodox, but closing off all future opportunities for effectively witnessing to the Orthodox faith in this American society.

4. Last, but not least, if we are serious about Orthodoxy in America, then we must seriously examine our financial com-

mitment to the Church and her future goals. This is necessary if we want to remain faithful to the Gospel's command to make disciples, baptize and teach. We have to be willing enough and generous enough to sacrifice some of our means in response to this challenging ministry. Church history teaches us that millions of martyrs faced martyrdom joyfully for the life of the Church, giving their blood for Christ's sake. Is it too much for us to give some of our material possessions for the cause of missions? We cannot evangelize and missionize America with empty words. It is unfortunate, indeed, that many of us on both the parochial and archdiocesan levels continue to contribute very little to our parishes and archdiocesan budgets.

Many of our parishes were established by early immigrants around the turn of the century, and some were also created during the Depression years. And yet, proportionately speaking, the early immigrants, despite their many hardships, planted the seeds of Holy Orthodoxy on this continent and were more generous than we are, our wealth and affluence notwithstanding.

In Malachi, the Scripture says:

Will man rob God? Yet, you are robbing Me. But you say, how are we robbing Thee? In your tithes and offerings. Bring the full tithe into the storehouse, that there may be food in My house; and thereby put Me to the test, says the Lord of hosts, if I will not open the windows of heaven for you and pour down for you an overflowing blessing (Malachi 3:8–10).

The Place of Tithing and Bearing Witness

Tithing was not invented by some Protestant group. It is as old as the Scripture itself. Both the Old and New Testaments testify to this reality. Moreover, early Christian documents support this practice beyond doubt. Tithing was and still is a sacred part of our worship. The faithful of the Old Testament brought to the temple one tenth of their harvest, and the early Christians brought to church the fruit of their labor. A portion of their offering, namely, bread and wine, was consecrated by the bishop, and the rest of their tithe was distributed to the poor by the deacons. Everything we have in this world belongs to God. "The earth is the Lord's and the fullness thereof, the world and those who dwell therein" (Psalm 24:1). Thus we give God a small portion of what He has given us. "Thine own, of Thine own, we offer unto Thee." I pray from the depths of my heart for the day when all the faithful of this archdiocese will practice tithing. Is it too much to give God ten percent of what He gives you, and who could take with him or with her one penny to the grave?

Not only do we need to tithe in the Church, but also we must remember that we cannot bear witness to the Light and bring America to Orthodoxy unless we immerse our whole being in that Light, and bring Orthodoxy to ourselves first. Thus, evangelism must begin within each and every one of us as individuals, families and communities. In his book, *Eastern Orthodox Mission Theology Today*, James Stamoolis says:

> What better way to see the missionary work of the Church than to see it in the development of the life of its members. Note two facts about this concept: First, that Mission is seen as the role of each individual, not of some special person or group; second, that it again illustrates the corporate view of the Church. The sanctification of the individual is in the context of the local Church, and the result of the individual sanctification is the extension of the Church's mission in the world.

Individual sanctification, family sanctification and community sanctification must be our first and foremost goal, if we hope to bring America to Orthodoxy. The early Christians were not known by their highly developed theology, but rather by their exemplary life, and because of that, many pagans were converted to Christianity. I realize that our Orthodox communities cannot be isolated entities in this ocean of Americanism, yet I strongly believe that we can make a difference in this society by daring to be different. Who wants to be a part of the herd? And why should we accept the distorted values of this sick environment? In his Epistle to the Ephesians, St. Paul says: "Look carefully then how you walk, not as an unwise man but as wise, making the most of the time because the days are evil. Therefore, do not be foolish but understand what the will of the Lord is" (Ephesians 5:15–17).

Bearing Witness in the Contemporary Culture

The days are indeed evil. Look around you and what do you see—crime, drugs, abortion, rented wombs, racism, injustice, homelessness, world hunger, pornography, rape, etc. Last April, a young woman was jogging in New York City's Central Park in the evening. A gang of teenagers who went to the park "wilding" attacked her, beat her savagely and raped her repeatedly, leaving her almost dead. When some of them were asked, "Why did you do that?" their answer was, "For the fun of it." This is just one example of the moral decadence which is eating at the heart of our society.

Bear witness to the Light by daring to be different and, with the grace of God, you will make a difference. I call on Orthodox parents to exercise—not dictatorship—but loving parental authority over their children. Please stop psychoanalyzing them; instead give them some doses of that old-fashioned medicine which our parents and grandparents called "common sense." Our children and young people are the most precious gifts which we have received from God and we must do everything we can, through the family and the Church, to protect them, "because the days are evil."

There is so much emphasis in our society on ecological pollution, and rightly so, because God did not give us this beautiful earth to be polluted and raped. When the unfortunate oil spill polluted the beautiful shores of Alaska a few months ago, Ted Koppel justifiably devoted so many "Nightline"s to this problem. But what about that spiritual pollution which is blackening the soul of America? How come this kind of pollution is not properly addressed? The American family is polluted, our schools are polluted, our movies and TV programs are polluted, our streets are polluted, our music is polluted, our literature is polluted, our businesses are polluted, our politics are polluted and even religion in America is polluted.

The task of Orthodox evangelism, therefore, is not to glorify the past in a triumphalistic attitude, but to humbly proclaim Orthodoxy as we received it from the Apostles, the Fathers, the saints and martyrs for the past two thousand years. Believe me, brothers and sisters, America may be in some sense polluted, but it is also truly thirsty for the Living Water and the Heavenly Bread. America is waiting for us. Let us go forth and do the job: "As the Father has sent Me, even so I send you."

Finally, my friends, I beseech you to bear witness to the Light; the Light which darkness cannot overcome. Orthodoxy with its rich spirituality and sound teachings can transfigure this world and inaugurate a new day, a new age and a new creation, as the author of Revelation wrote:

> I saw a new heaven and a new earth, for the first heaven and the first earth had vanished, and there was no longer any sea. I saw the Holy City, new Jerusalem, coming down out of heaven from God, made ready like a bride adorned for her husband. I heard a loud voice proclaiming from the throne: 'Now at last God has His dwelling among men. He will dwell among them and they will be His people, and God Himself will be with them' (Revelation 21:1–3).

Part III

The Third Decade
The 1990s

Chapter 16

TO THY NAME GIVE GLORY:
The Twenty-fifth Anniversary

> *Jesus said, "In Me you may have peace. In the world you will have tribulation; but be of good cheer, I have overcome the world" (John 16:33). The history of this world is full of war, tragedy and catastrophe. Christ did not overcome the world with guns, tanks, missiles. . . . On the contrary, he overcame the logic of this world by His most effective weapon: love.*
>
> Metropolitan Philip

- *A Storm in the Desert, 1991*
- *Our Hearts in Flames: Address to President Hraoui, 1991*
- *God as Witness to My Vow, 1991*

AND HE LEADS THEM

Philip's twenty-fifth anniversary in 1991 found the world in turmoil, and the three pieces of literature included in this chapter clearly reflect this state.

Metropolitan Philip writes the first piece immediately before the war which became known as Desert Storm, and Philip honestly addresses the disturbing events which are on the horizon in the Arabian Desert: "It is a real threat to the peace of the world and to the fragile peace in the Middle East . . . We do not condone the Iraqi invasion of Kuwait . . . Nor do we condone the massive American buildup in Saudi Arabia and the Gulf." The reader will see how Philip is not only warning about "winning the battle but losing the war"; he is praying also that "the peace from above" will prevail. His warning was correct and his prayer continued.

The second entry of 1991 is his address to President Elias Hraoui of Lebanon. While the Middle East is caught in "the war in the desert," Lebanon has begun to be restored after decades of the torment and destruction created by civil war. Philip delivers this address at the archdiocese headquarters where he welcomed the president, the prime minister, various foreign ministers, and other honored guests during an elaborate evening dinner. The metropolitan, however, not only speaks in thankfulness and joy that "the tempest has subsided and the clouds have dissipated"; he also reflects philosophically on those dark nights, hoping that they will teach the lessons which lead to new dreams and challenges for Lebanon, and indeed, the entire Middle East.

The third address of 1991 is precisely focused on Philip's twenty-fifth anniversary, as he addresses the Archdiocesan Convention gathered in Washington, D.C. Patriarch Ignatius IV, while originally intending to be there for this occasion, could not be present because of unforeseen reasons. Nevertheless, Philip begins the address with a focus on the University of Balamand, the present project of the patriarch, one to which Philip has given so much over the years. In general, however, the metropolitan quickly moves to reviewing the twenty-five years in light of his vow at his consecration: "It is up to God who sees the secrets of the heart, and it is also up to you, His Church, to judge whether or not I remained faithful to my vow."

Philip then moves on to review the latest projects of his administration for the good of the Church and archdiocese: the Antiochian Village, the West Coast Chancery, the Antiochian Christian Orthodox Radio Network, etc. Each project is cause for Philip to ponder with his people the past twenty-five years. This ends, however, not in pride and arrogance, but in praise for God: "O Lord, let Your name, not mine, be praised."

J. J. A.

A Storm in the Desert
1991

While the world is preparing to celebrate Christmas, we see a storm brewing in the Arabian Desert and we hear the drums of war beating everywhere. It is sad, indeed, that as we celebrate the birth of the Prince of Peace we look around to find no peace and no "good will toward men." We have failed utterly to find "that peace from above," because we have been trying in vain to attain it through so-called peace treaties, which, very often, create more problems than they solve. Any peace which is not based on Christian values and principles is doomed to failure.

Jesus said: "In Me you may have peace. In the world you will have tribulation; but be of good cheer, I have overcome the world" (John 16:33). Christ is speaking here about that inner peace which the world cannot give—the peace which springs from the hearts of people. Only in Him will we find peace, "and in His light shall we see light." Unfortunately, the history of the world is full of war, tragedy and catastrophe. Christ did not overcome the world with guns, tanks, missiles, chemical and atomic weapons. On the contrary, He overcame the logic of this world by His most effective weapon: *love.* How easy it is for nations to wage war against nations and how difficult it is to invade our inner beings and discover within us the peace of Christ.

What is happening in the Arabian Desert is very disturbing, to say the least; it is a real threat to the peace of the world and the fragile peace in the Middle East. We do not condone the Iraqi invasion of Kuwait and the misery which was inflicted on the Kuwaiti people. Nor do we condone this massive American military buildup in Saudi Arabia and the Gulf. I hope that we have not reached a dead end, because a dead end means catastrophe. It is alarming that the position of our government continues to be "either or" and the Iraqi position "neither nor."

I wonder what happened to the art of diplomacy. Webster's Dictionary defines diplomacy as "the art and practice of conducting negotiations between nations." Why then do we not give diplomacy a chance? Why do we not encourage the Arab people to solve their own problems? Saddam Hussein must realize that he cannot defeat the United States militarily. By the same token, the United States must realize that it will undoubtedly win the battle, but it will ultimately lose the war. After almost a century of betrayal, mistrust and unfulfilled promises, the Arabs no longer trust the intentions of the West. Thus, the majority of them consider this Western jingoistic policy in the Middle East as a new crusade. If we are in Saudi Arabia to secure the flow of oil to the industrialized world, we have already achieved that goal, and in this case a military attack against Iraq, which will cost us many American lives, is unjustifiable. Blood is more precious than oil.

The Arabs are tired of our double-standard morality in the Middle East. And in this respect, one might ask: Where was our military might when Turkey invaded Cyprus and divided that beautiful island? Where was our military might when Israel invaded Lebanon, unprovoked, in 1982 and continues to occupy South Lebanon? Why does our military might not protect the little Palestinian children who are being shot daily by Israeli bullets? I am afraid that a military confrontation with Iraq might cost us tens of thousands of American lives. We certainly do not want our young men and women to come home in body bags. Nor do we want hundreds of thousands of innocent Iraqis to be incinerated by our bombs and missiles. Is this the kind of legacy we want to leave in the Middle East? The Arab masses in general, and the Muslim people in particular, will never forgive us. Instead of waging war, let us give economic sanctions against Iraq a chance. Negotiation is more prudent than military confrontation.

Let us fervently pray during this season of hope and reconciliation that the Prince of Peace will instill His love in our hearts

AND HE LEADS THEM

and grant our leaders enough wisdom to understand that "nation shall not lift up sword against nation, neither shall they learn war any more" (Isaiah 2:4).

Our Hearts in Flames: Address to President Elias Hraoui of Lebanon
1991

Mr. President, Mr. Prime Minister, Foreign Ministers, Your Eminences, Ladies and Gentlemen:
On behalf of myself, and of my brothers, the leaders of the Christian and Islamic communities, I would like to welcome you warmly into this Lebanese home, hoping that your visit has fulfilled its objectives in the interest of Lebanon.

Our beloved country, Lebanon, has experienced many lean years and many devastating storms which almost destroyed its independence and its very existence. We give thanks to the Almighty God, however, because the tempest has subsided and the clouds have dissipated. And through your great efforts and your sincere and wise leadership, Lebanon has begun to be restored.

What Was Lost

The immigrants and displaced Lebanese are still deeply rooted in the Lebanese soil. We therefore watched the unfolding of its tragedy with great agony, despite the enormous distances separating us from our tormented homeland. Whenever we saw a house, a store, or a factory consumed by fire, *our hearts burst into flames*. Whenever we saw a bullet rupturing a Lebanese artery, the very arteries of our hearts ruptured with it.

Mr. President and distinguished guests: Now that the cannon has fallen silent, and the sound of the bullet has been hushed, we must examine ourselves and deeply contemplate the factors which have led us to the edge of the abyss. In my opinion, the crisis in Lebanon was not only political, but cultural, educational and ethical as well. Politics became decayed, corrupting everything. Culture lost its authenticity and became Westernized. Education lost its direction and morality collapsed. Thus, the saying of an Arab poet has proven to be true in us: "Nations survive, if their morality remains alive, but if it vanishes, then they themselves also vanish."

The English historian, Arnold Toynbee, describes history as *challenge and response*. Consequently, the nations which respond to history and face its challenge will live, but those which do not face the challenges of history, do not deserve to live!

The precious treasure which Lebanon possesses is neither oil, nor silver, nor gold, but the person himself. Give me a noble, upright, faithful and honest Lebanese, and I will give you a country shining as a beacon of light which all countries will emulate.

In his book, *We and History*, Dr. Constantine Zreik said:

> Our guarantee is in the honesty of our determination, provided that we do not remain compliant and passive, i.e., allow others to affect us and dominate us, while we do not affect anyone. It is in the sublimity of our longing for creative and historical action. It is in the unity of our yearning to hold the judgment of history in our hands, and not to hold it against us. It lies, firstly and finally, in the extent of our evaluation of the conditions which are required by these preeminent goals, and of the responsibilities which are laid on us, and in our honest readiness to make the needed sacrifice. It is in the extent to which we ascend to the level of the important and serious challenge and of our response to it by something more significant and more splendid.

What We Hope: The Taif Accord

Mr. President and esteemed guests: We, the majority of the Lebanese Arab immigrants, have a burning desire to see Lebanon sound and intact, independent within its internationally recognized borders, interacting with its neighbor Syria and the Arab world, predominant in social justice, and liberated from political sectarianism. No privilege should be given to any Lebanese except for his service to Lebanon. We are anxious, Mr. President, to see the displaced allowed to return to their homes, which they built by the sweat of their brows—and we mean *all* the displaced, from *all* regions, regardless of their political and religious affiliations. Social integration among the Lebanese will not happen unless all the displaced return to their homes. And we hope that they will return in the very near future! We also look forward to the implementation of Resolution 425 of the United Nations, so that South Lebanon is liberated from foreigners and agents. Likewise we would like to see that the Taif Accord is implemented. This accord is an important step towards rebuilding a more stable and beautiful country.

The whole world supported the Taif Accord, particularly the United States of America. President George H. Bush, addressing the Fortieth Convention of the Antiochian Orthodox Christian Archdiocese in North America, during July 1991 in Washington, D.C., stated the following:

> In Lebanon, we see the first tangible signs of political progress, of domestic reconciliation and restored order, after a decade and a half of nightmarish civil war. Thanks to the Taif Accord, a truly sovereign Lebanon, one free of all armed militia and foreign forces, is no longer just a dream.

Ladies and gentlemen, we supported the Taif Accord before it was born, in spite of its shortcomings. When the Taif assembly was in session, a friend of mine who is a member of the Lebanese Parliament called me from Saudi Arabia and asked my opinion about the proposed accord. After he had briefed me about it, I said to him: *"Agree to it without hesitation."* I said this because there was no other alternative, except more destruction and devastation. What did the "war of liberation" and the "war of extermination" achieve, other than the liberation of the nation from many of its young people, and the

extermination of its cultural role—by which Lebanon was distinguished from the very beginning of this century?
Had it not been for the Taif Accord, the two Beiruts would not have become one. Had it not been for the Taif Accord, the militias would not have dissolved, and the sniping and the snipers would not have disappeared. Had it not been for the Taif Accord, the Lebanese army would not have entered South Lebanon. Had it not been for the Taif Accord, Lebanon would not have become close to Syria and the Arab world, liberating itself from the complex of fear vis-à-vis Arabism and Islam. Ultimately, had it not been for the Taif Accord, the treaty of cooperation and brotherhood between Lebanon and Syria would never have been signed; this treaty should have been signed fifty years ago!

Lebanon in Unity with Arab Neighbors

In spite of all these achievements, there is yet a group of Lebanese who continue to curse the Taif Accord and to demonstrate their hostility to Syria and the Arabs, as if they wanted to weave a cocoon around themselves in which they become strangled, exactly as silkworms. These people still ask what connects Lebanon with Syria, or Lebanon with Jordan, or Lebanon with Egypt? To these people we say: what connects Lebanon with Syria or any Arab country is much more than what connects Florida with Alaska, or New York with Hawaii, despite the fact that to fly from Florida to Alaska takes more than thirteen hours, and to fly from New York to Hawaii takes more than ten hours. Do those who cry over Lebanon forget the ties of kinship, of history, of geography, of language, of culture, and of economy which connect Lebanon with the Arab world? We live today in the era of economic integration and social openness between nations, in spite of their differences in historical and geographical nature. Is it not more appropriate for the Arab world to adopt this integration and openness, especially when we stand at the threshold of the twenty-first century?

Mr. President, toward the end of the last century, and at the beginning of the twentieth century, our Lebanese forefathers played a distinguished cultural role in creating the modern Arabic renaissance. Today the Lebanese people are called once again, after the complete restoration and healing of Lebanon, to create a unique political and democratic renaissance which will unite the Arab world into one entity, which might be appropriately called: *The United Arab States*. These states should be free and democratic and should adopt one foreign policy, one economic policy, and one military policy, provided that each state retains internal independence and its distinguishing cultural characteristics. Some people may think that this thinking is an idealistic dream, but the great revolutions which have changed the course of history started as idealistic dreams, and were then realized through sound planning, right thinking, intense striving and clear vision.

The Future of Lebanon: Response and Challenge
The future of Lebanon about which we dream is the Lebanon of intellectual pioneering in all fields, the Lebanon of creativity and originality, the Lebanon of civilization and illumination, the Lebanon of freedom and democracy, the Lebanon of cleanliness from bribery, corruption, patronage and favoritism. If these unique characteristics cease to exist, there will be no reason for Lebanon to exist.

This, finally, is the great challenge to which the Lebanese should respond, and Lebanon will exist only if the response is equivalent to the challenge. I believe that Lebanon will continue to exist because of your leadership, wisdom, boldness and patience.

God as the Witness to My Vow
Washington, D.C., 1991

*"Not to us, O Lord, not to us,
but to Thy Name give glory" (Psalm 115).*

Before I share with you some thoughts about the state of the archdiocese since the Anaheim Convention, I would like to express my deep regrets that, because of unforeseen circumstances, our Father in Christ, His Beatitude, Patriarch Ignatius IV, could not be with us for this very special convention.

An Orthodox University for the Middle East
I wonder how many of you have read about the ambitious project which His Beatitude has been undertaking for at least the past three years. He is building the University of Balamand, an institution which has been the dream of our people since the inception of the Holy See of Antioch. Some people reiterate history, and some make history. Patriarch Ignatius is making history by building this university, which is a defining moment in the history of Antioch and the Middle East. He has been busy raising funds, examining architectural drawings, organizing a Board of Trustees and appointing various committees to implement this project.

The progress has been amazing, despite the long, dark years of the Lebanese uncivil war. Unfortunately, we have never had an Orthodox University in the Middle East. Perhaps, if we had one, the Lebanese Civil War and other tragedies which have plagued the Middle East, especially during this twentieth century, could have been avoided. There are other universities in Lebanon, but most of these universities were established by foreign money and foreign missionaries in order to propagate their particular brand of Christianity. Very often, I feel that the intellectual chaos and the many philosophical contradictions which have exploded in the Middle East are the result of the competing ideologies of these universities.

In this respect the University of Balamand is different and unique. It is a university built and financed by our own people, thanks to the vision of Patriarch Ignatius IV. Our university is being built to serve all the people of the Middle East, Christians and Muslims, the rich and the poor alike. Its philosophy is not imported from any foreign land; on the contrary, it stems from our long historical experience in the Middle East and our most significant interaction with Islam for many centuries. I want you to know that as a member of the Board of Trustees of this institution, I am totally committed to its success and I want all of you to join me in this sacred commitment. If you think that I will let you rest after twenty-five years of struggle, you are mistaken.

Refusing the Grave of History: Twenty-Five Years Later
This year has special significance for us because we are celebrating the twenty-fifth anniversary of an unprecedented era of relentless struggle and progress. It is a good time for us to reflect on where this archdiocese was and where we are today. Twenty-five years ago, on a mountain which overlooks the valley where I was born, and on a bright, sunny August day, at the beautiful Church of St. Elias Monastery where I began my ecclesiastical life, I made the following vow before the Holy Synod of Antioch and the Holy Church:

> I promise to visit and watch over the flock now entrusted to me, after the manner of the apostles, whether they remain true to the faith, and in the areas of good works, more especially the priests; and to inspect with diligence that there may be no schisms, superstitions and impious veneration, and that no customs contrary to Christian piety and good morals may injure Christian conduct. May God, who seeth the heart, be the witness of my vow.
>
> It is up to God who sees the secrets of the hearts and it is

also up to you, His Church, to judge whether or not I remained faithful to my vow.

It is not my intention, today, to elaborate on the accomplishments which we have achieved, together, for the glory of God, during the past twenty-five years. Nor do I want to take you on a journey to the past. Let the record speak for itself; if the past does not point to the present and shape the future, the past is dead. I refuse to live in the grave of history. For many years, we Orthodox have lived with an inferiority complex and have underestimated our capacity for greatness. What our beloved patriarch is doing at Balamand and what you have done for this archdiocese proves beyond doubt that with the proper leadership, our people can indeed move mountains.

Reviewing the Latest Accomplishments
Since I addressed you last in Anaheim, California, the following projects have been realized:

First, the completion and dedication of the second phase of our building program at *the Antiochian Village.* We can now house a minimum of two hundred people in hotel-like rooms with all the proper conveniences. We can seat comfortably, in our new dining room, a minimum of four hundred people. We have provided space for our growing museum and the School of Iconography. We have provided more spacious rooms for our meetings, workshops and seminars. This center has become a haven for our clergy and all the organizations of this archdiocese. I have been informed that the center is ninety per cent booked for this year and next year. When we plan seminars and workshops for our choirs, church schools, parish councils, etc., it is imperative that every parish send its church school superintendent, choir director and chairman of the parish council to attend and participate in this sacred work. Unfortunately, some parishes are not taking advantage of these wonderful opportunities. We still have a few rooms available for sponsorship; thus, if you want to memorialize a love one, you cannot find a better place than the Heritage and Learning Center. We hope that within three years, the second phase will be completely debt-free.

The camping facilities are now some of the best, not only in the state of Pennsylvania, but in the whole country. During last year and this year, the archdiocese has spent large sums of money to renovate all facets of the camp, because I want our children to have the best. It is important for you to know that we do not make money from the Village Camp. As a matter of fact, we have been subsidizing this camp since its inception. I cannot describe to you in words the tremendous impact which our camp is making on our children. Once again, I urge parents, grandparents and parishes to send their children to the Village and give us the pleasure of serving them.

Second, the completion and dedication of the *archdiocese chancery on the West Coast.* Our chancery on the West Coast is located in Hancock Park, one of the most beautiful areas in the city of Los Angeles. When you visit the West Coast, stop and see this beautiful chancery. Last September I had the pleasure of dedicating this chancery and I am happy to inform you that it is completely debt-free.

Now, since we have this residence, we need a bishop to reside in it. During the past twenty-five years, the archdiocese has grown from sixty parishes to one hundred sixty. Due to the vastness of the North American continent and the tremendous growth which we have experienced, it became evident to me that three bishops can no longer adequately serve you. It takes five and one-half hours to fly from New York to Los Angeles or San Francisco, and even more hours to fly to Alaska. Furthermore, in 1966 we had only four parishes on the West Coast; today, we have thirty parishes and a number of missions. Hence, the importance of having a bishop on the West Coast to watch over our flock. I would like to emphasize, however, that we are not nominating a bishop for the West Coast. Nor are we dividing this archdiocese into bishoprics. We are nominating another auxiliary bishop to reside part of the year on the West Coast and the other part at the archdiocesan headquarters. I want to assure you, however, that there will always be a bishop in residence on the West Coast.

My dear friends, the nomination of a bishop to minister to you, after the manner of the Apostles, to preach, to teach, to organize and to heal, is a very sacred and bright moment in the history of this archdiocese. We do have the right to nominate because this is an ancient practice in the Church. The names of the nominees will be submitted to His Beatitude and the Holy Synod of Antioch and the ultimate decision will be made by them. May the All-Holy Spirit guide us and enlighten our minds to do what is pleasing to His Holy Church.

Third, the Antiochian Christian Orthodox Radio Network. Last year in March, while in Beaumont, Texas, the possibility of starting our own Orthodox Radio Network on a national level was brought to my attention. Needless to say, this was very interesting and at the same time, very challenging. I liked the idea so much that a month later we were on the air, despite the fact that we did not budget for this program during the past fiscal year. To "make disciples of all nations" is one of the most important commissions of the New Testament.

For many years, our people have been asking, "How come we do not have our own Orthodox TV program?" The answer is simple: because we do not have the funds. We are even struggling to keep ACORN on the air. This Orthodox program is the first of its kind in North America and it deserves our financial and moral support. I heard that a good number of people in Oklahoma City have been converted to Orthodoxy through this program. I want you to publicize this program by putting it in your church bulletins and monthly newsletters. We know that our radio program is not yet perfect. Please help us to make it perfect through your participation and constructive criticism.

Fourth, the restructuring of our Youth Department. Last year, during the spring meeting of the Archdiocese Board of Trustees, the youth ministry of our archdiocese was discussed in depth. We found many things lacking in our youth programs and goals. Because of the seriousness of this situation, I immediately called for a decisive meeting on youth ministry in early November at the Antiochian Village Heritage and Learning Center. I invited to this meeting the leadership of both Senior and Teen SOYO, all the spiritual advisors of SOYO, the Chairman of the Campus Ministry, the Director of our Camping Program and the Director of the Department of Christian Education. The meeting was very well attended and everything related to youth ministry was put on the table.

After four days of meetings, and sometimes heated discussions, our young people and spiritual advisors agreed on a new platform which they presented to me, and which I endorsed, entitled, "Living the Orthodox Faith in Christ through Worship, Witness, Service and Fellowship." In their Statement of Purpose, our young people said: "We believe that the goal of Orthodox Christian Youth Ministry is the integration of each young person fully into the total life of the Church. We believe that Orthodox Christians must commit themselves to living the Orthodox faith daily. Worship, witness, service and fellowship are the natural expressions of that commitment." The Statement of Purpose concludes as follows: "Our plan integrates the Camping Program, Teen SOYO, Campus Ministry and SOYO Programs designed to meet the need of varying age groups. We will attain these goals by training youth ministers, both clergy and laity, to serve at all levels, and by developing and providing relevant resource materials."

We are proclaiming 1992 as the Year of Youth Ministry in our archdiocese and we have allocated the sum of $100,000 to help achieve this goal. I would like to caution you, however, that no youth director, regardless of his brilliance and energy, can achieve this goal alone. We can provide you with a very adequate budget and with the most creative programs on the archdiocese level, but if we do not have your full cooperation on the regional and parish levels, all our efforts on the national level will be for naught. I am convinced that if you do not respond to our youth program on the parish level, our young people will remain in the marginal life of the Church. I, therefore, call

all my coworkers, the reverend clergy, to work with the youth department and initiate meaningful spiritual programs for our young people. It will be sad indeed to face the twenty-first century without young people in our parishes.

Fifth, the Order of St. Ignatius of Antioch. The day we established the Order of St. Ignatius of Antioch was one of the brightest days in the history of this archdiocese. Since its inception, fifteen years ago, the Order has raised five million dollars for the enhancement of the spiritual life of our archdiocese. In some instances, the charitable deeds of the Order have transcended the boundaries of our own archdiocese. The Heritage and Learning Center, the camping program and facilities, the Department of Missions and Evangelism, campus ministry, Christian education, sacred music, and the clergy retirement fund, just to mention a few, have all benefited from the fruit of the Order of St. Ignatius.

More significantly, the Order has taught us the art of giving. The Order has instilled confidence in us that we can achieve greater goals and support institutions. Furthermore, the Order has helped us discover much, much hidden talent in this archdiocese and has become an example which the future generations, hopefully, will emulate. Fifteen years ago, some people said: "The metropolitan will be lucky if he can find fifty people who will join the Order of St. Ignatius." How wrong they were! I have so much confidence in our people that if you provide them with the proper leadership and show them what you are doing with their money, they will give you their money and their hearts. In 1976, our goal was to recruit five hundred men and women to the Order. This goal was reached. Our new goal is two thousand members by the end of this century, and we will reach it.

Sixth, Metropolitan Philip's Endowment Fund. Last year, at the Spring Meeting of the Board of Trustees, there was some whispering about celebrating my twenty-fifth anniversary in the holy episcopacy. Subsequently, I learned that our good trustees wanted to do something to honor me. I told the members of the Board, "Please do not do anything for me personally. If you really want to celebrate this occasion, I would like to see you establish an Endowment Fund to secure the future of the Heritage and Learning Center and to provide more scholarships for needy children to go to the Village Camp." The campaign has started, and we have almost reached our goal.

Seventh, Orthodox unity in America. Perhaps my biggest disappointment during the past twenty-five years is Orthodox unity in America, which remains an elusive dream. Modern history moves so fast that we cannot keep up with it. But we Orthodox seem to be living outside history. I wish I could report to you something positive about Orthodox unity in America; unfortunately, I have nothing to report because nothing is happening. His Beatitude, Patriarch Ignatius, has made many positive statements vis-à-vis this question and you know exactly where I stand, but Antioch, alone, cannot achieve this goal.

I am deeply convinced that the inter-Orthodox system does not work despite our sound theology and the eternal principles which we represent. After more than sixty years of meetings to prepare for the Great Orthodox Synod, we are still debating whether or not we should put the problem of the diaspora on the agenda of this Great Synod, when and if it convenes. I want to assure you, however, that with the blessings of His Beatitude, Patriarch Ignatius, we will continue to reach out and be a catalyst for Orthodox unity in this hemisphere. No one can turn back the wheels of history; thus I firmly believe that Orthodox unity on this continent, despite our monumental difficulties, is inevitable.

Finally, some *personal reflections*. As we travel through the journey of life, all of us experience hours of joy and hours of sorrow. We have a tendency to forget the hours of joy and remember the hours of sorrow because sorrow affects us more deeply. It was in this city on a cold, gray day of January, 1968, when I suffered my heart attack, while working for peace and justice in the Middle East after the June War of 1967. I was rushed to the hospital where I learned the next day that I had had a heart attack. Needless to say, I was disappointed, frustrated and very depressed. I said to myself, "If this is true, what is going to happen to my agenda and all my dreams?" For fifteen days, I did not make any progress at all. On the sixteenth day, the doctor walked into my room and said: "We must talk." "Talk about what?" I said. "You are not making any progress," the doctor said, "because you refuse to believe that you had a heart attack." He was right. I was young, strong, athletic and had much pride in my youth. Hence, my refusal to believe that I had a heart attack.

After a long talk with the doctor and seeing the X-ray pictures of my heart, I realized once and for all that I could no longer deny the reality of my illness. The question was, how to turn that defeat into a victory. The doctor departed and left me alone with my thoughts.

Have you ever talked with God? I did. "Lord," I said, "You know the secrets of my heart and You know that You have chosen me to serve Your Church. You are the Lord of history and master of my destiny. My life belongs to You and You can do with it whatever You want. Thy will be done." As I finished my conversation with God, the following words from Psalm 118 flooded my mind. "Out of my distress, I called on the Lord; the Lord answered me and set me free."

The Lord, gently and lovingly, said to me, "You have your plans, your dreams and your agenda, but you must learn that nothing will happen according to your plans and calendar. Things will happen according to my time and not yours. I am the Alpha and the Omega. I am the Lord of history, not you."

I was not ready to wrestle with God any more. I had wrestled with Him enough in my youth. The best thing for me to do was to surrender completely to His will. "The Lord answered me and set me free." It is indeed ironic that only when we surrender, we become liberated. I looked through the window and saw a few scattered snowflakes falling on the city, and suddenly was overwhelmed by a sense of peace—peace with God and peace with myself. There was no more tension, no more frustration and no more depression. After that encounter with God in 1968, my whole attitude toward life has changed. My basic philosophy now is: "Do your best and leave the rest to God."

What was more significant is that during this period, I came to terms with the whole question of life and death. As I began preparing myself for life, I began preparing myself for death at any moment. This seems paradoxical, but the logic of God transcends the logic of this world. We are alive now, but what guarantee do we have that we are going to be alive tomorrow? This is precisely why every moment of my life has become an urgent moment and every day I live has become a precious day.

Four years later, I began to experience significant chest pain. After some medical tests, the doctors recommended that I undergo open heart surgery at the Miami Heart Institute. There was no anxiety, no fear and no depression. And once again, I said: "Thy will be done." Thanks be to God, to Dr. Eugene Sayfie and to your prayers, the operation was a tremendous success, and nineteen years later, I am still around. I want to assure you that whenever I feel I can no longer serve you as you deserve, I will say with Simeon: "Lord, now lettest Thou Thy servant depart in peace; according to Thy word; for mine eyes have seen Thy salvation" (Luke 2:29).

Why the Success: The Gift of "the Father of Lights"
Ladies and gentlemen: During the past twenty-five years, I have told you on many occasions that the Church is not the bishop alone, nor the priest alone, nor the laity alone. The Church is the bishop, the priest and the people working together. This very important principle has guided us in the past and will continue to guide us in the future. The success which we have achieved during the past twenty-five years is, first and foremost, a precious gift from God. "For every good and perfect gift is from above, coming down from the Father of lights" (James 1:17). Second, it is the result of the magnificent cooperation between us on the archdiocesan level and you on the parish level.

Finally, however, lest we become puffed up with our own

achievements, I would like to conclude this message with this prayer by Thomas á Kempis from his book, *The Imitation of Christ.*

> O Lord, let Your name, not mine, be praised
> Let Your work, not mine, be magnified.
> Let Your holy name be blessed, but let no human praise
> Be given to me. You are the joy of my heart.
> In you, I will glory and rejoice all the day,
> And for myself, I will glory in nothing but my infirmities.
> All human glory, all temporal honor, all worldly position
> Is truly vanity and foolishness compared to Your everlasting glory.
> O my truth, my mercy, my God, O Blessed Trinity, to You alone
> Be praise and honor, prayer and glory, throughout all the ages of ages. Amen.

Thank you, and God bless you all.

Editor's Endnotes

1. *As the new decade begins, Phase II of the Heritage and Learning Center is dedicated in June of 1990 and the new West Coast Chancery is dedicated in September of that same year; Philip reorganizes some of the departments and declares his aim of establishing full-time directors for various positions.*

2. *In 1991 Philip meets with President George H. Bush, who is invited to the Archdiocesan Convention in Washington, D.C. President Bush addresses the Convention at the metropolitan's invitation.*

3. *In honor of Philip's twenty-fifth anniversary, a biographical book is published on his life by Father Peter Gillquist, entitled:* **Metropolitan Philip: His Life and Dreams** *(Nashville: Thomas Nelson Publishers).*

Chapter 17

MISSION AND EVANGELISM

> *The Lord's command was to go to all nations, and He promised that He will be with us until the end of time. This means that the missionary works of the Church did not end in eleventh-century Byzantium or nineteenth-century Russia. ... "I will be with you always" (Matthew 28:20). As He was with Peter and Paul, with Cyril and Methodius, He will be with us at this very moment if we obey His command.*
>
> Metropolitan Philip

- *Mission and Evangelism: Address to the First Orthodox Episcopal Conference in North America, 1994*
- *On the Nativity of the Lord, 1994*

AND HE LEADS THEM

History was made in 1994 when the first Orthodox Episcopal Conference was held at the Antiochian Village Heritage and Learning Center. Key papers were delivered by the American hierarchs of the various jurisdictions under SCOBA. The "fall-out" of this conference has never left the history of Orthodoxy in North America. At the time of the editing of this book, one still cannot predict if that conference will bear the fruit for which it hoped.

Philip delivers one of the three major papers, entitled "Missions and Evangelism." After reviewing the two major missionary periods in Church history, he brings the theme directly to the conference members: "The Church is not a museum for historical nostalgia . . . it is rather a living body . . . dynamic and permeated by the power of the Holy Spirit . . . therefore we must 'go' and never stop until the end of time." In the end, Philip reminds them that America, too, must be won for the Gospel of Jesus Christ, but that can only happen when, as he says, we unite.

This more academic paper is presented in its entirety.

Also in 1994 Philip pens a moving meditation, the third of its kind, on the Nativity of the Lord. We present that meditation in this chapter.

J. J. A.

Missions and Evangelism: Address to the First Orthodox Episcopal Conference in North America
1994

Your Eminence, my beloved brothers in Christ,

I was indeed delighted when the venerable Chairman of SCOBA, His Eminence, Archbishop Iakovos, asked me to deliver at this first Orthodox Episcopal Conference in North America a paper on Missions and Evangelism, a topic which is significant to Orthodox Christianity in this hemisphere. The biblical text which I chose for this paper is Matthew 28:18, "And Jesus came and said to them, 'All authority in heaven and on earth has been given to Me. Go, therefore, and make disciples of all nations, baptizing them in the name of the Father and of the Son and of the Holy Spirit, teaching them to observe all that I have commanded you; and lo, I am with you always, to the close of the age.'"

Our Lord Himself was indeed the missionary *par excellence*. In Matthew 4:23 we read: "And He went about all Galilee, teaching in their synagogues and preaching the gospel of the kingdom, and healing every disease and every infirmity among the people." And in the "fullness of time,"[1] the "Word became flesh"[2] and entered time on a mission of salvation. He was sent by the Father to make us "partakers of the Divine Nature."[3]

In John 20:21, Christ said: "As the Father has sent Me, even so I send you." The Church, which is the extension of Christ in time and space, was sent by Christ to missionize and evangelize. Evangelism means to preach the Gospel. "Woe unto me if I do not preach,"[4] said St. Paul. After the birth of the Church

---
[1] Galatians 4:4
[2] John 1:14
[3] 2 Peter 1:4
[4] 1 Corinthians 9:16

AND HE LEADS THEM

on Pentecost Day, the Apostles and early Christians went about the *oikomene*, the known world at that time, preaching the Gospel and missionizing, despite their persecution and the monumental difficulties which they had to face. Although the Church was born in Jerusalem, Antioch became the greatest center for missionary activities. It was in Antioch that the disciples were first called Christians.[5] For more details on the role which Antioch played in evangelism, I recommend the *History of the Church of Antioch* by Chrysostomos Pappathopoulos, Professor of History of Athens University.[6]

There are many stories about the missionary travels of the Apostles.[7] It is clear, however, that Christianity did not spread throughout the entire Roman Empire until after the Edict of Milan. The *Pax Romana* presented what Michael Green[8] describes as both opportunities and difficulties for evangelism. Some of the opportunities were (a) peace and unity; (b) philosophical hunger; and (c) religious dissatisfaction.
Some of the difficulties were:
a. the cultural offensiveness of the Gospel, i.e., the Jewish communities and their Gentile adherents were openly affronted by the central language of the Gospel: God's Incarnation and death;
b. political considerations, i.e., the Christian unwillingness to participate in the state cult of the emperor was seen as political treason[9] and the closed nature of the Christian gatherings likewise led to charges of cannibalism.

---

[5] Acts 11:26.
[6] This volume was written in Greek and was translated into Arabic by Bishop Estephanos Haddad.
[7] Aziz S. Atiya, *A History of Eastern Christianity*, second ed., Millwork, NY, reprint 1980. Egypt was evangelized by St. Mark; Armenia by Ss Thaddaeus and Bartholomew, ibid.; Scythia between the Caspian & Black Sea, by St. Andrew; South India, by St. Thomas, ibid.; Proconsular Asia (Mysia, Lydia and Cosia) by St. John the Evangelist; Arabia, Asia Minor, Macedonia, Italy, and Spain by St. Paul.
[8] *Evangelism in the Early Church*, pp. 13–47.
[9] Paul D. Garrett, Memo to Metropolitan Philip, p. 5.

After A.D. 313 circumstances changed radically, and organized missionary enterprises became normal. Metropolitan Anastasios divides the history of Byzantine missions into two major periods:
1. The fourth to the sixth centuries witness the Christianization of the empire and its immediate peripheries.
2. The ninth to the eleventh centuries, Byzantium's classic outreach into the Balkans and Russia.

The First Great Missionary Period:
The Fourth to Sixth Century
The post-Constantinian emperors concentrated on removing all vestiges of paganism from the empire. By this time, the urban centers of Spain, Southern Gaul, Germany, Italy, Macedonia, Greece, Central Asia Minor and the Black Sea Region, greater Syria, lower Egypt and Africa had all received the Christian witnesses, as had Armenia, the Arab Peninsula[10] and India, outside the empire boundaries.

In Palestine, at the close of the fourth century, St. Hilarion mobilized some two thousand monks to preach the Gospel to the inhabitants, many of them nomadic Bedouins, not easily reached. He used his monasteries in Gaza as a missionary center, and it became the norm of the Church for monks to have a larger portion of the responsibility for missions.[11]

Both in Antioch as a presbyter, and in Constantinople as patriarch, St. John Chrysostom was an outspoken and enthusiastic supporter of missions.

In 380–381, Emperor Theodosius outlawed heathen sacrifices, and mission became extended to the hinterlands. Emperor Justinian (527–565) was instrumental in many ways in

---

[10] Atiya writes: "In 225, a bishopric was in existence at Beth Katraye, the country of Qatar in Southeast Arabia, opposite the island of Bahrain. Christianity had found its way to the tribes of Himyar, Ghassan, Taghlib, Tannukh and Quda'a, long before Islam." Ibid.
[11] James J. Stamoolis, *Eastern Orthodox Mission Theology Today*.

spreading Christianity outside the boundaries of the empire. He even directed that missions be dispatched into the Berber region of North Africa. Georgia had become familiar with the Gospel through the life of faith and complete virtue of a Cappadocian captive, St. Nina.

The Non-Chalcedonian churches made tremendous missionary strides, especially at the hand of Jacob Baradeus, who wandered all his life from Egypt to the Euphrates preaching and founding churches. It is significant here to note that the Non-Chalcedonian missionaries had reached India and China.

The Second Great Missionary Period:
The Ninth to the Eleventh Century

In 862, the Moravian ruler, Rostislav, approached Emperor Michael III about receiving Slavic-speaking Greek missionaries to enlighten his people. War broke out between the Byzantine Army and Boris of Bulgaria. "Boris capitulated, abandoned the Franks and promised to accept the Byzantine form of Christianity."[12] Boris was baptized in 864, taking the name Michael in honor of his imperial godfather. A missionary company of bishops and priests, aided by Archbishop Joseph, was dispatched to Bulgaria. They were accompanied by a corps of architects, painters and other artisans needed to build and adorn churches.

Under Boris' son, Symeon, Greek theological books were translated into the vernacular Slavonic. Further north in Moravia, mission work was proceeding well under Prince Rostislav, who wrote to Emperor Michael III:

> Our people have renounced paganism and are observing the Christian law, but we do not have a teacher to explain to us the true Christian faith in our own language in order that other nations even, seeing this, may emulate us. Send us therefore, Master, such a bishop

---

[12] Francis Dvornik, *Byzantine Missions Among the Slavs, Ss. Cyril and Methodius*, pp. 126, 27.

and teacher, because from you emanates always the good law.[13]

The Moravians were not immediately granted a bishop,[14] but they received two remarkable evangelists, Ss. Cyril and Methodius. The two brothers were raised in Thessalonica, a region with a large minority concentration of Slavs, whose dialogue they learned from childhood. The two brothers were highly educated in theology and philosophy and they mastered the Greek, Hebrew and Syriac languages.

In 863, Cyril invented an alphabet perfectly suited for the phonology of the old Slavonic language and began the task of translating the Scriptures and liturgy.

The body of literature in Slavonic, including the Bible and the liturgy, played an important role in the Christianization of Russia. The influence of Ss. Cyril and Methodius far outlasted their own efforts. It is no wonder that they are commemorated in the Liturgy as *equals to the apostles,* evangelists of the Slavonians.[15]

I would like to emphasize here that the genius of Cyril and Methodius lies in the fact that they did not impose the Greek language on the Slavs. They used the vernacular for worship, and taught converts to praise God in their own language. The second distinct element of the Slavic mission was the use of indigenous clergy. Instead of imposing foreign clergy on the Slavs, converts were ordained to care for the spiritual needs of the people. I wish that the Patriarchate of Jerusalem would learn this valuable lesson from Cyril and Methodius before it is too late.

[13] Quoted by Dvornik, p. 73, Ibid.
[14] Methodius refused the episcopal dignity following his return from the Khazar mission, preferring to return to a monastery. Dvornik, p. 104, Ibid.
[15] James J. Stamoolis, *Eastern Orthodox Mission Theology Today,* p. 21.

The emphasis on indigenization led to the third element, which is selfhood of the Church. Orthodox canon law permits the establishment of local churches, but there has not always been agreement between the Mother Church and the mission Church over when self-government is granted. Unfortunately, this problem continues to disturb the peace of the Church today.

After the fall of Constantinople in 1453, a dark night settled on the mission of the Orthodox churches of Byzantium. The Lord, however, works in mysterious ways. The light which was extinguished in Byzantium continued to shine brightly through the deep spirituality and missionary zeal of the Russian Church. Missions were established in Northern Russia, and Alaska was missionized in 1794. The nineteenth century was called the "great century of Russian Orthodox missions."[16] Missions were established in Japan, Korea and China. In all their missions, the Russian missionaries followed the example of Cyril and Methodius.

Not a Protestant Concept; a Gospel Concept
I have presented this historical survey on Orthodox mission and evangelism in order to reemphasize that mission and evangelism is not, by any means, a Protestant idea. Long before the Reformation, Orthodox missionaries preached the Gospel to hundreds of millions of people. "You shall receive power when the Holy Spirit has come upon you; and you shall be My witnesses in Jerusalem and in all Judea and Samaria and the uttermost ends of the earth."[17] The Church, therefore, is divinely sent to the nations that she might be "the universal sacrament of salvation." She, in obedience to the command of her Founder, and because it is demanded by her own essential universality, strives to preach the Gospel to all men. The Apostles, following the footsteps of Christ, "preached the word of truth and begot

---

[16] Stamoolis, pp. 28–49.
[17] Acts 1:8.

churches." It is the duty of their successors to carry on this work so that "the word of the Lord may spread and triumph," and so the "Kingdom of God [may be] proclaimed and renewed throughout the whole world."[18] It is obvious then that the Church on earth is, by its very nature, missionary. Missionary activity is nothing else, and nothing less, than the manifestation of God's plan, its epiphany and realization in the world and in history.

Reflecting on the theme of this paper, which is "Mission and Evangelism," in Matthew 28:16-20 we find that our Lord told us clearly and plainly that He received "all power on heaven and on earth," and because of that power over the universe, He can initiate a universal mission. He commanded us, through His disciples, to do three things: (a) to make disciples, (b) to baptize, (c) to teach.

To make disciples is the first part of the divine command. In Matthew 10:6, our Lord told His disciples to go only to the people of Israel. The mission is now to the whole world; the Gentiles are now included. The eleven Apostles are to make disciples of all nations; the Jews are not excluded, but they no longer enjoy a privileged status as the Chosen People. Christ died for all men.

The process begins with the proclamation of the Gospel: "Make disciples." The process continues with baptism in the name of the Father and of the Son and of the Holy Spirit. Although the Church may have initially baptized in the name of Jesus, by the time Matthew wrote his Gospel, the Trinitarian formula had already been in use.[19] Matthew conceives a baptism as incorporation into the life of God and of His Church. It is no longer circumcision that makes a person a member of the Church of God, but it is baptism.

As the process continues, Jesus sent His Apostles to "teach,"

---

[18] Decree on the Church's Missionary Activities, Vatican 11, 7, December, 1965.
[19] John P. Meier, Michael Glazeer, Inc., Wilmington, DE, p. 371.

and they are instructed to teach humanity to "observe all things I have commanded you." It is Jesus, Himself, who is the norm of all truth and all morality. It is what He has commanded that must be taught. The ministry of Word and Sacrament of the Church is rooted in this sacramental mission given to the Apostles. This very ministry of Word and Sacrament is what distinguishes Orthodox Christianity from superficial evangelism which has already severed all connections with the historic Church. Mission and evangelism, therefore, in the Church is not a matter of choice. It is a divine command. Jesus did not say, "Make disciples if you want," or "Please baptize and teach if you wish"; He said "Go," and the disciples obeyed and became fishers of men.

St. John Chrysostom said:

> For not to one, or two or three cities shall you preach, says Christ, but to the whole world. You will traverse land and sea, the inhabited country and the desert, preaching to princes and tribes alike, to philosophers and orators saying everything openly and with boldness of speech.[20]

This divine lesson transcends time and space. We cannot just seek the comfort of a past period in our history and freeze there. Nor can we remain within a geographic area like Byzantium or Russia. The Lord's command was to go to all nations, and He promised that He will be with us until the end of time. This means that the missionary work of the Church did not end in the eleventh-century Byzantium or the nineteenth-century Russia. Furthermore, this means that mission and evangelism must continue until the end of time, the *Parousia:* "And I will be with you always."[21] As our Lord was with Peter and Paul and Cyril and Methodius, He will be with us at this very moment if we obey His command.

[20] Chrysostom on Matthew 20:23.
[21] Matthew 28:20.

My dear brothers in Christ, the Church is not a museum for historical nostalgia. Nor is the Church an archeological site from the time of Justinian. The Church is indeed the living body of Christ. She is dynamic and always permeated by the power of the Holy Spirit, who descended on the disciples like a mighty wind. The Church must live with the conviction that she is always sent. Therefore, we must "go" and never stop until the end of time. As we prepare to face the challenges of a new century, we Orthodox of North America must ask ourselves: "To whom are we sent?"

This Nation, Also

If the Lord has commanded the Church to make disciples of all nations, He must have meant this nation, also. Consequently, Orthodoxy has a mission to this country. We do have a special ministry to those who came from Greece, the Middle East, Eastern Europe and Russia. But we also have a special mission to all the people of North America, and they are men and women of every race and people on earth.

Looking at the religious scene in America today, one would think that we are living in a post-Christian era. Some American Christians no longer believe in the Virgin Birth. They say that the Virgin Mary was raped by a Roman soldier. Some do not believe in the Resurrection of Christ. A so-called Christian bishop claims that St. Paul was a homosexual. Some denominations are marrying people of the same gender. If you pray in an ecumenical gathering, you must not mention the name of Jesus Christ, let alone the Triune God. Some Christian denominations no longer baptize in the name of the Father and of the Son and of the Holy Spirit, but rather in the name of the "Creator and Redeemer." Many Christians believe that religion is a private matter and everything is relative. Thus, the absolute truth does not exist, and the Good News which was preached by our Lord was, perhaps, good for His time, but not ours.

Do we have an Orthodox response to spiritual decadence? Of course we do; but only if we put our house in order—only if we could create one strong and well-financed Department of Mission and Evangelism. We need missionaries and evangelists who know this country, its language, its history, its ethos, its problems, and its religions. In summary, we need Orthodox missionaries who know how to communicate with America.

> For these reasons, communication of the Gospel in a foreign culture can no longer be a superficial presentation of biblical Christianity. Instead, it must be a careful, thoughtful and precise cross-cultural communication which speaks in such a way that the biblical Gospel is understood within the culture and native framework of thought.[22]

This year, we are celebrating the two-hundredth anniversary of the evangelization of Alaska, and next year the Antiochian Archdiocese will be celebrating the centennial of Antiochian Orthodoxy in North America. These are significant occasions for us to reflect on the past, meditate on the present, and focus on the future.

Ten years ago in Worcester, Massachusetts, I delivered a message to the Orthodox on the Sunday of Orthodoxy. I said:

> We have a tremendous opportunity in this land to dream dreams and to see visions—only if we can put our house in order. Where in the whole world today can one find seven million free Orthodox except in North America?
>
> We are no longer a Church of immigrants; the first Orthodox liturgy was celebrated in this country before the American Revolution. Many of our Orthodox young people have died on the battlefields of various wars, defending American ideals and principles. We have contributed much to the success of this country in the fields of medicine, science, technology, government, education, art, entertainment and business. We consider

---

[22] *Common Roots, A Call to Evangelical Ministry*, by Robert E. Webber, p. 170.

ourselves Americans and we are proud of it—except when we go to church, we suddenly become Greeks, Russians, Arabs, Albanians and so forth. Despite our rootedness in the American soil, our Church in America is still divided into more than fourteen jurisdictions, contrary to our Orthodox ecclesiology and canon law, which forbid the multiplicity of jurisdictions in the same territory.

Individually, Orthodox jurisdictions have done much for themselves. . . . Collectively, however, we have not been able to rise above our ethnicity and to work together with one mind and one accord for the glory of Orthodoxy. Our efforts continue to be scattered in different directions. Why should we have fifteen departments for Christian education, media relations, sacred music, youth ministry, clergy pensions and so forth?

Where is our spiritual and moral impact on the life of this nation? . . . Why is it that every time there is a moral issue to be discussed, a Protestant, a Roman Catholic and a Jew are invited for such discussions? How can we explain our Orthodox absence, despite the authenticity of our theology and moral teachings? . . .

We cannot be agents of change in full obedience to the truth unless we transcend ethnicism and establish a new Orthodox reality in North America. . . .

The mission of the Church is not to be subservient to any kind of nationalism. The mission of the Church is the salvation of souls—all souls. In his Epistle to the Galatians, St. Paul said, "There is neither Jew nor Greek, there is neither slave nor free, there is neither male nor female; for all are one in Christ Jesus" (Galatians 3:28).[23]

Let Us Unite

Yes, we can missionize and evangelize America, but only if we unite. We pray that the mother churches will soon realize that

[23] This complete address is found in Chapter 12 of this book.

we are no longer little children and that the Preparatory Commission for the Great Synod will stop discussing the diaspora *in absentia*.

My dear brothers, America is searching for the New Testament Church. America is searching for the Church which was born on Pentecost Day. America is ready and waiting for us, but are we ready for America?

Finally, I would like to conclude with these words from the Perfect Missionary, our Lord and Savior, Jesus Christ.

> Do not say, "There are yet four months, then comes the harvest." I tell you, lift up your eyes and see how the fields are already white for harvest. He who reaps receives wages and gathers fruit for eternal life, so that the sower and reaper may rejoice together (John 4:35, 36).

On the Nativity of the Lord
1994

What is a merciful heart? It is a heart that burns with love for the whole creation—for men, for birds, for beasts, for demons and for every creature. —St. Isaac the Syrian

Christmas music is filling the air. In every home there is a Christmas tree; some are real and some are plastic. Lights of every color are glittering in windows, shops, bars and even the discos. Some people are selling, some are buying, some are eating, some are drinking and some are starving to death.

I put a "Do Not Disturb" sign on my door because Christmas Eve is a very special and private time to me. I want to be alone in order to embrace all men and love all things. In the depths of my aloneness, the past, the present and the future become one single moment. In the depths of my aloneness I experience that boundless love which encompasses the whole creation. I am alone on Christmas Eve but not lonely, because in Christ Jesus there is no loneliness and there is no separation. The walls are destroyed and the barriers are no more. The Child of the manger has reconciled everything to Himself; henceforth, there is no race, no color, no conflict and no hatred; in Him there is "a new heaven and a new earth."

Christmas Eve, to me, is a time for reflection. The year is slowly sinking into the ocean of eternity, and in my reflection there are painful questions:

Did I love Him enough? Did I serve Him enough? Did I suffer enough? Did I forgive enough? How many tears did I dry? How many wounds did I bind? Was I faithful to Him who loved me beyond measure? How loving and compassionate is God, that despite my sinfulness and unworthiness, He "became flesh and dwelt amongst us." What an unfathomable condescension that He assumed our nature in order to make us partakers of His nature. Despite His Incarnation, He will always remain incognito in this world if we don't care for each other. But do we really care? Have we seen the starving children on our television screens? Have we ever seen so much despair, so much misery and so much helplessness? These are our brothers and sisters, His brothers and sisters. How sad it is that we do not see the tragedy unless it is projected for us on the screen!

Tonight the Body and Blood of this tender Child will touch millions of lips throughout this troubled world. This divine touch will make us Christlike if we care and respond to His love. To be Christlike, we must be born with Him in the manger, crucified with Him on the Cross and resurrected with Him from the dead. The manger, the Cross, and the empty tomb—these are one single event which sums up the entire history of salvation.

It is Christmas Eve, and another year is about to dawn on us. Let Your light shine upon us so that we may see a new vision, sing a new song and dream a new dream. And if we live to celebrate another Christmas, give us courage to love You more, serve You more and worship You more "in spirit and in truth."

Editor's Endnotes:

1. In 1992, the first Parish Council Symposium is held at the Heritage and Learning Center; additions are made to the archdiocese headquarters; the Antiochian House of Studies is established.

2. In 1994, a record number of churches are established (23); the fundraising drive begins for the Balamand University in Lebanon; Philip receives the Ellis Island Medal of Honor.

3. Philip meets with President William Clinton in 1994 at the signing of the Jordanian-Israeli Peace Accord at the White House.

Chapter 18

THE LEGACY OF ANTIOCH FOR NORTH AMERICA

The insights which come to us from the past provide a guide that can illuminate the present and help us chart a course for the future. If we do not learn from the mistakes of the past, we will be condemned to repeat these very same mistakes.

Metropolitan Philip

- On the Immigration: Pursuing Their Dreams across the Sea, 1995
- A Day of Joy and Anticipation: The Reception of the Third Doctorate Degree, 1995
- The Suffering Orthodox of Jerusalem, 1995
- The Challenge of Another Century: The Centennial Address, 1995

AND HE LEADS THEM

1995 marks the one-hundredth anniversary of the Antiochian Orthodox Christian Archdiocese in North America, and everything included in this chapter is related to that anniversary. Indeed, Philip's talks and writings are permeated by this historical occasion.

The first of our entries is Philip's Introduction to the book he commissioned for publication, **The Centennial Anthology.** *The book is a compilation of articles by distinguished scholars, focused not only on the history of the archdiocese, but also on "the legacy of the Arab immigrants . . . the rich and the poor, the clergy and the laity, the literate and illiterate alike."*

The second address is given in 1995 on the occasion of Philip receiving a doctorate degree **honoris causa** *from the Holy Cross Greek Orthodox School of Theology. It is presented by his long-time friend, Archbishop Iakovos. In his acceptance address, he focuses upon the* **kerygma,** *the proclamation of the Word, by reminding the graduates of three considerations:* **where** *you are preaching,* **when** *you are preaching and* **to whom** *you are preaching. Measuring these three against his own personal experience, Philip then tells the students what the Lord said to Peter: "Feed my sheep."*

The third address during this centennial year is indeed a new focus for Philip, one which "bears much weight," and still provokes lively discussion throughout the Orthodox **Oikomene:** *Jerusalem and Orthodoxy. Philip establishes, and then gives the main address at the First International Conference, the Task Force for Palestinian Orthodox Christians living in the Patriarchate of Jerusalem. This Conference is gathered at the Heritage and Learning Center and sets the tone for the action of helping the Church survive in the most dire circumstances. It is certainly not the last time Philip will have to deal with this problem; this is merely the beginning, and at the time of this publication the end is still not in sight.*

The fourth and final piece is Philip's centennial address to the Archdiocesan Convention gathered in Atlanta, Georgia. Here he turns to those factors which have shaped the Church of Antioch in America. "We cannot honestly say that everything during the past one hundred years of our Antiochian history in North America was glorious and magnificent." He then goes on to cover both "the bright moments

... and the blind moments." The reader will find each of his points full of both honesty and hope.

J. J. A.

On the Immigration:
Pursuing Their Dreams Across the Sea
1995

Emma Lazarus (1849–1887) wrote the following words inscribed on the Statue of Liberty which stands, majestically, in the harbor of New York City like a beacon of hope:

Give me your tired, your poor,
Your huddled masses yearning to breathe free,
The wretched refuse of your teeming shore,
Send these, the homeless, tempest-tossed, to me:
I lift my lamp beside the golden door!

Around the turn of this century, thousands of tired and poor people sailed from the sunny shores of the Eastern Mediterranean, seeking economic opportunities, social justice and freedom in the United States of America and Canada. They were told the streets of America were paved with gold. Thus, they left the simplicity of their villages in Lebanon, Syria and Palestine, *pursuing their dreams across the sea*. Some of them were left to die from starvation in the seaports of North Africa. Some were left in Marseilles, France, thinking they were already in New York City. Some of them were lucky to land in South America, not by design, but rather by accident. Many, however, were fortunate enough to reach these blessed shores of the United States of America and Canada. Perhaps very few of them were able to read these immortal words inscribed on the Statue of Liberty: "Give me your tired, your poor. . . ."

They were tired, poor and mostly illiterate. They had neither relatives nor friends to welcome them at Ellis Island. But despite the foreign environment and the monumental difficulties which they faced, they were determined to challenge the unknown and leave heroic marks on the plains and prairies of

America. It is evident, therefore, that the early immigrants did not bring with them any material wealth; they brought something more precious than gold and silver. They brought their social and spiritual values, which left lasting marks on the soul of America.

It did not take them long to discover that the streets of America were not paved with gold. And nothing was going to save them except their faith in God, hard work, honesty and decency. They peddled their merchandise from city to city and from town to town, to the point of exhaustion. When they could no longer walk, they stopped and established a worshipping community, very often without the help of priests and bishops. Their two most cherished institutions were the Church and the family.

In 1895, the Antiochian Orthodox Christians in North America were fortunate to have Archimandrite Raphael Hawaweeny in charge of their spiritual life. This saintly, scholarly and mission-minded priest became their bishop in 1905, and laid the foundation of Antiochian Orthodoxy in this hemisphere. He founded the *WORD Magazine,* translated many liturgical books, authored many religious articles and served his flock with apostolic zeal until he fell asleep in the Lord in February 1915. The seeds which Bishop Raphael planted in the North American soil germinated and flourished through the splendid efforts of his successors. Thus, the Antiochian Archdiocese grew from thirty parishes in 1915 to 190 parishes in 1995. The decade of the sixties was a defining moment in the direction which this archdiocese was destined to take. The doors were open for indigenous Americans who were seeking refuge, theological meaning and stability in the Orthodox Church; they were welcomed home.

Besides the spiritual legacy which Bishop Raphael Hawaweeny and the early pioneers left, there is a literary legacy which must be celebrated as well. Although most of the first immigrants were illiterate, nevertheless, some of them were men of letters who have left their indelible marks on the Arabic language and literature. No one can write the history of Arabic literature in the twentieth century without devoting many pages to the Pen Bond (Al-Rabita Al Qalamiyya). The Pen Bond was founded in 1920 by the distinguished poets and writers such as Khalil Gibran, Mikhail Nuayme, Iliyya AbuMadi, Nasib Arida, Nadra and his brother, Abdal-Masih Haddad and others.

The decline of the Arab Empire was paralleled by a tremendous decline in Arabic literature, which became mere forms, void of substance, i.e., words, words, words, just boring verbosity. The members of the Pen Bond and their companions revolutionized Arabic literature and created a new school of literary expression which will continue to influence Arabic literature and language for many years to come. Their poetry was marked by a strong sense of longing for the villages and simple life which they left behind. Moreover, it expressed the eternal tensions of the immigrant who constantly lives with two halves—one in his new country and the other in the old country.

This Centennial Anthology is written to celebrate the memory of all Arab immigrants: the rich and the poor, the clergy and the laity, the literate and the illiterate alike. In this volume, you will read about the legacy of the immigrants and the rich heritage which they have inherited from past generations. I am eternally grateful to the distinguished scholars who have contributed to this anthology. We hope that you will enjoy reading it, lest we forget.

A Day of Joy and Anticipation: The Reception of the Third Doctorate Degree
1995

Ladies and gentlemen:

I am indeed delighted to share this podium with my beloved brother in Christ, Archbishop Iakovos, Primate of the Greek Orthodox Archdiocese of North and South America. During the past twenty-nine years, I have had the distinct honor and pleasure of working with him as vice-chairman of the Standing Conference of Canonical Orthodox Bishops in the Americas. Throughout the years, he has led SCOBA with much patience, wisdom and vision, despite the monumental difficulties which we are facing from within and without this continent. I do not know of any Orthodox hierarch who has sacrificed more of his time, energy and health for our Church in this hemisphere than Archbishop Iakovos. May God grant him many years.

I would like to convey very special gratitude to the president of this fine institution, my dear brother, Bishop Methodios, and all members of the faculty for the love and care which they continue to express to our Antiochian seminarians and all seminarians.

It Seems Like Yesterday: I Was Where You Are
Though unworthy, I am most honored indeed to receive this honorary doctorate degree from this fine institution which gave our Orthodox Church so many of its leaders on the parochial, diocesan, national and international level. It seems like yesterday when, thirty-nine years ago, I received some of my theological education in this school.

Many of these beautiful buildings which adorn this holy hill were not here in 1956. This tremendous progress which you have made since then is indicative of the dynamic leadership of your great archbishop and his faithful coworkers.

Commencement Day belongs to the graduates. It is a day of great joy and great expectation. Joy, because after years of theological study and spiritual preparation, you have realized your academic goal. And expectation, because sooner or later, you will be ordained to shepherd the flock of Jesus Christ in this broken world. In his first letter, St. Peter said: "Tend the flock of God, that is your charge, not by constraint but willingly, not for shameful gain but eagerly, not as domineering over those in your charge but being examples to the flock" (1 Peter 5:2, 3).

I would like to remind you, my dear graduates in particular, and seminarians in general, that the communities which you will be serving in the future are not Holy Cross School of Theology. This beautiful hill where you received your theological formation is a spiritual island in a pagan ocean. Thus, in your future parishes, you will encounter the believer and the unbeliever, the sacred and the profane, the literate and the illiterate, the sick and the healthy, the rich and the poor, the good sheep and the black sheep; you must minister to all of them.

Communication and Proclamation

One of the most important ingredients for a successful ministry is communication. In order to communicate the good news to your future flock, you must take into consideration three things: (a) where you are preaching; (b) when you are preaching; (c) to whom you are preaching. When you preach to your flock, remember that you are not lecturing to the senior class at Holy Cross School of Theology.

Allow me to share with you the benefit of my experience. Two months after my ordination to the holy priesthood, around the end of the 1950s, I embarked on a series of sermons entitled, "Christ and Wealth." After my third sermon, I heard murmuring in the parish that "this new priest is a Communist." So on the following Sunday, I decided to do something else.

Instead of a sermon, I just made announcements, i.e., Monday evening, the teens will meet; Tuesday evening, the Fellowship of St. John will meet; Wednesday evening, the Ladies Society will meet; Thursday evening, the Parish Council will meet; Friday evening, the Brotherhood and the Sisterhood of St. George will meet. Saturday evening, Vespers at 6:00 P.M. After the dismissal, the Executive Committee of the Parish Council remained in the church to tell me, "Father, today you gave a wonderful sermon."

I am not asking you to water down your message and sacrifice your idealism and theological principles (God forbid). I am asking you to discern your situation and understand your flock. In other words, you will not be preaching to theologians and seminarians, but to average people. Try your best to avoid abstract theology, because we are not living in a theoretical world, but in a broken and sick world which is crying for healing.

In order to reach people, *all* the people, use simple and sincere words, and above all, get to know your flock. Reach down to them in order to uplift them. Do not preach to them from your ivory towers. You must relate your theology to their concrete problems. People are more than theories and concepts; thus, any theology which does not touch people in their life and death, in their illness and health, in their poverty and wealth, in their joy and sorrow and in their hope and despair is an abstract and meaningless theology. What is the use of your theology if you cannot communicate it to people? Consequently, if you cannot communicate what you have learned in this school to your flock, the years which you have spent in this fine institute would have been in vain.

Today, you have graduated from Holy Cross School of Theology. You will receive your real diplomas, however, if five or ten years from now, you graduate from the school of the parish. This will be your real graduation. May the life-giving Cross grant you wisdom and patience to face the difficulties which lie ahead. Finally, in addition to wisdom and patience, you must have the capacity to love. In the last chapter of John, there is the story of that beautiful encounter between our Lord and Peter, a story which every priest and every bishop must always remember. It is recorded as follows:

> When they had finished breakfast, Jesus said to Simon Peter, "Simon, son of John, do you love Me more than these?" He said to Him, "Yes, Lord; You know that I love You." He said to him, "Feed My lambs." A second time, He said to him, "Simon, son of John, do you love Me?" He said to Him, "Yes Lord, You know that I love You." He said to him, "Tend My sheep." He said to him the third time, "Simon, son of John, do you love Me?" Peter was grieved because He said to him the third time, "Do you love Me?" and he said to Him, "Lord, You know everything; You know that I love You." Jesus said to him, "Feed My sheep" (John 21:15–17).

My dear graduates, I know you too love Him. Go feed His sheep.

The Suffering of Orthodox Jerusalem
1995

It gives me great pleasure to welcome you to the Antiochian Village, your home in North America for your first International Orthodox Conference to discuss the tragic conditions of the Arabic Orthodox Christians within the Patriarchate of Jerusalem. I believe that the grace of the Holy Spirit has gathered us from Palestine, Jordan, Canada and the United States during this Centennial Year of Antiochian Orthodoxy in North America to stop the continued hemorrhaging of the Orthodox Patriarchate of Jerusalem.

Keeping the Proper Perspective
I would like to state from the outset that our struggle is not directed against the Greek people with whom we are united in one bread and one chalice. Nor is our struggle against the Ecumenical Patriarch, or the Archbishop of Greece or the Greek Archdiocese of North and South America. I want you to know that we enjoy the best of relations with the aforementioned hierarchs. As a matter of fact, some of my seminarians receive their theological education at Holy Cross Greek Theological Seminary, in Brookline, Massachusetts. Moreover, next Saturday, I will be receiving an Honorary Doctorate degree from the very same institution. Our struggle, then, is against a patriarch and a hierarchy who imposed themselves over the traditions of our Church and against the indigenous people of the Patriarchate of Jerusalem.

The Antiochian Orthodox Christian Archdiocese of North America was founded one hundred years ago to serve all our Arabic-speaking people whether they come from Lebanon, Syria, Palestine, Jordan, Egypt or any other part of the Arab world. I am delighted to tell you that among my new bishops is a bishop from Palestinian background, His Grace, Bishop Demetri Khoury, from Al-Taybeh near Ramallah. I am sure that the Brotherhood of the Holy Sepulchre would have vetoed his election because he is a highly educated bishop. And among my clergy, there are outstanding priests from Palestine and Jordan who are treated with utmost love and respect because of their unquestionable dedication to the eternal ideals and principles which this archdiocese represents.

The Creation of the Task Force for Jerusalem
The Task Force which was organized to preserve and improve the Orthodox presence within the Patriarchate of Jerusalem is a step in the right direction. Moreover, it is a continuation of the long struggle of our beloved people in Jordan and Palestine to liberate the Church from foreign domination and to lead her to the promised land of freedom, prosperity and justice. I do not know of any Orthodox people on earth today who are more neglected than the Orthodox people within the Patriarchate of Jerusalem.

Some might ask: Why is this archbishop so concerned with the Church of Jerusalem? I am concerned because of the following reasons:
1. The Church of Jerusalem is the Mother of all Orthodox Churches and non-Orthodox Churches alike.
2. I am an Arab Orthodox by origin and culture. Thus I cannot remain silent while my people in the Patriarchate of Jerusalem are despised and neglected by a patriarch and a hierarchy who do not fear God and continue to neglect His Church.
3. In our Orthodox traditions, no one can impose foreign patriarchs, bishops and priests on native peoples. We cannot and ought not impose an Arab archbishop on the Greek people and an Arab patriarch on the Russian people. What is happening within the venerable Patriarchate of Jerusalem is scandalous to say the least.
4. I am concerned with the conditions of the Patriarchate of Jerusalem because Orthodox Christianity transcends geography. Thus, all of us should be concerned with the

life of the Church in Greece, Russia, Romania, Serbia, the Middle East or any part of the globe.
5. The news which was published in the press that the Patriarch is selling the Waqf of the Patriarchate to the Jews and leasing the land for ninety-nine years is most disturbing and most shocking to all of us. We must put a stop to it.

What History Has Taught Us
I have stated that the Patriarchate of Jerusalem is the Mother of all Churches. When you read the New Testament you notice that all the saving events of Christ took place in Palestine, i.e., the Annunciation, the Incarnation, the Crucifixion, and the Resurrection from the dead, just to mention a few. All of us know that the Church was born on Pentecost Day in Jerusalem. The first converts to Christianity were Palestinians. The first bishop of Jerusalem was St. James the Apostle who presided over the first Church council. During the era of persecution, the Church of Jerusalem suffered much and gave Christianity many of its saints and martyrs. After Emperor Constantine embraced Christianity, the Church of Jerusalem entered its golden era. Most of the Christian historical sites in Palestine were erected after the Christianization of the empire. During the Fourth Ecumenical Council in A.D. 45, the Church of Jerusalem was declared and independent patriarchate, i.e. an autocephalous Church.

History tells us that some of the most outstanding patriarchs who occupied the Throne of Jerusalem were Arabs such as Peter, the Bishop of the Arab Tribes; Elia who was from Najd and founded the Monastery of Constantine; John III and Peter II, the Bishop of the Arab Tribes.

This is just to mention a few. The claim of the Brotherhood of the Holy Sepulchre that the Orthodox Christians and the Patriarchs of Jerusalem were always national Greeks is false, and does not withstand historical scrutiny. Even the Greek historical sources contradict this claim. The Greek historian,

Chrysostomos, quotes Kostandios, the Patriarch of Constantinople: "That after the defeat and retreat of the Latins from Jerusalem until 1534, all the patriarchs and bishops of Jerusalem were Arabs nominated and elected by the Arab clergy and people" (Kostandios, pg. 23).

In the year 638, when the Arab Muslims invaded the Eastern Mediterranean, it was the Arab patriarch, Sofronios the Damascene, who received the famous charter from Caliph Omar Ibn-Al Khattab guaranteeing the safety of the Orthodox Christians of Palestine and their holy shrines.

The scope of this address does not permit me to mention all the names of the Arab patriarchs who reigned over Jerusalem. The last Arab patriarch, however, in that golden chain was Patriarch Atallah who succeeded the Arab patriarch, Mark III.

In 1517, the Ottomans conquered the Arab world and due to political circumstances, especially the influence of the Ecumenical Patriarchs of Constantinople over the "Salateen," the Greek Patriarch Germanos succeeded Patriarch Atallah and this was the beginning of the Greek domination of the Greek Patriarchate of Jerusalem. Since the last century, the Arab Orthodox of the Patriarchate of Jerusalem have been meeting in various conferences to convince the Greek hierarchy of the Patriarchate of Jerusalem to change its ways and return to the Arab Orthodox what rightly belongs to them, but to no avail. Again, the political circumstances worked in favor of the prevailing hierarchy.

Continue Our Struggle

I believe that what is built on falsehood is false, and the day will come when the Patriarchate of Jerusalem will be liberated just as Antioch was in 1899. History did not freeze in 1517. History is a dynamic force which cannot be measured by one hundred or even five hundred years. I, therefore, urge you to be united, organized and relentless in your struggle to free the Church of Jerusalem from the bondage of evil. Otherwise, the blood of your martyrs would have been shed in vain.

The Challenges of Another Century: The Centennial Address
Atlanta, 1995

In Psalm 102, the Prophet David said: "The children of Thy servants shall dwell secure; their posterity shall be established before Thee." Around the turn of the century, thousands of our people, driven by socioeconomic factors, sailed from the sunny shores of the Eastern Mediterranean, seeking economic opportunities, social justice and freedom in the United States of America and Canada. They were told that the streets of America were paved with gold. Thus, they left the simple life of their villages in Lebanon, Syria, and Palestine, pursuing their dreams across the sea.

The early immigrants did not bring with them material wealth, such as gold and silver. Instead, they carried with them the seeds of the Holy Orthodox Faith, which left, and continues to leave, everlasting marks on the soul of America. It did not take them long to discover that the streets of America were not paved with gold. And nothing was going to save them except their faith in God, perseverance, hard work, honesty and decency. They peddled their merchandise from city to city and from town to town, to the point of exhaustion. And when they could no longer walk, they stopped and founded worshipping communities, very often without the help of priests and bishops. Their most cherished institutions were the Church and the family.

The Peace of the Archdiocese and Orthodox Christianity
In 1895, the Antiochian Orthodox Christians in North America were very fortunate to have Archimandrite Raphael Hawaweeny in charge of their spiritual lives. This saintly, scholarly and mission-minded priest became their bishop in 1904 and laid the foundation of Antiochian Orthodoxy in this hemisphere. He

founded *AL-KALIMAT* (the *Word Magazine*), translated many liturgical books, authored many religious articles and served his flock with an apostolic zeal until he fell asleep in the Lord in February, 1915. The seeds which Bishop Raphael planted in the North American soil germinated and flourished, through the splendid efforts of his coworkers and successors. The Antiochian Archdiocese grew from thirty parishes in 1915 to sixty-six parishes in 1966 under the leadership of Metropolitan Antony, of blessed memory, and to 195 parishes in 1995. This unprecedented growth could never have been realized without the tireless efforts of many of our clergy and laity on the parochial, regional and North American level.

If we reflect on our Orthodox Christian history in North America in general, we will discover an awesome phenomenon. Was it a sheer accident that most of our Orthodox people immigrated to North America around the turn of this century? I do not believe so. In the history of salvation, there are no accidents. The world was not created by accident. Abraham did not leave Ur for the land of Canaan by accident. Moses did not receive the Ten Commandments by accident. The Incarnation did not happen by accident. The Crucifixion and Resurrection from the dead did not happen by accident; nor did the events of Pentecost happen by accident.

And consequently, the immigration of our Orthodox people, almost at the same time, from the Middle East, Greece, Russia and Eastern Europe to North America, surely did not happen by accident. I believe it was Divine Providence which brought Orthodoxy to North America to transform this culture and bring it back to God. The history of salvation is more than statistics, dates and a mere record of the past. Therefore, we must discern the past, find meaning and significance for the present and discover a common vision for the future in the light of the Scriptures. For "only in His light, shall we see light."

I told you once that history is full of "bright moments and blind moments." We Orthodox, however, have a strong tendency to magnify and glorify history, sometimes to the point of idolatry. Thus, we cannot honestly say that everything during the past one hundred years of our Antiochian history in North America was glorious and magnificent. Yes, we have experienced many bright moments, but at the same time we have had our share of blind moments. Our archdiocese has suffered the tragedy of division for sixty years: first between Russi and Antaki, and second between New York and Toledo. This unfortunate division began after the death of Bishop Hawaweeny and lasted until 1975, when Archbishop Michael, of blessed memory, and I put an end to our conflicts and inaugurated a new era of Orthodox history in North America.

As we reflect on the past, I appeal to our beloved hierarchs, clergy, trustees and faithful people not to permit Satan to divide your ranks again. Even if the angels tell you division is good for you, do not believe them. The insights which come to us from the past provide a guide that can illuminate the present and help us chart our course for the future. If we do not learn from the mistakes of the past, we will be condemned to repeat these very same mistakes.

Where Do We Go From Here?

After an eventful century of mission, service and witness, where do we go from here? I am sure all of you have various answers. What we need, however, is a common response to this question. Two years ago, on July 22, 1993, I appointed a task force on the Church in the twenty-first century, and I prefaced this appointment with the following:

> *Seven years from now, the twentieth century will be history and a new century will dawn on us. The question is: are we prepared, as the Church, to face the challenges of the new century? In order to find answers to this question and define our goals for the years to come, I am appointing a Task Force.*

I am delighted that this task force acted swiftly and did not procrastinate. Many meetings were held, many thoughts were exchanged and many ideas clashed. It was indeed a healthy process which resulted in a very good document entitled, "An American Orthodox Vision: Charting a Course of Action for the Church in the Twenty-First Century."

The task force report states that we should start implementing its recommendations beginning 1996–97, 1998–99 and 2000–2001. Since time is of the essence and every moment is an urgent one, I believe we can start implementing some of the recommendations of this report immediately and not wait until next year. If we want to implement all the recommendations of this report, we will have to raise almost an additional two million dollars. Thus, instead of implementing all the recommendations of the report at once, we can implement them gradually. I believe between now and next year, we will have achieved the following:

More Bishops
The report recommends that we have an additional four bishops. The Board of Trustees and I do not think, at this point in time, we need four bishops. We need two and we already have them. As you can see, we did not wait until next year. How did that happen? Last year at the fall meeting in Phoenix, Arizona, the Board of Trustees voted unanimously to ask the Holy Synod of Antioch for two additional bishops and the Synod responded positively. Thus, we welcome to our fellowship two beloved brothers in Christ: His Grace, Bishop Joseph (Zehlaoui) and His Grace, Bishop Demetri (Khoury).

For the first time in our history, you now have five bishops at your service. Bishop Antoun will remain with me at the main headquarters in New Jersey and Bishops Joseph, Basil and Demetri will be serving you from Los Angeles, California, Wichita, Kansas, and Toledo, Ohio. Parishes on the West Coast, for example, will seek the service of the bishop who happens to be in California, and so forth. It is not practical or economically feasible for parishes in the Midwest to invite a bishop from the West or from the Southwest when they have a bishop next door to them in the Midwest. Parishes in Canada and in the East will be served primarily by His Grace, Bishop Antoun, and myself. I want our bishops to be very busy. Thus, I strongly recommend that every parish should be visited by one of our hierarchs at least once every year.

The Southwest Chancery
To have more bishops is to have more regional chanceries. I am delighted to inform you that last month I visited our parish in Wichita and blessed the new, beautiful chancery which consists of four bedrooms, a large living room, a dining room, a finished basement, first floor and second floor. It stands on one and a half acres of land.

Missions and Evangelism
One of the most important departments of our archdiocese is the Department of Missions and Evangelism. In John 22:21, our Lord said: "As the Father has sent Me, even so I send you." And in Matthew 4:23, we read, "And He went about all Galilee teaching in their synagogues, and preaching the Gospel of the Kingdom and healing every disease and every infirmity among the people." Our Lord Himself was the missionary par excellence. He commissioned His disciples "to teach and baptize all nations." Consequently, the Church, which is the extension of Christ in time and space, is sent by Christ to make "disciples of all nations." If the Church loses this missionary dimension, she loses the raison d'etre for her existence.

Some of our Orthodox people are under the impression that missions and evangelism is a Protestant idea. This is far from being true. During the pre-Islamic era, millions of people were converted to Orthodoxy through evangelism; and who can forget the heroic efforts of Cyril and Methodius in spreading the Gospel to the Slavic nations. We thank God, through the efforts of our Department of Missions and Evangelism, thousands of people have been converted to Orthodoxy, both in the Byzantine and Western Rites. In the report, it is recommended that we should have four full-time missionary priests, at a cost of $200,000 a year. We now have three full-time missionary priests, and if you approve the proposed increase in the assessment, I will appoint an additional priest to the Department of Missions and Evangelism, beginning in our next fiscal year. I believe that in our missionary thrust, we must target the following groups: (a) people who are searching for the One Holy Catholic and Apostolic Church; (b) lapsed Orthodox within our own parishes (there are thousands of Arab-American Orthodox who do not know anything about their Church); (c) immigrants who came to North America as a result of the unfortunate wars in the Middle East and other parts of Eastern Europe and Russia. (Such immigrants need a special ministry and must not be neglected. I hope that our Arabic-speaking bishops will pay special attention to these immigrants who feel alienated within our North American culture.) And (d) it is time to start thinking seriously about a mission to our Afro-American and Hispanic brothers and sisters. You can see that we have unlimited possibilities if we have the financial resources.

The Department of Planning and Future Development
I am delighted to inform you that I have already established this department. Some of its main functions will be: (a) to find major donors to help us fund some of the recommendations of the task force; (b) to develop long-range financial plans such as wills, legacies, annuities, trusts and endowments, such as Endow Orthodoxy for Tomorrow; (c) to recruit qualified people on the regional and North American level to help implement this program; (d) to assist our parishes in finding new ways and means of raising funds with an emphasis on tithing.

Orthodox Unity in America
Last year, 1994, between November 30 and December 2, an unprecedented Episcopal Orthodox Conference was convened, at the Antiochian Village, Western Pennsylvania. Twenty-nine hierarchs from the United States and Canada met for the first

time in our North American history to discuss and discover a common vision for Orthodoxy in this hemisphere. The Antiochian Archdiocese played a pivotal role in this historical event. I wish that all of you could have been with us to witness the harmony, peace and love which prevailed throughout the conference. All hierarchs, especially Archbishop Iakovos and Metropolitan Theodosius, contributed to the success of our assembly. We did not have one single misunderstanding, even when Bishop Maximos of Pittsburgh advocated in his paper that all Orthodox in the diaspora should be under the omophorion of the Ecumenical Patriarch. I was amazed at the generous silence of the OCA bishops, who did not challenge Bishop Maximos' view for the sake of peace.

What amazed me most, however, was the anger and unwarranted reaction of certain patriarchal headquarters across the ocean. Despite the monumental difficulties which we are facing from within and without, the Antiochian quest, or rather obsession, with Orthodox unity in America will persist and never be stopped. We shall never rest until the Orthodox canonical chaos in this country is normalized. I long for the day when we can have one bishop, in one city, over one territory. Without Orthodox unity in North America, our spiritual and moral impact on this culture will remain marginal and ineffective. Just think how much we can do in the fields of missions and evangelism, youth ministry, Christian education, communication, spiritual renewal, clergy pensions, etc. if we can put our house in order. I strongly believe that Orthodox unity is inevitable because the All-Holy Spirit continues to work in the Church and He will lead us from the wilderness of disunity to the promised land of unity and fulfillment.

As We Begin the Next Hundred Years

In closing, as we begin another one hundred years of mission, witness and service, let us reaffirm what St. Paul wrote in his Epistle to the Hebrews: "Jesus Christ is the same yesterday, today and forever." God is present in history, not only in past events and present experience, but also as a future hope. He who is Alpha, is also Omega. In Him all things hold together.

On this one-hundredth year, God bless this archdiocese, and God bless you all.

Editor's Endnotes:

1. In his Centennial address in Anaheim, California, Philip also reorganizes the Youth Department; calls for a review of clergy stipends, and the clergy insurance and retirement fund; raises the assessment per baptized member from $20 to $25 to pay for increasing needs, e.g., additional auxiliary bishops; remembers the departed clergy on the centennial anniversary; thanks the retired clergy for their service. Finally, he welcomes Bishop Joseph and Bishop Demetri to the hierarchy of the archdiocese, which now includes the metropolitan and four auxiliary bishops.

Chapter 19

FAITH AND WORKS:
Whose Feet Will I Wash?

> *If we claim that we love God and our neighbor, but fail to translate that love into acts of mercy and compassion, we are living a false faith, a dead faith. This is why St. Basil the Great says, "If I live alone, whose feet will I wash?" The Lord washed the feet of the disciples; whose feet will you wash?*
>
> Metropolitan Philip

- *The Right Faith, the Wrong System, 1996*
- *Created to Serve: The Twentieth Anniversary of the Order of St. Ignatius of Antioch, 1996*
- *Woe to the Shepherd Who Leaves the Flock: The Second Address to the Task Force on Jerusalem, 1997*
- *Faith Without Works Is Dead, Toronto, 1997*

The components of this chapter rightly belong under the title "Faith and Works," because in some way each entry refers to the devastating effect of separating of faith and works. At times, this is expressed as a separation of the faith we proclaim and the works we actually accomplish; at other times, it is expressed as a separation of what we say and what we do.

The first article is a poignant but truthful editorial which speaks precisely about faith and works; Philip writes about "The Right Faith, the Wrong System." It is written in light of the strained relations between the Patriarchs of Constantinople and Moscow. Philip clearly proclaims: "Our system does not work!" For Philip, this is merely another example which calls Orthodox scholars and theologians "to come down from their ivory towers" and to deal honestly with the antiquated system prevailing in the Orthodox Church. He proclaims this, despite the fact that it is "the right faith!"

*The second piece from 1996 is Philip's address delivered in Montreal, Canada, at the twentieth anniversary of the Order of St. Ignatius of Antioch. He reviews the challenges of the Order as the "philanthropic arm" of the archdiocese, created to serve, and **only** to serve, following the Lord who referred to Himself: "I have come not to be served, but to serve" (Mark 10:45). He then lists the innumerable ways in which the Order helps the Church and archdiocese in reaching its goals.*

The third piece, given in Los Angeles, California, is his address in 1997 to the Task Force to Jerusalem. This comes two years after his first address in 1995. However, by this time things have started to escalate. Therefore, Philip turns to the Scriptures and the Fathers to justify his action on behalf of the Arab Orthodox; "it is based on the theology of our Church." In this way, he calls those present to "raise their voices" at the unjust treatment of the Palestinian Orthodox Christians.

The fourth and final piece is Philip's 1997 address to the Archdiocesan Convention meeting in Toronto, Canada. The theme of the Convention is precisely "faith without works is dead" (James 2:26). In this address, Philip shows his lifelong focus on "incarnational theology" by first theologically explaining the scriptural debate about faith and works, then by explaining to the listeners how the Orthodox Faith gets translated into proper **praxis**. *Although he reviews some of the practical decisions he has made since the previous convention in 1995, Philip never leaves the strong scriptural and patristic roots which, in the end, teach one of his favorite quotes of St. Basil the Great: "If I live alone, whose feet will I wash?"*

J. J. A.

The Right Faith, the Wrong System
1996

Words are inadequate to describe the depth of my sorrow when I read about the suspension of brotherly relations between the Moscow Patriarchate and the Patriarchate of Constantinople. According to the press release issued by the Patriarchate of Moscow, it seems relations were suspended because of a canonical dispute over the Orthodox faithful in Estonia. Moreover, the Ukrainian problem has, undoubtedly, contributed to such strained relations between these two patriarchates after 1,008 years of normal relations. This tragic situation could have been avoided had we developed an effective Orthodox system to mediate disputes among sister patriarchates. The Ecumenical Patriarch is supposed to be, traditionally speaking, the spiritual leader of world Orthodoxy, but since His Holiness is part of this dispute, how could he preside in love as "first among equals"?

Four years ago Diodoros I, Patriarch of Jerusalem, flagrantly interfered in the internal affairs of our archdiocese by dividing our St. Nicholas Parish of San Francisco. We strongly protested his uncanonical interference by appealing to the Ecumenical Patriarch, the Antiochian Patriarch and all Orthodox Patriarchs, but to no avail. The answer was dead silence. *Our system does not work.*

The International Task Force to Support the Orthodox People of Palestine and Jordan has persistently and strongly protested the actions of Patriarch Diodoros I against the indigenous people of the Patriarchate of Jerusalem. Many letters were sent to the Ecumenical Patriarch, the Antiochian Patriarch and all Orthodox Patriarchs. Again, the answer was dead silence. *Our system does not work.*

Last October, I brought to the attention of the Holy Synod of Antioch the strained relations between Moscow and Constantinople. The reaction of Antioch was simply inaction.

We Orthodox consider ourselves, and rightly so, the inheritors of the Faith which "once for all was delivered to the saints." And yet, we cannot solve our problems peacefully because we do not have a referee. *Our system does not work.* During the Byzantine era, the emperor often presided over the meetings of the Ecumenical Councils and enforced their decisions. Consequently, the emperor was the referee, and such a system did work despite its pitfalls. Today we do not have an emperor; therefore we do not have a referee.

Our sacred canons have very well addressed inter-Orthodox relations. Our problem is: When we disagree on the interpretation of the canons, and in the absence of pan-Orthodox Great Synods, who will referee our disputes? It is embarrassing indeed that in this age of the global village and excellent communications, we Orthodox cannot solve the problem of Estonia and stop the Patriarch of Jerusalem from meddling in the affairs of the Antiochian Archdiocese of North America. Since we live in a highly organized society, is it impossible to form a pan-Orthodox Commission, representing all autocephalous churches, to mediate inter-Orthodox disputes?

It is a shame that on the eve of celebrating the two-thousand-year anniversary of Orthodox Christianity, two prominent Orthodox Patriarchates suspended brotherly relations because we do not have a mechanism to deal decisively with such problems. We invite Orthodox theologians and thinkers to come down from their ivory towers and address this urgent matter objectively and without any racial or historical bias.

Finally, let us stop using lofty words such as "the most Holy Synod," "most beloved brother," and "most venerable Patriarchate" while stabbing each other in the back. This is not Orthodoxy.

Created to Serve: The Twentieth Anniversary of the Order of St. Ignatius of Antioch
1996

The twentieth anniversary of the Order of St. Ignatius of Antioch coincides with the thirtieth anniversary of a special era in the life of this God-protected Archdiocese. Some refer to this occasion as the anniversary of my consecration to the Holy Episcopate. I would rather refer to this as the anniversary of a distinct and unique period in our history as a Church in North America. In 1966, by the power of the Holy Spirit and your "amen," I was consecrated metropolitan archbishop to serve you as long as God wills. Life in the Church can be summarized in one word: service. If we do not serve each other lovingly, sincerely and with compassion, then we lose the raison d'etre of our existence. Our Lord said: "The Son of man came not to be served, but to serve, and to give His life as ransom for many" (Mark 10:45).

The formative years of this thirtieth anniversary were most difficult, to say the least. Time does not permit me to elaborate on these difficulties. In January of 1968, I suffered a health setback while in Washington, D.C., working for a just peace in the Middle East. Suddenly my dreams were shattered and my visions were blurred. For a while I thought that my ministry to this archdiocese was over. Despite my miraculous recovery, four years later, I underwent open-heart surgery in the Miami Heart Institute. The Miami experience was a tremendous spiritual transformation. Doubt, despair and uncertainty were conquered by faith, hope and complete surrender to the Will of God. It is ironic, indeed, that in order to be liberated, we must completely surrender. Christ said to me what he said to St. Paul: "My grace is sufficient for you, for My power is made perfect in weakness"

(2 Corinthians 12:9). There is no doubt that God works through us; thus what we have achieved, after 1972, in this archdiocese, was a perfect gift from God. For His grace is sufficient for us. Just think that most of our accomplishments happened after a shattered heart was repaired. "For when I am weak, then I am strong" (2 Corinthians 12:10).

In 1973, the Antiochian Orthodox Christian Women of North America (AOCWNA) was founded. Today the women of this archdiocese are a tremendous source of spiritual and financial power for our Church. In 1974, I began to dream of the Order of St. Ignatius of Antioch. In 1975, I met with a dedicated group of this archdiocese to lay down the foundation of this revolutionary movement. Also in 1975, our Antiochian people in the United States and Canada were reunited into one strong archdiocese, after sixty years of division.

In 1976, this great Order of St. Ignatius of Antioch was born. I want to emphasize before you tonight that the success of the Order is indeed a miracle. Someone might ask, why a miracle? It is a miracle because our people in general do not like to be organized; we are very individualistic. And second, we do not like to pay; i.e., we are not that generous with our money when it comes to charity. The miracle of the Order proved otherwise. You proved beyond doubt that you can be organized and that you can be generous. The fact that in twenty years you have raised more than eight million dollars for worthy projects, nationally and internationally, speaks louder than words.

In his Epistle to the Ephesians, your patron St. Ignatius of Antioch said:

> *Pray, then come and join this choir, everyone of you; let there be a whole symphony of minds in concert; take the tone all together from God, and sing aloud to the Father with one voice through Jesus Christ, so that He may hear you and know by your good works that you are indeed members of His Son's body. A completely united front will help to keep you in constant communion with God.*

Members of the Order of St. Ignatius: A few weeks ago, in Detroit, Michigan, I said: "When future historians write the history of this archdiocese, they will divide it into two eras: before the Order and after the Order. Today the Order consists of almost 1,600 women and men who are totally committed to the eternal ideals and principles of St. Ignatius of Antioch. St. Paul admonishes us to 'give thanks always for all things.' "

Tonight, I want to thank you on behalf of the Heritage and Learning Center, which has become the spring of our spiritual renaissance. I want to thank you on behalf of thousands of our children who have benefited from your scholarships to our camp. I want to thank you on behalf of the clergy who are benefiting and will benefit from our retirement fund. I want to thank you on behalf of our young people throughout the United States and Canada for the Youth Department and Campus Ministry. I want to thank you on behalf of the Department of Missions and Evangelism for bringing thousands of non-Orthodox to the promised land of Orthodoxy. In 1966, we had sixty-five parishes. Today, we have 205 parishes.

I want to thank you on behalf of Christian Education, Antiochian House of Studies, Teen SOYO, Project Mexico, Prison Ministry, victims of natural and social catastrophes, the task force to help liberate our Orthodox people within the Patriarchate of Jerusalem, the West Coast Chancery, the Southwest Chancery, St. George Hospital of Beirut, and the University of Balamand. Last June, I visited Lebanon in the aftermath of that savage and barbarian attack against South Lebanon. For the help which you have offered to thousands of orphans, I bring to you messages of thanks from little children written with the blood of their fathers and mothers.

These are but some of your achievements. Now, when some people ask what the Order is all about, we tell them, "Come and see." Christianity, my friends, is more than speculation and theories. Christianity, in the final analysis, is love translated into action. During the past twenty years, some members of the Order have fallen asleep in the Lord. May their souls rest in peace.

Finally, I would like to leave you with these words from the Epistle of St. Ignatius to the Smyrneans. "As the tree is known by its fruit, so they who claim to belong to Christ are known by their actions; for this work of ours does not consist in just making professions, but in a faith that is both practical and lasting."

Congratulations on your twentieth anniversary!

Woe to the Shepherd Who Leaves the Flock: The Second Address to the Task Force on Jerusalem
1997

Last year in May, we had a most successful gathering in Chicago, Illinois, to discuss the past, present and future of our Orthodox people within the Patriarchate of Jerusalem. I remember vividly the talks which were delivered at that gathering, the enthusiasm which permeated your hearts and the great banquet which was a true expression of our commitment to the eternal ideals and principles which the Task Force represents.

Why Antiochians are Concerned
Some people might ask, why are we, Antiochians, concerned about the plight of our brethren within the Patriarchate of Jerusalem? The answer is simple and it is based on the theology of our Church. Our Creed states, "And I believe in One Holy Catholic and Apostolic Church." And in the first letter of St. Paul to the Corinthians, we read, "The cup of blessing which we bless, is it not a participation in the blood of Christ? And the bread which we break, is it not a participation in the body of Christ? Because there is one bread, we who are many are one body, and we all partake of one bread" (1 Corinthians 10:16, 17).

Therefore, the Church is one and this oneness is expressed through our participation in the same cup and in the same bread regardless of whether we are in Antioch, Jerusalem, Istanbul, Greece, Moscow or the United States of America. We are many members in the same Body of Christ which is the Church; thus if one member of this body suffers in Palestine or in any part of this world, naturally, the rest of the members of this body will feel the same pain. Our Lord did not establish different churches.

On the contrary, He established one Church and said, "I will build My Church and the gates of Hell shall not prevail against her."

The Church is holy because her founder is the absolute holiness. The Church, as the extension of Christ in time and space, must incarnate this holiness and make it a reality in our daily life. The Church is Catholic because it transcends all geographic boundaries and human barriers. And finally, the Church is Apostolic because it is based on the treasured teachings of the holy Apostles and fathers.

This is precisely why, as members of the Body of Christ which is the Church, we are concerned with the plight of Orthodoxy in the Holy Land, that land which was stained by the blood of our Lord and many martyrs, saints and confessors. The Patriarchate of Jerusalem has had a glorious history. Its early fathers such as Saint Sava, Saint Cyril and many others have enriched our spirituality by their tremendous contribution to our theological thoughts. From the first Christian century to the Muslim conquest of the Holy Land, Jerusalem and the entire Holy Land was inhabited by Orthodox Christians. After the Muslim conquest, however, the population of Jerusalem and the Holy Land consisted mainly of Orthodox Christians and Muslims. This demographic fact continued until the era of the Crusades. Most of the holy places in Jerusalem and the Holy Land were controlled by the Orthodox.

With the rise of the Western Missionary movement, Latins and Protestant began to invade the Holy Land and proselytize the Orthodox people. Thus, through monies and different kinds of bribery, many of the Orthodox deserted their faith and joined various Christian denominations. Today, I am sorry to tell you that, according to statistics, only two thousand Orthodox Christians are left in the city of Jerusalem. So many of our people in the Holy Land have deserted the Orthodox faith because their hierarchs, their shepherds, did not care for the flock. Our Lord, through the power of the Holy Spirit, has ordained apostles, and subsequently bishops, to protect and serve the flock.

Therefore, the main responsibility of any patriarch or any bishop is to minister to his people and to protect his flock from ravaging wolves.

In Ezekiel, we read:

> Son of man, prophesy against the shepherds of Israel, prophesy and say to them, thus says the Lord God to the shepherds: Woe to the shepherds of Israel who feed themselves! Should not the shepherds feed the flocks? You eat the fat and clothe yourselves with the wool; you slaughter the fatlings, but you do not feed the flock. The weak you have not strengthened, nor have you healed those who were sick, nor bound up the broken, nor brought back what was driven away, nor sought what was lost; but with force and cruelty you have ruled them. So they were scattered because there was no shepherd; and they became food for the beasts of the field when they were scattered. My sheep wandered through all the mountains, and on every high hill; yes, my flock was scattered over the whole face of the earth, and no one was seeking or searching for them (Ezekiel 34:2-6).

Two Kinds of Imperialism

Do not these screaming words of Ezekiel describe the Orthodox shepherds in the Holy Land and paint a tragic and dark picture of what happened to the flock? The Orthodox people of the Holy Land have been plagued by two kinds of vicious imperialism: one is *political*, represented by international Zionism and the other is *spiritual*, represented by Hellenism. I realize that the political situation in the Holy Land is confused and uncertain, but that does not prevent us from working hard to preserve the remnants of this glorious Orthodox faith which "once and for all was delivered to the saints."

The Prophet Zechariah said:

> Woe to the worthless shepherd who leaves the flock! A sword shall be against his arm, and against his right eye;

his arm shall completely wither and his right eye shall be totally blinded (Zechariah 11:17).

Apostolic Canon 38 states:

Let the bishop have the care of all ecclesiastical matters and let him manage them on the understanding that God is overseeing and supervising. Let him not be allowed to appropriate anything therefrom, or to give God's things to his relatives. If they are poor or needy, let him provide for them as poor and needy, but let him not trade off things of the Church under this pretext.

What We Must Do
All of us are responsible for this precious heritage which we have received from our forefathers. How can we remain silent when we see the wealth of the Church which is supposed to be distributed to the poor, being spent on palaces, villas and worldly pleasures by selfish shepherds who do not even speak the language of the flock.

In conclusion, as members of the "One Holy Catholic and Apostolic Church," regardless of where we live, we must raise our voices, use our God-given talents and direct all our efforts to save the Orthodox Church in the Holy Land so that when we stand before the Judgment Seat, at the second coming of our Lord and Savior, Jesus Christ, we will hear these divine words: "Well done, thou good and faithful servants."

Faith Without Works Is Dead
Toronto, 1997

The theme of our Convention this year is chosen from the Epistle of St. James (2:26): *"Faith without works is dead."*

Some Christian denominations, however, believe that works are not necessary for salvation, and that we are saved by "faith alone." Their point of reference is St. Paul's letter to the Romans. The Orthodox theological position is clearly against reducing the Christian message to salvation through good works alone or faith alone. St. James did not emphasize the importance of "good works" at the exclusion of faith. In the first chapter of his epistle, he says, "if any of you lacks wisdom, let him ask God, who gives to all men generously and without reproaching, and it will be given him. But let him ask in faith with no doubting" (James 1:5).

In Chapter 5, he again says: "And the prayer of faith will save the sick man, and the Lord will raise him up; and if he has committed sins, he will be forgiven" (James 5:15).

Ss. James and Paul: What They Mean

Religion to St. James is not something abstract, nor is it an intellectual adventure, nor can it be reduced to a mere philosophy. In James' own words, "Religion that is pure and undefiled before God and the Father is this: to visit orphans and widows in their affliction, and to keep oneself unstained from the world" (James 1:27).

"Be doers of the word and not hearers only, deceiving yourselves" (James 1:22). Therefore, if you have faith, translate it into concrete actions on behalf of your neighbor, for a dead faith can save no one.

> What does it profit, my brethren, if a man says he has faith but has not works? Can his faith save him? If a brother or sister is ill-clad and in lack of daily food, and

one of you says to them, go in peace, be warmed and filled, without giving them the things needed for the body, what does it profit? So faith by itself, if it has no works, is dead (James 2:14–17).

In his explanation of the Orthodox Faith, St. John of Damascus says: "Because faith without works is dead, likewise works without faith are dead, because true faith is tested through works." Some Christian denominations, unjustifiably, find contradictions between James and Paul. The Church, however, does not find any such contradictions. It is inconceivable that the emphasis of James on good works excludes faith, and by the same token, it is inconceivable that St. Paul's emphasis on faith in his letter to the Romans, Chapter 5, excludes good works. James and Paul wrote to two different kinds of people. I read and reread St. Paul's letter to the Romans and discovered, once again, that St. Paul never said that we are saved by faith alone.

James was concerned with the dead and legalistic approach to faith, while Paul was concerned with the self-righteousness of the Judaizing elements in the early Church. Their basic teaching was that salvation can be achieved through the legal piety of the law. Paul emphasized that we win salvation only through Christ and in response to divine grace, apart from the Mosaic Law. "Therefore, having been justified by faith, we have peace with God through our Lord Jesus Christ, through whom we have access by faith through grace" (Romans 5:1, 2). There is a fundamental difference between the old law and the grace brought by Christ. "For what the law could not do . . . God did by sending His own Son" (Romans 8:3).

In John 1:17, we read, "For the law was given through Moses; grace and peace came through Jesus Christ." In all the letters of St. Paul, faith and good works cannot be separated, even in his letter to the Romans.

Glory and honor and peace for everyone who does good (Romans 2:10).

Contribute to the needs of the saints, practice hospitality (Romans 12:13).

If your enemy is hungry, feed him; if he is thirsty, give him drink (Romans 12:20).

In Galatians 6:2–4 we read, "Bear one another's burdens and so fulfill the law of Christ. . . . Let each one test his own work." In First Thessalonians 1:2, 3, St. Paul says: "We give thanks to God always for you all, constantly mentioning you in our prayers, remembering before our God and Father your work of faith and labor of love." In Hebrews 6:10: "For God is not so unjust as to overlook your work and the love which you showed for His sake in serving the saints, as you still do." In 2 Corinthians 6:1: "Working together with Him, then, we entreat you not to accept the grace of God in vain." This is a wonderful example of that synergy, that cooperation with God which is necessary for salvation. And in Galatians 5:6: "For in Christ Jesus neither circumcision nor uncircumcision is of any avail, but faith working through love." Any faith which does not work through love is no faith. In fact, it is a dead faith.

In the Gospel of St. John 5:17, Christ said: "My Father is working still, and I am working." And in the same Gospel, 9:4, our Lord said: "We must work the works of him who sent Me, while it is day; night comes when no one can work."

In Ephesians 2:10, we read:

For we are what He has made us, created in Christ Jesus for good works, which God prepared beforehand to be our way of life.

Scripture and the Fathers

The focus of the entire New Testament is on the incarnate and resurrected Christ and good works. History, from an Orthodox perspective, does not move in a vicious circle. It began with the creation of man and it will end with the Second Coming of Christ. "And He shall come again with glory, to judge the living and the dead, whose kingdom shall have no end." And so, my friends, according to our Nicene Creed, Christ shall come again to judge us, "the living and the dead." What kind of criteria will He use to judge us? Let us for a few moments examine Matthew 25:31, the most moving lesson which we read on Meatfare Sunday and which depicts the Last Judgment.

> When the Son of man comes in His glory, and all the angels with Him, then He will sit on His glorious throne. Before Him will be gathered all the nations, and He will separate them, one from another, as a shepherd separates the sheep from the goats, and He will place the sheep at His right hand, but the goats at the left. Then the King will say to those at His right hand, Come, O blessed of my Father, inherit the kingdom prepared for you from the foundation of the world.

Please listen carefully to these words which scream at us:

> For I was hungry and you gave me food, I was thirsty and you gave me drink, I was a stranger and you welcomed me, I was naked and you clothed me, I was sick and you visited me, I was in prison and you came to me. Then the righteous will answer Him, Lord when did we see Thee hungry? ... And the King will answer them, truly, I say to you, as you did it to one of the least of these, my brethren, you did it to Me.

I am sure you know the rest of the lesson, which makes all of us tremble. He did not say: I was hungry and you just prayed for me. Nor did He say, I was thirsty and you told Me to buy bottled water. Nor did He say, I was a stranger and you showed Me the inn. Nor did He say, I was naked and you wished Me warm weather. Nor did He say, I was sick and you lit a candle for Me.

I quoted this particular lesson from Matthew to emphasize that faith in the Risen Lord and good works are inseparable and complement each other. The most important commandment in the Scripture is to love God and your neighbor. Listen to these words from the First Epistle of John: "For if any one says 'I love God' and hates his brother, he is a liar; for he who does not love his brother whom he has seen, cannot love God whom he has not seen" (1 John 4:20).

If we claim that we love God and our neighbor, but fail to translate this love into acts of mercy and compassion, we are living a false faith, a dead faith.

Beloved children in Christ, our Church is called the Church of the Fathers, and rightly so, because our theology is deeply rooted in patristic thoughts in interpreting the Scripture and the history of salvation. Therefore, let us turn now to those great and inspired minds to see what they have said about good works.

In his homily on 2 Timothy, John Chrysostom said:

> Do you see that the failure to give alms is enough to cast a person into hell, for where will he avail anything who does not do good works? Do you fast every day? So also did those foolish virgins, but it availed them nothing. Do you pray? So did they. Prayer without almsgiving is unfruitful.

To this Chrysostom adds: "Let us not, then, beloved, think that faith suffices for our salvation." In the same vein, St. Basil the Great states: "He who fails to clothe the naked, if he could, deserves to be called a thief."

St. Clement of Alexandria said: "When you see your brother, you see God." Likewise, Evagrius taught: "After God, we must count all men as God Himself." Paul Evdokimov adds: "The best icon of God is man."

St. Anthony the Great put it this way: "From our neighbor is life, and from our neighbor is death. Therefore, if we win our neighbor, we win God, but if we harm our neighbor, we sin against Christ."

And in the following paragraph, St. Basil the Great expands

on this theme even more graphically, when he asks:

> If I live alone, whose feet will I wash? What scope will a man have for showing humility if he has no one before whom to show himself humble? What chance of showing compassion, when cut off from the fellowship of other men? The Lord washed the disciples' feet. Whose feet will you wash?

I would like to reemphasize here that the purpose of all these quotations from the Fathers is not to impress on you that we are saved by good works alone. If good works are not a genuine response to the divine grace and an expression of our deep faith in Christ Jesus, then such good works are to no avail.

Professor John Karmiris put it this way:

> Generally, then, we can say that man's justification and salvation is first and foremost an action and a gift of the divine grace; secondly, it is by the intention and free cooperation of man in the form of concrete faith and good works. While, to the contrary, a fall from faith and good works entails a fall from Divine Grace.

Faith and Works in the Archdiocese

This archdiocese has been sustained throughout the years by two ingredients: an abiding faith in the Risen Lord and good works. Where would this archdiocese be without the faith and good works of our clergy, our Board of Trustees, our Order of St. Ignatius of Antioch, our Antiochian Women, our Fellowship of St. John the Divine, our Teen SOYO, and members of our parish councils, ladies' societies, choirs and church schools? Where would this archdiocese be without the millions of dollars which our Trustees, the Order of St. Ignatius and the Antiochian Women have raised for projects and charity within and without this archdiocese?

A good example of faith and good works is our Food for

Hungry People program. Since its inception, this program has raised more than two million dollars for the needy in North America, Latin America, Africa and the Middle East. And what about all the new parishes which have been planted throughout the continent? Or we could ask: where would this archdiocese be without the Antiochian Village, which has left and continues to leave a lasting impression on the youth of our Church?

Simply said, a faith will remain abstract and empty if we do not put flesh on it. We indeed have put flesh on our theology in many ways. For example, we have established four endowments; one of them, Metropolitan Philip's Endowment for the Antiochian Village, in the amount of one million dollars, has reached its goal. We can spend only the interest of this endowment without touching the principal. The three other endowments, which are still far from reaching their goals, are: Youth Ministry, Christian Education and Missions and Evangelism.

Last but not least, the Order of St. Ignatius of Antioch, which as the philanthropic arm of the archdiocese exists solely for the faith and works of the Church, continues to grow. Thanks be to God, as of this date, the number of women and men who have joined the Order is 1,745. Remember our goal is 2,000 by 2000.

Ladies and gentlemen, despite some disappointments which we have experienced from time to time, if we want to remain faithful to our calling, we must continue our struggle for the well-being of this archdiocese and the glory of God.

I would like to take this opportunity to thank my brother hierarchs who continue to work and travel tirelessly, watching over the flock, namely: His Grace Bishop Antoun, His Grace Bishop Joseph, His Grace Bishop Basil and His Grace Bishop Demetri.

In conclusion, I would like to leave you with these words from the martyr, St. Ignatius of Antioch: "As the tree is known by its fruit, so they who claim to belong to Christ are known by their actions; for this work of ours does not consist in just making professions, but in a faith that is both practical and lasting."

Editor's Endnotes:

1. *In 1996, the archdiocese celebrates the thirtieth anniversary of Metropolitan Philip's Episcopate. Celebrations are held in various locations throughout the archdiocese.*

2. *In 1997, Philip is invited and accepts an invitation to Moscow. There he celebrates, for the second time, in many of the cathedrals, and meets with Patriarch Alexei II.*

3. *In the 1997 address to the convention in Toronto, Philip announces that twenty-two new parishes are accepted; a full-time director is hired for the Christian Education Department; eighteen new seminarians are accepted to Holy Cross and St. Vladimir's Seminaries; the Antiochian House of Studies is expanded with the educational forum of Applied Theology in the form of an accredited Doctor of Ministry Course with Pittsburgh Theological Seminary; a record number of campers attended the Summer Camp at the Antiochian Village; a full-time director for Camp Programs and Campus Ministry is established.*

Chapter 20

KEEPING HEARTS AND MINDS IN CHRIST JESUS:
Endings and Beginnings; a New Millennium

> *It is very important to preach the Gospel, but it is even more important that we become the Gospel. It is important to preach a sermon, but it is even more important that we ourselves become a sermon.*
> Metropolitan Philip

- *Tending the Flock, 1998*
- *Keeping Our Minds and Hearts in Christ Jesus, Chicago, 1999*

AND HE LEADS THEM

We close out the final decade of this book, the 1990s, with two most fitting addresses; they are those with which we also end this presentation of "The Mind and Heart of Philip Saliba." This can be said because in both addresses he summarizes the many messages leading up to his thirty-fifth anniversary, thus fulfilling the role given to him in our title, **And He Leads Them.**

In 1998, Philip addresses his clergy at the Antiochian Village Heritage and Learning Center. It is fitting that his message during this last Clergy Symposium of the twentieth century would be that his clergy, many of whom he ordained over his many years, should "tend the flock of God that is in your charge" (1 Peter 5:2). Philip, however, does not hide his disappointment—and sometimes anger— over those who blatantly disobey that command. Indeed, the reader will see that the sensitivity and pain endured by all parties involved in the Ben Lomond crisis is obvious. The crisis which had to be faced is finally resolved as Philip turns to St. Paul's words to Titus.

The final piece of literature included in this chapter is Philip's 1999 address to the Archdiocesan Convention gathered in Chicago, Illinois. It is delivered in the presence of Patriarch Ignatius IV, who is making his second official visit to the archdiocese. Being that this is the last convention, not only of the century, but also of the millennium, Philip uses the occasion to reflect on the deepest lessons of the Christian faith and life: endings, beginnings, signs, prophecy, history, the **parousia** *(the Second Coming), etc. But he also turns to the particular problems with which the Orthodox Church continues to be faced, i.e., the multitude of pan-Orthodox problems in the world. As he speaks of these conditions, Philip, although referring to some things during his own episcopate, is brutally honest.*

We present this last talk **in toto**, *believing it to be a striking end to the faithful service of a striking man, one who is well described by the title of this book:* **And He Leads Them** *(John 10:3).*

J. J. A.

Tending the Flock
1998

Beloved clergy, my coworkers, in this sacred vineyard:
Since the theme of this Symposium is most pastoral, I would like to begin my short remarks with this admonition from First Peter, Chapter 5:

> Tend the flock of God that is in your charge, not by constraint, but willingly, not by shameful gain, but eagerly, not by domineering over those in your charge, but by example to your flock. And when the chief shepherd is manifested, you will obtain the unfading crown of glory.

In the past few days, I have been fortunate to spend some time with our children at the camp. Their laughter, their innocence, their music, their love, and their prayers have energized and rejuvenated my soul, during this difficult year in the life of our archdiocese.

I am sure you are aware that since we last met on this mountain three of our clergy have violated their ordination and are no longer with us. They did not "take heed to themselves and the flock" (Acts 20:28). Last year in Toronto, Ontario, at the Archdiocesan Convention, I told you that "any priestly misconduct will be dealt with severely and swiftly." If I do not attend to that, I will put this archdiocese, which we built with our sweat and tears, at a great risk. I would like to share with you these awesome words on the priesthood from St. John Chrysostom.

> The priestly office is indeed discharged on earth, but it ranks amongst heavenly ordinances; and very naturally so, for neither man, nor angel, nor archangel, nor any other created power, but the *paraclete*, the Holy Spirit

Himself, instituted this vocation, and convinced men to represent the ministry of angels.

I do not know how many deacons and priests I have ordained during the past 32 years of my Episcopate, but I know one thing: at every priestly ordination, when I give the lamb to the newly ordained priest, asking him to "preserve this gift pure and undefiled until the second coming of our Lord and Savior, Jesus Christ," I go through the most moving spiritual experience possible.

The priesthood is not a "job" or "profession;" it is a life and vocation. Therefore, yes, it is very important to preach the Gospel, but it is more important that we ourselves *become* the gospel. Even the Devil can preach the gospel. It is important to preach a sermon, but it is more important that we ourselves *become* the sermon.

Some of the most dangerous temptations which we face on a daily basis as bishops and priests, are always about us: pride, self-sufficiency, self-glory, disobedience, lack of discipline, etc. When God created the universe, He created it with order; "and everything was good." Can you imagine this cosmos, with all its billions of galaxies, without order? The alternative would be destruction and utter chaos. By the same token, no government, no society, no archdiocese, no institution, and no parish can survive without order. Since last February, I have been distressed and agonizing over the tragic problem in Ben Lomond, California. I am sure that all of you have heard or read about it, especially on the Internet. Please do not believe everything you read on the Internet, but rather depend on the news which you receive from the archdiocese regarding this case, lest you become confused and deceived.

I believe it was the devil himself, the master of deceit and dissention, who divided our parish in Ben Lomond. What happened in that parish was a complete breakdown of law and order. On February 12, 1998, the priests and parishioners were summoned by the then-pastor to a meeting. I believe he told them all kinds of lies to the point of insulting the hierarchy and some of the clergy of our archdiocese. Moreover, that particular pastor, in a rebellious manner, asked all the clergy and people present to sign a petition to join the OCA (that is, the Orthodox Church in America). The patience which I exercised, and the many attempts which I made to reconcile these people to the Church, were to no avail. Therefore I did what St. Paul ordered Titus to do:

> As for a man who is factious, after admonishing him once or twice, have nothing more to do with him, knowing that such a person is deceitful and sinful; he is self-condemned (Titus 3:10).

We thank God that a portion of the parish remained obedient to the metropolitan and faithful to the Church. We are delighted that a clergy delegation from Ben Lomond representing the canonical Church remained with us.

Let me say as a close to my portion of this discussion, if you ask me whether or not I regret accepting the former Evangelical Orthodox into our archdiocese, I want you to know that I would say and do the same thing a million times! This is all for the greater glory of God.

Keeping Our Minds and Hearts in Christ Jesus
Chicago, 1999

First and foremost, I would like to extend a very warm and sincere welcome to our Father in Christ, His Beatitude, Ignatius IV, Patriarch of Antioch and all the East. The presence of His Beatitude adds to this convention a special Antiochian flavor. I have told you many times in the past that Antioch is not a nationality, nor is it a race; Antioch is an idea, a school of spirituality with emphasis on incarnational theology which was best expressed by Saints Ignatius of Antioch, John Chrysostom and other confessors and martyrs.

Ladies and gentlemen, this convention is not only our last convention of this century; it is our last convention of this millennium. Two thousand years have elapsed since Jesus of Nazareth preached the "good news" to this fallen and broken world. We thank God that the Church which He established with His precious blood and glorious resurrection continues to be faithful to the truth which is the "same yesterday, today and forever" (Hebrews 13:8). "The faith which once for all was delivered to the saints" (Jude 3).

The Millennium and Time

There has been so much excitement and speculation about the end of this millennium. One might ask, "Why do we make so much fuss about time?" If you compare one thousand years with the eternity of God or even with this cosmos, which is billions of years old, you find that one thousand years pass like the twinkling of an eye or the fluttering of a wing. In Psalm 90, Verse 4, the Prophet David said: "For a thousand years in Thy sight are but as yesterday when it is past, or as a watch in the night." I remember when I was a student at Holy Cross, Brookline, Massachusetts, I asked the great Father George Florovsky,

"What is time?" He paused for a while and said: "I knew what time was until you asked me." God is timeless and does not follow our Julian or Gregorian calendars. This is precisely why we become frustrated and disappointed when some historical events do not happen according to our plans and expectations. There has been so much hype and so much excitement about the end of this millennium, to the extent that some Christian sects and cults speak with certainty about the Second Coming of Christ. Even one of our United States Presidents was concerned about the imminent end of history.

In 1983, before I traveled to the Middle East, I visited President Ronald Reagan to discuss with him the explosive situation in that region. After some discussion, he suddenly changed the subject and out of the blue, he asked: "Your Eminence, do you think that history is going to end soon?" Needless to say, I was puzzled by his question and said: "Mr. President, why did you ask me this question and what made you think that history will end soon?" He said, "Well, we have floods in Louisiana, earthquakes in California, wars and starvation in Africa, social upheaval in Latin America, tension in the Middle East and apprehension about the Soviet Union, etc. Are not these signs of the approaching end?"

I said, "Mr. President, we do not know when history will end. We have always had floods in many parts of the world; we have always had earthquakes, wars, starvation, upheavals and social problems. We have had these phenomena since the beginning of history and the world did not end. We believe that some day history is going to end with the Second Coming of Christ. Every time we recite the Creed in the Orthodox Church, we say, 'and He shall come again with glory to judge the living and the dead, whose kingdom shall have no end.'"

But when will this Last Judgment take place? No one knows. In Mark 13, Jesus tells Peter, James, John and Andrew:

> Take heed that no one leads you astray. Many will come in my name saying: I am He! And they will lead many

astray. And when you hear of wars and rumors of war, do not be alarmed; this must take place, but the end is not yet. For nation will rise against nation, and kingdom against kingdom; there will be earthquakes in various places, there will be famine; this is but the beginning of the sufferings (Mark 13:5, 6, 8).

These signs are typical of this sinful and fallen world. The Second Coming may happen at any moment, and it may not. Millennia may come and go and still no one can determine when Christ will come again. Nevertheless, we must be always prepared for His Second Coming. In Luke, our Lord said: "Blessed are those servants whom the master finds awake when He comes. You must be ready; ... For the Son of man is coming at an hour you do not expect" (Luke 12:37–40).

History, Time and the Orthodox Church

Some time ago, I wrote that history consists of many bright moments and many dark moments. The first Christian millennium was one of those long, bright moments. Despite the persecution endured during the first three Christian centuries, many saints, confessors, evangelists and martyrs witnessed to the eternal truth of Christ with their own blood. I believe that the greatest and most precious testimony is the testimony of blood. Another bright moment was the era of the great Ecumenical Councils, which extended from A.D. 325 to 787, the last Ecumenical Council. Thus, the Church of the first millennium was alive, dynamic and courageous in her response to the monumental challenges which she faced. Fortunately, most of the Byzantine emperors were faithful persons who believed in God, protected the Church and executed the decisions of the Councils.

In 1923, a Pan-Orthodox Congress convened in Constantinople and decided that the Gregorian calendar is more correct than the Julian calendar and we must follow the Gregorian calendar. This was not a dogmatic issue, and yet a great misunderstanding occurred which resulted in some

Orthodox celebrating the feasts according to the Gregorian calendar and some according to the Old Calendar. Why? Because we do not have a central authority in the Orthodox Church, a referee, if you please, someone to whom canonical matters are referred for investigation and settlement.

A few years ago, my beloved children who have their spiritual roots in Palestine and Jordan approached me and complained bitterly about the conditions of the Patriarchate of Jerusalem, i.e. about Church land (*wafq*) being sold or leased for ninety-nine years to the Israelis; about Orthodox children being lost to other Christian sects; about so much corruption in that Church. Needless to say, I was shocked and saddened because the Church is One, Holy, Catholic and Apostolic, because the unity which binds us together as Orthodox transcends jurisdictionalism. Thus I promised my spiritual children that I would write, on their behalf, to the Ecumenical Patriarch, who is supposed to be our traditional referee, which I did, five years ago; I am still waiting for an answer.

This millennium is coming to an end, and we still do not have a viable mechanism through which we can solve our pan-Orthodox problems. A few years ago a jurisdictional dispute arose between the Patriarchate of Constantinople and the Patriarchate of Moscow over the Orthodox of Estonia. Finally, they agreed to solve the problem this way: let the parishes of Estonia choose between Moscow and Constantinople. They did. The result was two jurisdictions over the same territory, which is typical of our uncanonical situation in the Americas.

I am not advocating some kind of papacy here. If we need a pope, we know his address. I am simply asking for some kind of a mechanism to bring the Orthodox together in order to settle their differences. One of the few occasions in which the Orthodox meet is during the assemblies of the World Council of Churches. Bringing the Orthodox together with a well-planned agenda to put our Orthodox house in order must be one of our main priorities in the new millennium. It is inconceivable that in this age of jet travel, computers, fax machines, e-mail and excellent communication, we Orthodox do not meet annually or biennially on the patriarchal level, or on any level, to discuss problems which the Church is facing on the threshold of a new millennium.

The Second Millennium
The second Christian millennium has not been very kind to the Church. It began with the decline of the Byzantine Empire, which ultimately fell in 1453. Constantinople was conquered by the Turks, and thus one of the brightest chapters in world civilization ended. For political reasons, the Turkish Sultan put the Patriarch of Constantinople in charge of the rest of the Eastern Patriarchates, and thus Antioch, Jerusalem and Alexandria became captive to foreign hierarchy. Fortunately, Antioch was liberated in 1898, and now this patriarchate is experiencing an educational and spiritual renaissance under the leadership of His Beatitude, Patriarch Ignatius IV.

In the meantime, Jerusalem, Alexandria and Constantinople are still in captivity. We know from reliable sources that the number of Orthodox faithful remaining in Istanbul is less than two thousand. We also know that the number of Orthodox left in the Patriarchates of Jerusalem and Alexandria is dwindling day by day and year by year. We are called, especially as the new millennium dawns on us, to help the spiritual leaders of these patriarchates realize that we are living in a post-Byzantine era and that the emperor is not returning in the foreseeable future to liberate Constantinople.

Another dark moment of this century was the Communist Revolution of 1917 and the Stalinist persecution of the Russian and Slavic churches which lasted for seventy years. Thousands, if not millions of faithful clergy and laity received the honor of martyrdom, refusing to compromise the Holy Orthodox Faith. I am happy to tell you that two years ago, when I revisited Russia, I noticed that a special renaissance was taking place, under the very able leadership of His Holiness, Patriarch Alexei II, and that thousands of churches and monasteries are being rebuilt and reopened. This confirms the biblical saying: "I will build my Church, and the powers of hell shall not prevail against it" (Matthew 16:18).

Beloved in Christ, perhaps the brightest moment during the last quarter of this millennium was the planting of the seeds of Holy Orthodoxy in this fertile North American soil. Driven by poverty, social injustice and economic deprivation, thousands of Orthodox arrived on these blessed shores from the Middle East, Turkey, Cyprus, Greece, Eastern Europe and Russia. Next to survival in this new environment, their first and foremost concern was building churches to perpetuate their Orthodox heritage. Prior to the Bolshevik Revolution, however, there was a semblance of canonical order in the North American Church. After the revolution in Russia, ethnicism became the norm and thus Orthodoxy in North America became divided into various jurisdictions according to ethnic background.

Unity in America: The Antiochian Perspective
I believe that the most difficult challenge which the Church will be facing in the new millennium is Orthodox unity in this hemisphere. I would like to state for history's sake that Antioch was never a stumbling block to Orthodox unity. Two of our illustrious and venerable patriarchs of this century have made crystal-clear statements on behalf of Orthodox unity in North America.

In 1977, the late Patriarch Elias IV, in an interview published in *A Man of Love,* was asked: "What do you foresee for the future of Orthodoxy in the diaspora, particularly in North America?"

His Beatitude answered:

> In preparation for the upcoming Great Council, the Antiochian Holy Synod has studied in depth the situation of Orthodoxy in the diaspora. Our position is clear. There must be established independent churches in Eastern Europe, North America, etc. The possibility for

such an autocephalous church is greatest in North America. However, the decision to create such a church must be done with the blessings of all mother churches which have dioceses on this continent.

We are all well aware of the canons of the Church which, among other things, say that there cannot be many bishops in one city. The Antiochian See is ready to do her part to rectify this unfortunate situation of Orthodoxy in North America. We affirm that in North America there should be an autocephalous church with its own patriarch and Holy Synod. However, all mother churches must agree on this point, and more importantly, the faithful in North America must do their part to make independence and unity a reality and not just a written Tomos.

In 1985, the position of Antioch was again stated on the pages of the *WORD Magazine* by our beloved Patriarch Ignatius. In anticipation of the Great and Holy Synod, His Beatitude said:

1. The Orthodox diaspora has reached such a maturity that it is necessary to consider it from a new viewpoint in such a way that leads to resolution.
2. We must see it as the vocation of the Orthodox diaspora, not only to preserve the present, but to become a dynamic and creative element in its own environment.
3. It is desirable that the Council should recognize all the Orthodox churches in the diaspora provided there is no serious cause not to do so.
4. It is desirable that local synods should be created, comprising the bishops of the Orthodox churches of the area in question and their members. This should be realized especially in Western Europe, America, Australia and also elsewhere, as far as necessary.
5. Autocephaly should be granted to all the churches of

the countries mentioned above. The local synods of the autocephalous mother churches should decide on it and determine its boundaries.
6. The traditional apostolic and catholic regulations of the Orthodox Church should be followed so that in each city there would be only one bishop, and in each province there would be one metropolitan.
7. The relationship between the mother churches and the diaspora churches are to be kept brotherly and cordial, as is natural to the Orthodox spirit and to the extent that all is for one and one is for all.
8. Within the churches, there should be preserved the cultural, linguistic and other national elements, insofar as they do not disrupt the unity of the local church or the wholeness of the local diocese.

I believe that these two explicit statements of our venerable patriarchs speak for themselves. My predecessor, Metropolitan Antony Bashir, was a staunch advocate of Orthodox unity in North America, and has made many statements in this regard. In 1976, speaking in Pittsburgh, Pennsylvania, on the Sunday of Orthodoxy, I said: "We Orthodox have a tendency to glorify the past and feel proud of ourselves. There is no doubt that the church of the Ecumenical Councils was glorious and courageous in responding to the challenges of her time. Have we responded to the challenges of our time? As individual jurisdictions, I believe we have succeeded in building beautiful churches, in educating young priests and organizing good choirs and church schools, etc., but collectively, we have done absolutely nothing."

The tragedy of Kosovo clearly revealed our nakedness and ineffectiveness as Orthodox in this country. We have no clout in Washington, D.C., whatsoever, because we are still speaking to the State Department and the White House as Greeks, Russians, Antiochians, Serbians, etc., instead of speaking to Washington with one voice. Even Madeline Albright refused to talk to us during the dark days of that unfortunate war. We cannot be agents of change in full obedience to the truth unless we transcend ethnicism and establish a new Orthodox reality in North America. I am not asking anyone to deny his or her own history and culture. What I am asking is to blend the old and new cultures into some kind of integrated reality.

You see, my friends: Antioch is not the problem. The problem lies elsewhere. A few years ago, we in North America experienced a moment of transfiguration when thirty Orthodox bishops gathered at the Antiochian Village to know each other, pray together, and discuss common Orthodox problems. At that time, I delivered a paper on "Missions and Evangelism," and Metropolitan Maximos of Pittsburgh delivered a paper on "Orthodox Unity in North America." That was all. The news of this brotherly, long-anticipated and unprecedented meeting caused an earthquake in certain Orthodox quarters, which sent shock waves all the way to North America. How dare we meet and say, "We are here in America to stay and we are not in diaspora!"

Finally, I firmly believe that Orthodox unity in North America is inevitable and such unity will strengthen the mother churches, spiritually and otherwise. No one can stop the wheels of history and no one can reverse the course of a mighty river.

Our Archdiocese: Sad Moments, Joyful Fruits
Let us now reflect for a moment on the state of our archdiocese. In 1998, we experienced some deep sadness and disappointment because of the tragedy in Ben Lomond, California. I do not intend to go into details because you know this whole painful story. I would like, however, to take this opportunity to thank those who gave countless hours defending the integrity of our archdiocese. During this tragedy, a former evangelical priest asked me, "Are you not sorry for accepting us in the Antiochian Archdiocese?" I said: "No, and if I have to say 'Welcome Home' again, I will say it a million times." The overwhelming majority of the former evangelicals are faithful Orthodox and I am proud of them. We have received hundreds and hundreds of letters

supporting the position of the archdiocese vis-à-vis the dissidents of Ben Lomond. If they ever repent and decide to return home, we will receive them with open arms.

Despite some insignificant distractions, our archdiocese continues to flourish spiritually and otherwise. Let the facts speak for themselves: we now have 320 priests, 144 deacons, 18 seminarians and 220 parishes and missions. One can see we have come a long way since 1966. Most of our missions receive some financial assistance from the archdiocese and our seminarians are the envy of all seminarians from other jurisdictions. We have full-time directors for the departments of Youth Ministry, Christian Education, Missions and Evangelism and a full-time director for the Heritage and Learning Center. Our camping program, since its inception in 1979, has hosted thousands and thousands of young people and impacted their lives. Thank God for the Antiochian Village! The other departments of the archdiocese have either volunteers or part-time directors.

I am very happy to inform you that the Antiochian House of Studies, combined with St. Stephen's Course of Studies in Orthodox Theology, is at the cutting edge of contemporary theological education. The combined program seeks to apply Orthodox theology to the practice of the priestly ministry. Indeed, this is the program for which we are currently seeking accreditation to offer a Master of Arts Degree in Applied Orthodox Theology. We are beginning this process of accreditation in the states of New Jersey and Pennsylvania, and with the St. John Damascene Patriarchal School of Theology, Balamand University, in Lebanon.

I am grateful to the chairpersons of our departments for their splendid efforts. Four years ago, we set a goal for the Order of St. Ignatius of Antioch. The goal was 2,000 members by the year 2000. I am happy to tell you that we have exceeded our goal one year ahead of time; 2,000 by 2000 is no longer a dream, but a reality. The Fellowship of St. John the Divine has made tremendous progress and I want to thank all their leaders for their good work.

I am very grateful to the Antiochian Orthodox Christian Women of this Archdiocese who continue to dedicate their efforts to charity. Last year, under some brilliant leadership, the Antiochian Women raised $90,000 for orphans in Latin America and the Middle East.

And speaking about charity, I am most thankful for your genuine concern with the plight of the poor and needy of this world. During the past thirty-three years, between Food for Hungry People and other charitable drives which we conducted on behalf of victims of earthquakes, floods, hurricanes, tornadoes, civil wars, social upheavals, hospitals and universities, especially in the Middle East, we have raised millions of dollars to alleviate some of the suffering of our brothers and sisters in humanity, regardless of race, religion or political affiliation.

Giving With Cheerfulness

The Lebanese poet, Gibran, said, "Some people give with joy and joy is their reward, and some people give with pain, and pain is their reward." From the beginning, the Church was rooted in charity, and the Scripture testifies to this fact. If the Church does not care for the poor and the needy, then what is the purpose of the Church? In his Epistle, St. James the Apostle said: "Faith without works is dead" (James 2:17). And I say to you, the Church without charity is dead. "Do not give grudgingly, but cheerfully, for God loves a cheerful giver" (2 Corinthians 9:7).

Ladies and gentlemen, this archdiocese has not been a one-man show. The progress which we made during the past thirty-three years is the result of team effort. *All* of you have contributed to our success according to your means, and I am thankful to you.

I would also like to thank our clergy for their dedication to the eternal values which our Church represents. I would like to thank our esteemed members of the Board of Trustees for their time and generosity to the archdiocese. I would like to thank the Order of St. Ignatius of Antioch, the Antiochian Women,

Keeping Hearts and Minds In Christ Jesus

the Fellowship of St. John the Divine, and Teen SOYO for remaining faithful to the Church in these troubled times. I would like to thank our parish councils and all parochial organizations for their faith and work.

Finally, as this century and this millennium draws to an end, I would like to remind you of the following biblical admonitions:

Do not ignore this one fact, beloved, that with the Lord one day is as a thousand years, and a thousand years as one day (2 Peter 3:8).

Have no anxiety about anything, but in everything by prayer and supplication with thanksgiving let your requests be made known to God. And the peace of God, which passes all understanding, will keep your hearts and minds in Christ Jesus (Philippians 4:6, 7).

AND HE LEADS THEM

Editor's Endnotes:

1. *In 1998, Patriarch Ilia of Georgia, who is visiting America, is invited to the archdiocese, where Philip welcomes him to speak at a special dinner given in his honor.*

2. *Also in 1998, Philip meets with President Yasser Arafat in New York City.*

3. *In May of 2000, the glorification of Bishop Raphael Hawaweeny takes place.*

4. *In the winter of 2000, Philip suffers a heart attack while in Florida. He writes a letter to all the parishes explaining the events, and that he is undergoing therapy which leads to healing.*

5. *In July of 2001, Philip celebrates his thirty-fifth anniversary during the Archdiocesan Convention which is planned for Los Angeles, California. This book,* **And He Leads Them: the Mind and the Heart of Philip Saliba,** *is published in honor of His Eminence.*

May God Grant Our Master Many Years!
Eis Polla Eti Dhespota!

APPENDIX

SELECTED LETTERS OF METROPOLITAN PHILIP

- *To Carol, After Open Heart Surgery, 1972*
- *Thanksgiving Letter to St. George of Cleveland, 1973*
- *To the Child Chrissy, Who Requested a Poem, 1973*
- *To the Priest Gregory, after the San Francisco Convention, 1976*
- *To the Child Stephanie, after Lunch Together, 1986*

December 21, 1972

My Dear Carol,
Have you ever felt sad at Christmas? I always do; but it is a strange kind of sadness. It is a mixture of joy and sorrow which sometimes fills your heart with happiness and sometimes fills your eyes with tears.

Christmas intensifies my feelings about everything. With the year breathing its last breath, Christmas reminds me of the years which have already vanished in the abyss of time. Christmas makes old friends, old places, old cities, old sorrows and old joys vivid realities.

In the past years I used to dream of my first Christmas. This year I can hardly dream of my next Christmas because tomorrow is so uncertain.

Well, enough of this. Take care of yourself and may the Divine Child of Bethlehem continue to embrace you now and throughout the New Year.

With much love,
Metropolitan Philip

Thanksgiving, 1973

Dear Father and Parishioners of St. George,
 For the past forty-five years, you have been solemnly gathering to break bread with Thanksgiving to the Almighty God. Thanksgiving season is a time to remember:

> I remember you constantly in my prayers because through you I discovered the beauty of God.

> I remember the innocence, laughter and embraces of your little children which, oftentimes, transformed me to heaven.

> I remember the beautiful years which I spent with you sharing your joy and sorrow.

> I remember and pray for the souls of your fathers and mothers who have fallen asleep in Christ after an historic struggle to establish a community of love.

My friends, as we remember with gratitude God's love for us, let us beseech Him to be mindful of our troubled nation, our people in the Middle East who have been suffering the scourge of war and injustice. Let us pray that peace, justice, decency and honesty will reign in this world so that God's name may be glorified forever and ever more.
 Metropolitan Philip

AND HE LEADS THEM

December 24, 1973

To my little friend, Crissy,

Once you asked me to write you a poem. I smiled and said: "Crissy, I will, some day."

Little did I know that my poem will be a tearful good bye.

In my dark moments, when life became hopeless and unbearable, you and my other little friends have always given me hope, joy and courage to live.

Tonight, Crissy, a little friend of ours will be born in a lowly manger. He will be very much loved by his parents, but he will suffer and die in his youth the way you did, and his friends will ask—Why? Why? Only heaven knows the answer; we do not know. This little friend, Crissy, will open his arms to you and embrace you eternally.

Crissy, from one convention to another and with much longing, I always waited for your innocent laughter, your embrace and your bright face.

Conventions will come and conventions will go but they will never be the same because you will not be there.

Snow will come and snow will go. Many little friends will be born and many will die and we will continue to ask, Why?

I will miss you Crissy.
    Your friend,
    Metropolitan Philip

Summer, 1976

Dear Gregory,

I am in the sky, two hours away from home and I feel like writing. I only write when I am very sad or very happy. I have a deep feeling of inner satisfaction, which I have not experienced for a long time.

The time which we spent together, and that glorious Convention which was the transfiguration of the archdiocese, is the source of my happiness.

Many times, during the past four years, I felt the pain of my doctor's knife go through my shattered heart.

However, the San Francisco Convention with all its emotional events made me forget the agony of January 5, 1968,[1] and September 18, 1972.[2] The beautiful memories of Thursday evening, July 29, will remain with me forever. It was indeed an outpouring of much love, which I cannot find in the marketplace. And, perhaps this is what made me give away the money to the wretched children of Lebanon.

Thursday evening, Gregory, I was in ecstasy; thus, it was impossible for me to remember how poor I was. It was impossible for me to remember that at one time in my life I walked the streets of London with one shilling only in my pocket. It was impossible for me to remember that Alexander III and the Holy Bishops of Antioch refused to send me a penny to live on while in England, desiring to be fed from the crumbs which fall from their richly laden tables.

I cannot tell you, Gregory, how many nights I washed my pillow with tears. I cannot tell you how many times I desired to buy a coat to protect me from that bitter, biting and cruel

---

[1] January 5, 1968, is when Metropolitan Philip had his first heart attack in Washington, D.C..
[2] September 18, 1972, Metropolitan Philip had his open-heart surgery at the Miami Heart Institute.

English weather. The most precious thing, which I could have in England, was a hot cup of tea.

My father and mother were poor; they could not give me money. Instead they gave me love; that kind of love which I experienced in San Francisco. I could have sent that money to my father but it would not have made any difference to him. He would continue to embrace the trees and immerse his mighty fingers in the sacred soil of his beloved Lebanon.

When I left California, I had mixed feelings of happiness and sadness. Happiness because I was coming home to my peaceful hermitage, and sadness because I left room 107, which was bathed with the California sun every morning.

Now, life must continue; I don't know how long, and I don't know either whether I will live to celebrate another decade. One thing I know is that I am a fighter and the struggle to realize the eternal values which this archdiocese represents must continue.

May God surround you with His love.

Metropolitan Philip

June 2 1986

Dear Stephanie,

Like the twinkling of an eye, the years will swiftly pass and you will be able to read this love letter. I loved you, Stephanie, when I married your Mom and Dad in my little chapel. I loved you even more on the day of your baptism when you were born of "water and spirit."

Some day, if I am around, I will remind you of the day when we had lunch together. It was one of the happiest days of my life. Although I do not speak your language and you cannot speak mine, we had no problem communicating. Love, my dear little Stephanie, transcends all languages and overcomes all barriers. The gestures of your little hands were like the fluttering of a bird's wings and your angelic smile was as beautiful as God's smile when He created the world and "everything was good." When I look at your face, Stephanie, I remember the moments when the world was pure and innocent. It is a pity that we have to grow old and lose that innocence.

Two years ago, Stephanie, you were a beautiful dream. Today, you are even more beautiful because the dream is real. I am happy, Stephanie, because I prayed for that dream and when we pray for something, we become united with it.

Stephanie, you have visited me on a spring day and you brought me the "lilies of the field." May all your future dreams be as beautiful as these lilies. Thank you for the gift, dear one. When I wear it some day on a lonely shore or in a lonely field, I will look at the lilies and think of you.

Love,
Metropolitan Philip